Fables, Fashions, and Facts About Advertising

For Henrietta, Philip, and Mary

Fables, Fashions, and Facts About Advertising

A Study of 28 Enduring Myths

John Philip Jones
Syracuse University

SAGE Publications
International Educational and Professional Publisher
Thousand Oaks ▪ London ▪ New Delhi

For information:

Sage Publications, Inc.
2455 Teller Road
Thousand Oaks, California 91320
E-mail: order@sagepub.com

Sage Publications Ltd.
6 Bonhill Street
London EC2A 4PU
United Kingdom

Sage Publications India Pvt. Ltd.
B-42, Panchsheel Enclave
Post Box 4109
New Delhi 110 017 India

Printed in the United States of America

Library of Congress Cataloging-in-Publication Data

Jones, John Philip.
Fables, fashions, and facts about advertising: A study of 28 enduring myths / John Philip Jones.
    p. cm.
Includes bibliographical references and index.
ISBN 0-7619-2799-9 (pbk.)
   1. Advertising. I. Title.
HF5823.J7172 2004
659.1—dc21   2003013582

This book is printed on acid-free paper.

03   04   05   06   07   10   9   8   7   6   5   4   3   2   1

Acquisitions Editor:	Al Bruckner
Editorial Assistant:	MaryAnn Vail
Production Editor:	Diane S. Foster
Copy Editor:	Sally M. Scott
Typesetter:	C&M Digitals (P) Ltd.
Proofreader:	Scott Oney
Indexer:	Julie Grayson
Cover Designer:	Ravi Balasuriya

Contents

Epigraph

The most colorful description of advertising is the one attributed to George Orwell: Advertising is the noise of the ladle banging against the swill bucket to attract the pigs.

Although Orwell's statement is a delicious piece of prose, it bears no relation to reality. Far from being an insistent call to action, advertising attracts the full attention of only small numbers of people. It is looked at very casually by the rest. And the vast majority of goods and services for which advertising is used make a modest but not totally unimportant contribution to the welfare and happiness of society. Think of toothpaste, deodorants, disposable diapers, laundry detergents, frozen foods, canned soup, telephone services, credit cards, cars, and air travel, not to speak of Smoky the Bear and how he helps prevent forest fires.

Orwell's statement is palpably wrong. Nevertheless, many people agree or at least half-agree with it. These people even include some advertising practitioners who should know better. There is equally widespread agreement with many other misconceptions that surround advertising. The subject calls for a dispassionate and objective appraisal. This is why I have written this book.

Preface

Books about advertising in the mass media are plentiful, but their content varies greatly in quality and style. There has also been a good deal of interest in interactive communication, but this business sector is decidedly less dynamic than it appeared at the turn of the twenty-first century so that the originally intense fixation with it has not been sustained.

Most advertising books are attractively presented. Many are descriptive manuals for use in classrooms or for self-improvement; others are affectionate memoirs written by people who have spent careers in the business; yet others are propaganda for fashionable theories. I believe that there is a real need for a different type of work. This should not be written as a "how to" text or as a vehicle for war stories or as a sales pitch, but it should be a book that concentrates solely on describing how advertising works as revealed by the best research available.

For more than twenty years, I have taught graduate and upper-level undergraduate students in a highly selective communications school in a large independent university. My students have taken majors in advertising, in other communications disciplines, and in management (with an emphasis on marketing). This book, *Fables, Fashions, and Facts About Advertising* (*FFFAA* for short), has been planned with my own professional needs in mind. These needs are typical of professors in a similar position to mine in the many communications and business schools in the United States and abroad.

Students, even in highly selective schools, are no longer passionate readers. They do not read for pleasure; they read for duty, and this is not an inspiring experience. "Dumbing down" is a defeatist principle, and it has negative side effects. I have tried very hard to write a book that students will read without drudgery. Much of my teaching uses the principles of *Action Learning*, which I am convinced is the most productive method for teaching marketing and advertising. This is not a new technique but it is practiced surprisingly rarely in the United States. A footnote on *Action Learning* appears as a conclusion in the information about the author at the end of this volume. I hope that *FFFAA* will be particularly suitable for this teaching method.

This volume should also be very useful to the tens of thousands of businesspeople whose careers are directly or (more commonly) indirectly concerned with advertising. I see these people as working for manufacturing and service corporations, marketing and selling organizations, advertising agencies, media planning and buying companies, and the media themselves. Some members of the public are interested in advertising in a general way, but very few books on the subject have reached out to this nonspecialist audience. I hope this book might do better, because I have taken great pains to make it well informed but understandable.

Advertising has one unusual feature that has compelled me to use a special device to begin each chapter. This feature is strikingly obvious to people who have firsthand knowledge of the business, but it sometimes amazes people who do not. *We know less about the actual workings of advertising than about the workings of any other business activity that swallows so much money.* Until quite a late stage in the history of the advertising industry—about 1960—we knew virtually nothing. There was even some doubt about whether advertising worked at all.

In the absence of facts, it is not surprising that theories were thought up to fill the vacuum. These were soon developed into doctrines that became widely followed. These were fables that became fashions—fables like the Hierarchy of Effects, the Unique Selling Proposition and Usage-Pull, the Slice of Life, the cumulative effect of repetition, Impact Scheduling, Effective Frequency, Adstock and Half-Life, Day-After-Recall testing, advertising cut-through, and others. Note the vigor of these concepts. The words themselves seem to signal a strong, confident, successful business. The reality of advertising is quite different, as readers will see from the discussions of advertising effectiveness in this book.

These theories came from a fusion of common sense and imagination, supported by market research (but not all of it very good research).

Such theories caught on fast, because advertising agencies and advertisers were thirsting for guidance to help them with the difficult tasks of producing advertising ideas and also evaluating them before large dollar sums were committed. The path from fable to fashion was unimpeded, and the theories that emerged became instantly popular, although there was a turnover as more fashionable theories ousted less fashionable ones. This process continues. Not many of these theories have ever been subjected to harsh scrutiny based on factual knowledge, mainly because not much factual knowledge was available—at least not until relatively recently.

This book, as the title indicates, is devoted partly to a study of these advertising fables and fashions. Each chapter begins with one or two examples that relate to the topic of the chapter. However, the real meat is *facts*, to help evaluate these fables and fashions objectively, and to illustrate their occasional incompleteness, inadequacy, and in some cases total wrongheadedness. Each chapter then attempts to describe one aspect of how advertising *really* works.

The twenty chapters in this book are relatively short, and they do not contain footnotes, endnotes, tables or figures, or statistical diagrams. But everything in this volume is underpinned with facts, and I have tried hard to ensure that these are accurate, well founded, and correctly interpreted. They are mostly, although not all, in the public domain. Chapter 20, "The Expanding Universe of Information," gives full details of the publications where most of these facts can be found, and the books and articles listed there include notes that refer to yet additional (mainly specialist) sources. The chapter goes into great detail, and I have written it in such a way that it is easy for readers to refer to the published sources that support everything I say in this book. The separate Bibliography of 107 items and the detailed Glossary will also help. I myself have spent many years in the advertising business, but I have resisted the temptation to use my personal opinions as evidence to defend or refute any theory—unless these are strongly rooted in empirical experience.

I hope readers will now forgive me if I make a qualification to what I have said in this Preface. There *is* one specialist type of advertising—mail order (more generally described as direct response)—about which a great deal has been known for many decades. We can maximize the efficiency of this type of advertising by selecting the most appropriate creative and media plans through a process of running alternatives experimentally and calculating the dollar value of the business generated by each. In

1923, a book was published entitled *Scientific Advertising*, devoted to this interesting example of the advertiser's art. The author was Claude C. Hopkins, the best known advertising agency copywriter of his day.

Nevertheless, despite Hopkins's reputation, most people employed in advertising assumed and still continue to assume, without any serious research, that the lessons from direct response are in no way applicable to advertising for goods and services sold through the retail trade. This attitude on the part of supposedly responsible businesspeople is very difficult to credit. This disregard of the opportunities of using simple marketplace testing to improve the efficiency of all types of advertising—including those campaigns that account for vast dollar expenditures—is an egregious and economically profligate example of an unsupported doctrine in action: a doctrine that is still widely believed. It has done more damage than even the worst of the other fables and fashions discussed in this book.

In this Preface, I have talked more about fables and fashions than about facts. Readers will find, however, that this book is much more positive than negative. As I have already mentioned, what I am aiming to do is to describe how advertising works—or as much about how advertising works as the most up-to-date research will tell us—in order to help those people who plan to make careers in advertising or who are already directly or indirectly involved in the business. I am aiming to improve their judgment of advertising and in general to help them do their job better. We still have a long way to go before we fully understand this strange but fascinating activity, but the reader can be sure of some surprises in this book. And he or she will discover that not too many of the fables and fashions that still populate the advertising business are able to stand up to serious scrutiny.

Here are some notes on how the book is organized.

Chapters 1, 2, and 3 describe a few important aspects of advertising's relationship to business and to the consumer.

Chapters 4, 5, 6, and 7 are devoted to the processes of planning and writing advertising campaigns.

Chapters 8, 9, 10, and 11 are concerned with calculating the most economic advertising budget and finding the best ways to deploy this in the mass media.

Chapters 12 and 13 reveal what we know about advertising's effect on sales—or precisely, on consumer behavior. Advertising *can* work over certain clearly defined periods—short term, medium term, and long term—but advertising does not always have these effects, and may not work at all. Much advertising is totally wasted.

Chapters 14, 15, and 16 discuss other types of research used to develop and evaluate advertising. These include pre-testing; and tracking studies, to follow the progress of brands. They also look at direct response: a class of advertising that produces clear lessons about effectiveness but whose relevance to other types of advertising is widely disputed. Or forgotten.

Chapters 17, 18, and 19 review the mechanics of the advertising business, focusing on the changes that are taking place quite rapidly in how clients manage their advertising and how agencies (and other parties) create it.

Chapter 20, as stated earlier, gives details of the substantial battery of source material used to support the generalizations in this book. The book also has a full Bibliography and Glossary.

Acknowledgments

The first person I wish to thank is, as always, my wife Wendy, who has lived with this book for two years. She has prepared the final manuscript with great skill, having taken every chapter through at least six series of amendments. I am always profoundly grateful for her expertise and even more amazed by her patience.

I also give my warmest thanks to my friend Erwin Ephron, who combines a youthful enthusiasm for new ideas about advertising with massive experience in the field. He has scrutinized every page of the manuscript and given me many wise observations that I have incorporated in the final draft. He is a remarkable discussion partner who not only provides many ideas himself but also has the knack of stimulating other people (including myself).

I also wish to thank other friends who have looked at large portions of the manuscript and given me their unfailingly helpful comments. In the United States, they are Beth Barnes, Mary Baumgartner Jones, Harry Clark, Allan Kuse, Robert Lauterborn, Wally O'Brien, Gerry Pollak, Jan Slater, and Anthony Viola; in the United Kingdom, Chris Baker, John Billett, Jeremy Bullmore, Philip Kitchen, Denis Lanigan, and Colin McDonald; in Australia, Michael Ewing and Max Sutherland; and in Germany, George Black. I am also grateful for the comments of three academics whose reviews of my manuscript were commissioned by the publisher.

Part I

Advertising's Relationship to Business Generally and to the Consumer

Five Myths:

"Consumers are our lifeblood, our entire reason for being."

"The company integrates and co-ordinates all the activities that will affect customer satisfaction; and the company achieves its profits through creating and maintaining customer satisfaction."

"Advertising can persuade customers to change their attitudes, beliefs, or behavior."

"Most products, today, are almost identical. Many clients throw two newly minted half-dollars on the table and ask us to persuade the public that one is better."

"Products have a limited life. . . . Most discussions of product life cycle portray the sales history of a typical brand as following an S-shaped curve. This curve is typically divided into four stages, known as introduction, growth, maturity, and decline."

1

The first two statements appear sensible yet do not describe how most business is actually practiced in the real world. The others are complete misconceptions of reality.

1

Why Advertisers Advertise

Myth:

"Consumers are our lifeblood, our entire reason for being."

Common Sense and Its Pitfalls

The quotation given at the start of this chapter seems so obvious that a typical CEO will nod in agreement without thinking too much about it. Yet if this CEO runs a major consumer goods company, he or she will know perfectly well that, in the process of bringing goods to the end-consumer, large roadblocks have to be overcome, and this can be done only by focusing on the roadblocks rather than on the consumer. Although consumers are always in decisive control of what really matters—whether or not any brand will succeed in the marketplace—consumer sovereignty is not quite so high on the typical CEO's agenda as it ought to be.

A major American consumer goods company markets six different (but not directly competing) brands in a single high-volume product category. Although the company's annual advertising expenditure in the category as a whole is decided by its projected profit, the division of the spoils—the advertising budget for each individual brand—is eventually arrived at by each brand manager making a pitch. Whether a brand receives above-average support, or average, or below-average, or zero support, depends essentially on how aggressively the brand manager makes his or her annual plan.

Inevitably a brand manager in this company will be driven by the following principle: "I spend money on advertising to increase sales, by gaining new consumers and persuading both old and new ones to buy more." Is this sound policy? Such a statement *sounds* like common sense. Yet it is only truthful as a statement of optimistic intentions. It is certainly not true of the outcomes of most advertising campaigns. Consider the following facts:

- In any year, less than 20 percent of brands increase their sales significantly. These include the very small number of new brands that succeed. In general, introducing new brands is a disheartening activity although most manufacturers feel forced to do it, both to steal a march on the competition and for fear that the competition will steal a march on them.
- Virtually all categories of products and services have stopped growing. This means that, in any market, the increased sales of the growing brands must be balanced more or less by the stagnant or falling sales of everybody else.
- Large brands are generally more profitable than small brands—*relatively* more profitable, ton for ton or gallon for gallon—a consequence of economies of scale in manufacture and marketing. At the same time, large brands, because they have such great mass, do not grow or decline much. With a relatively small brand, a sales increase of 1 percent may mean an extra 10,000 cases, and an increase of 5 percent only an extra 50,000 cases. But with a fairly large brand, a 1 percent boost can mean 100,000 extra cases, and there comes a time in the life of a successful brand when increases larger than this are extremely difficult and therefore rare.
- The main feature of brand leaders in all categories is the sluggishness of their sales, which is the result of their being bought out of habit by large numbers of consumers, who at the same time regard them as unexciting although indispensable. This is sometimes known as *buying inertia*. The advertising for such brands reinforces the status quo.
- Advertising influences the success of the 20 percent of brands that grow, and it also helps maintain and sometimes increase slightly the sales of another 20 percent of (mainly large) brands. The overall success rate is therefore about 40 percent.

When we compare markets year by year and see little total growth and only small changes in brand shares, we might conclude that there is a lack of marketing activity. But the truth is totally opposite. The general stability of markets is the end-product of frenetic competitive action, most of which is self-canceling. The aggressiveness of individual manufacturers is counteracted by the aggressiveness of the others. Large-scale and continuous effort on behalf of brands competing against one another produces little overall change.

Consumer-goods markets are mostly oligopolies. This ugly word describes a situation in which the majority of sales—normally at least two-thirds of the total—are made by a handful of competitors: two (as in soft drinks, mouthwash, and toothpaste); three (as in automobiles, beer, and fast-food hamburger restaurants); four (as in bar soaps, breakfast cereals, and credit cards). Categories dominated by one single organization are rare although they exist (Campbell's in canned soup and Kodak in camera film). Fields that are splintered into large numbers of small units are rarer still, especially in consumer categories, although they are more common in business fields (e.g., advertising agencies and firms of attorneys).

Organizations that market consumer goods nationally or in large regions of the United States make sales every year generally worth between $100 million and $20 billion and sometimes more. This is substantial business that needs protecting, and it means that marketers are invariably caught in a dilemma. To what extent should they embark on fresh ventures to expand their volume of sales? On the other hand, to what extent should they stay at home to protect their existing brands (and with them the value of their stockholders' equity)? When manufacturers make speeches to their annual company meetings or when they are interviewed in the business press, they tend to favor innovation and growth. However, *in their actions* they tend to favor stability, certainly when business is in recession. A recent inquiry published in the management journal *The Economist* reported that three times as many manufacturers are concerned with their core businesses as are interested in new strategies.

Consumer Orientation

As already explained, manufacturers will usually say that their eyes are always focused on their end-consumers. This is where their eyes *should* be directed, because consumers are after all in ultimate control of every manufacturer's destiny. Because of this, wise manufacturers should restage their brands at regular intervals, with functional improvements and new advertising campaigns, to make sure that their consumers are not lured away by the promises of superiority in the advertising for competitive brands.

But this last sentence gives the clue as to where manufacturers' attention is really directed. Marketing companies are more concerned with their competitors than they are with the people who actually buy their brands. The very size of the companies competing in the market-place—and the threat that each poses to the others—means that each spends most of its time looking over its shoulder. It will continually try to get in first, to preempt competitors; if it does not succeed in this, it will spend the rest of its time responding to what competitors are doing.

There is an additional complication. Marketing companies do not sell to the consumers of their brands. They sell to retail customers who in turn sell to the end-consumers. And the retail trade in the food and drug fields is also made up of national and regional oligopolies. On a local level, the situation is generally the same with bottlers in the soft drinks industry, with franchisees of fast foods, and with automobile dealerships. The result is that many retail organizations are as large as— and sometimes much larger than—the manufacturers who supply them. For example, the annual value of the domestic sales of Wal-Mart (a substantially American operation) is ten times the size of that of Procter & Gamble, and 17 percent of P&G's sales *worldwide* are made to Wal-Mart.

Substantial advertising campaigns directed at the consumer—but, more important, designed to make things easy for the retailer—are a condition for retailers merely to carry manufacturers' brands. Significant amounts of shelf space and in-store display have an even higher price. And although manufacturers' advertising campaigns are important bargaining counters for retailers' patronage, there is an even more important counter that must be played. This is cash paid out directly or indirectly. It takes two forms: trade promotions, which are another word for large discounts of various degrees of complexity; and consumer promotions (especially coupons), which are also very expensive and are directed less at the consumers they explicitly target than at retailers as a reassurance that they will generate business for them. Without these large bribes, retailers will allow manufacturers' brands to wither on the vine.

There is a trade-off between promotional expenditures and advertising investments: If there is more of one, there is less of the other. And because of the size and the negotiating muscle of the retail trade, it is not surprising that promotional spending has grown faster than advertising. The ratio of promotional money to advertising money is currently about three to one. This is a distribution of funds that would have been unthinkable to advertisers and advertising agencies during the 1960s, organizations whose main priority was to establish and build a body of buyers who used their brands regularly. As advertising pioneer David Ogilvy said at that time: "It is the total personality of a brand which decides its ultimate position in the market." Advertising is quite rightly seen as the primary means of creating and strengthening this personality.

Advertisers today—much more so than in the past—are assailed from two directions: from the competition and from distributors. Advertisers have to tread on eggs, for fear of stirring up competitive retaliation to their activities. At the same time, they must disburse large and increasing dollar sums to keep their brands on supermarket shelves.

These realities of the marketplace therefore force us to think more deeply about the question of why advertisers advertise. Manufacturers concern themselves, first, with competitive manufacturers; second, with the large retail chains; and only third with their end-consumers. Readers will remember the astonishing story of Coca-Cola when, during the 1980s, the brand was relaunched with a sweeter flavor modeled on Pepsi-Cola. Existing drinkers of Coca-Cola, who liked the existing formula and whom the company seemed not to care about, were outraged. As a result, the original flavor had to be reintroduced with much trouble and at great cost.

One Voice, Many Voices

Ninety percent of marketing companies base their advertising budgets on what they can afford: a percentage of the value of their sales. This means that a brand's share of consumer advertising in its category (described as share of voice, or SOV) more or less balances its share of market (SOM). If *total* spending in a category goes up or down but the individual brands' shares of voice remain intact, individual shares of market will not change much. At the same time, total category sales are unaffected by increases and decreases in total advertising spending. (This seems strange, but it is true.)

If it should so happen that all competitors in the market reduced their advertising budgets by 50 percent, it is very likely that each individual brand would remain where it started—although each would have become more profitable because it would be advertising less. However, this attractive outcome could be brought about only by collusion, which would incur the most serious displeasure of the Federal Trade Commission (FTC), which would quite rightly consider it anticompetitive.

The FTC should have no fear that such collusion is likely, however. The most striking feature of oligopoly is heated and occasionally ferocious competition among individual manufacturers. Any reduction in advertising on the part of one advertiser would certainly be met by *increased* expenditure by its competitors, who would immediately try to seize market share from the brave but ill-advised advertiser who is attempting to exchange advertising for profit.

Although manufacturers may start by spending what they can afford, they are perpetually driven to increase advertising expenditures to keep competitors at bay. At the same time, however, huge dollar sums are funneled into trade and consumer promotions to persuade retailers to support their brands. The size of these promotions tends to dampen the upward pressure on advertising expenditure, because manufacturers cannot afford both heavy promotions and vast advertising budgets. But since *all* manufacturers are subjected to the same pressures of retailing buying power, the effect on individual advertising budgets is felt the same way by everybody. Budgets do not go up as much as advertisers (and their agencies) would like.

After manufacturers have responded to the psychological pressure of competition with other manufacturers, and the continuous battles with the retail trade, the consumer is forced to the bottom of the manufacturer's list of priorities. But the consumer is not at the bottom of the retailer's. Retailers compete fiercely for the consumer's dollars through regularly repeated temporary price reductions, an activity that is very obvious from the retailers' advertisements that adorn every local newspaper in the United States: the unbeautiful inserts that appear on Sundays and the strident trumpet calls to "buy today" that are run later in the week.

Manufacturers' efforts to use advertising to enrich the personalities of their brands, in the way recommended by David Ogilvy, are largely negated by massive and continuous price cutting. This is not only because this price cutting is funded at the expense of manufacturers' advertising, but also because cheap prices degrade the image of a brand.

Retailers, who are skilled and tactically aggressive, evaluate the effects of their price cutting with great care. Sales of virtually all brands of consumer goods are sensitive to price changes. On average, a 10 percent price reduction will produce an 18 percent increase in sales. But the problem with price reductions is that they are unprofitable because the direct costs for the extra volume have to be paid for and, in addition, the price reductions themselves take a big bite out of the receipts from each unit sold. However, this unprofitability does not matter much to retailers because the cost of these reductions is being covered to a large degree by manufacturers.

Manufacturers are less skilled in measuring the effects of their advertising. It is admittedly a very difficult task. But the real reason why they do not make the great effort necessary to improve matters is that they are essentially more concerned with their direct competitors and the retail trade than they are with the effect of their advertising on their end-consumers. This is a shocking truth, and it helps to explain why the quantity of effective advertising is so small. As already mentioned, only about 20 percent increases the consumer purchasing of (generally small) brands and sustains this effect, and perhaps another 20 percent is able to maintain the buying levels of large ones and sometimes boost their profitability slightly by tapping into economies of scale. An even smaller proportion of brands benefit from the full range of longer-term effects of successful advertising.

Manufacturers still pay lip service to the importance of increasing their sales to consumers immediately and in the future, but they have too much to think about to devote attention and substantial resources to develop and test their campaigns, and at a later stage to take scrupulous care to monitor their effectiveness after they have been run.

In any case, we have been able to measure accurately advertising's immediate influence on sales for only about a decade. And for an even shorter period of time have we been able to construct statistical models to quantify its medium-term effect (i.e., the sales it produces over the course of the year). Not many manufacturers have the experience of—and confidence in—these systems to use them to determine how much they should be spending on advertising and sales promotions. But the problem stems more from the innate conservatism and skepticism of advertisers and their agencies than from the weaknesses in the research per se. The state of the art in advertising research is not nearly as developed as it will eventually become, but the existing methods are serviceable. In any event, they represent a great advance on unsupported judgment.

Can advertising perform better than a 40 percent success rate? This is what this book is all about; only the reader can judge, when he or she has finished reading it, whether or not advertising is capable of the qualitative and quantitative improvements necessary to justify fully the very large sums of money spent on it.

This chapter began with a myth and it will conclude with another one.

Myth:

"The company integrates and coordinates all the activities that will affect customer satisfaction; and the company achieves its profits through creating and maintaining customer satisfaction."

This chapter has disputed this notion. I have argued that marketing money is spent, first, to protect the brand from assaults from competitors, and second, to keep it in distribution and on display in the retail trade. Only when these needs have been satisfied do manufacturers think about how they will use advertising and promotions to influence their end-consumers. Far from single-mindedly focusing on consumers, manufacturers' attention is diverted to what they implicitly consider to be more urgent tasks connected with their relationship to their competitors and the retail trade. It should not surprise us, therefore, that only 40 percent of advertising effectively carries out the job of stimulating consumer demand. Is it too much to hope that at least some advertisers can be persuaded to reconsider their marketing priorities? This is the agenda for this book.

2

Overpromise and Underdelivery

Myth:

"Advertising can persuade customers to change their attitudes, beliefs, or behavior."

Advertising and the Consumer

Many members of the public would agree with the quotation given at the start of this chapter. But most people have never been directly concerned with advertising as a business and therefore have no firsthand knowledge of it. They may have seen lots of advertising and read something about the subject, but this is as far as they have gone. And although people who have opinions about advertising will always deny that it influences them personally, they believe nevertheless that it holds great sway over others—especially those who are less clever and less well educated.

The real problem with the quotation is the verb *change*. Although amateurs believe that advertising is a force for change—and a powerful one at that—this idea is a fallacy, as I hope to describe in this chapter. There is no doubt at all that advertising *can* have an effect and that it can help to build brands. However, it operates in a fashion that is not totally obvious, although the word "subliminal" does not describe in any way what it is all about. (This picturesque theory started as a journalistic hoax, but interest in it has never flagged despite the not unexpected lack of evidence for its existence.)

Advertising does not play much part in the lives of most people. They are admittedly exposed to quite a lot of it every day—something between

300 and 1,500 or more single advertising impressions, depending on which researcher one believes. (The vast range of these estimates says something about the difficulties of making this type of statistical estimate. Somebody has recently given a figure of 3,000, which must be fantasy rather than research.) People are confronted with such large numbers of advertisements because of their exposure to media every day. People listen to the radio when they are dressing and having breakfast, and often also when they are on their way to work. They read newspapers and magazines and pass countless numbers of billboards and outdoor signs. They are confronted with brand names with advertising messages on large numbers of packages in stores and at home. And, most important, they view on average at least four hours of television every day.

Yet, despite this huge volume of advertising messages, very few people take the trouble to "zap" television advertisements, because zapping is unnecessary. We are all adept at switching off our attention subconsciously, a process known to psychologists as "perceptual screening" or "selective perception." This quirk of the mind poses the greatest of all the problems facing the clever and imaginative people who spend their lives writing advertisements. They find it frustrating to devote their skill and energy to writing messages that their audience does not really want to see or hear, although a characteristic of perceptual screening is that people pay more attention to the advertising for the brands they use than for the brands they do not. This is a good reason for creative people to focus on users of the brand they are advertising.

Advertising is often referred to as "low-involvement communication." This means that people pay very little attention to advertisements, especially to those on television and radio. (These are also considered low-involvement media because members of the public do not pay much attention to the programs either.) Consumers must be half-inclined to buy the brand already before the advertising can be expected to work. It must strike a faint chord (at least) with the purchasers before it will nudge them into buying the brand. Low involvement also echoes consumers' lack of serious intellectual commitment in the choice of which brand to buy during any shopping trip. Note the natural "fit" between how such brands are advertised and how they are bought. People pay as little attention to the advertising as to the buying itself. All this emphasizes the fact that advertising must communicate with some subtlety if it is to work at all.

When members of the public are asked how many brands they can remember having seen or heard advertised yesterday, the answer they give is, on average, three. Perhaps they noticed many more advertisements than they were able to recollect the next day. But even if they actually noticed ten times the number they can remember, this still only means 30 advertisements—a very far cry from the 300 to 1,500 they might have been exposed to. The missing 270 (or 1,470) have effectively disappeared into the wide blue sky as far as most people are concerned. It is not surprising that they say that they are uninfluenced by advertising.

During the 1960s, when consumerism was at its height, the Harvard Business School carried out a sample survey to investigate public perceptions of advertising. It was found to come low on people's list of priorities: at the bottom of a list of ten factors that included religion, bringing up children, family life, and public education. People did not actually dislike advertising; nor did they positively enjoy it. Most were simply indifferent. (Different types of research bearing on the same question were carried out during the 1990s and reached similar conclusions.)

Even if we do not share George Orwell's cynical view of advertising (illustrated in the Epigraph at the beginning of this book), it is tempting to most of us to regard advertising as a rather superficial and self-serving activity. But such an appearance can deceive. Advertising is not trivial. If it is scrupulously planned, imaginatively executed, and exposed for long periods, it can contribute significantly to building brands. In fact, the brands that have become important and continue to hold leading positions in the marketplace—American Express and MasterCard, Budweiser and Coors, Cheerios and Kellogg's Corn Flakes, Coke and Pepsi, Colgate Toothpaste and Crest, Dial and Dove, Folgers and Maxwell House, Compaq and Dell, Toyota and Volkswagen, and many others—have invariably benefited from such advertising. But we must not forget the very much larger numbers of brands that have stagnated or sunk without trace; advertising was clearly not of much help to them.

The reality is that advertising is not a job for optimistic amateurs. Nevertheless, many such amateurs consider themselves experts. And they are not shy about expressing forceful opinions about the power of advertising's impact on society.

Advertising and the Amateur Experts

General and unsupported claims attesting to the great power of advertising are quite common. Here are two typical examples:

The first is from two journalists and authors of a book about advertising, in which they say, "The marketing process depends upon advertising and promotion for its dynamic energy."

The second is from the well-known academic economist and prolific author, John Kenneth Galbraith, in one of his most widely sold books (Galbraith's slightly archaic view is still widely supported in progressive circles): "Radio and more especially television have become the prime instruments for the management of consumer demand."

It is easy to see that the first quotation expresses very positive approval of advertising, and the second expresses sharp disapproval; note the chilling phrase "management of consumer demand." Note also how these opposing views are united by a common assumption that advertising produces a big effect: that it is persuasive and "hard selling." But to help us judge the value of these comments, we must remember that these experts had never actually practiced the trade of advertising. By merely looking at advertisements and making unsupported judgments about what these appear to be doing, these people seem perfectly confident to generalize about advertising's effects and to believe that promise leads to delivery (and perhaps overpromise leads to overdelivery). Researchers who have studied these effects empirically are more cautious about drawing such conclusions. The title of this chapter—Overpromise and Underdelivery—is nearer the truth.

Another person who wrote about advertising, the late and greatly lamented economist Julian Simon, had the benefit of having worked in advertising early in his career, so his words have some authority. Significantly, he gave up the business in the (partially justified) belief that it accomplishes very little for its users. Simon made the following statement in his autobiography, referring specifically to the pronouncements of Galbraith and other amateur experts: "Clearly, these people have never attempted to actually convince people to buy a commercial product with advertising; if they had, they would have known how difficult it is to do so."

Developing effective advertising campaigns is an exceptionally difficult task. It calls for three contributions, over and above what the client brings to the party, which is a brand that consumers find functionally effective, a brand that is in full retail distribution, and one that is available at a price acceptable to consumers. The first—and much the most important—contribution an advertising campaign must make is that it must embody an idea that indifferent consumers will not immediately pass by and that will help in some way to influence their preference for a brand. The second and third contributions are also important but they are more susceptible to rational management. The budget must be large enough for the campaign to make some impact in a competitive marketplace. And this budget must be employed in the best advertising media to reach a large audience, at the most appropriate intervals.

Even when all three contributions are as correct as human brains and ingenuity can make them, the advertising sometimes fails. One reason is preemptive competitive action, a result of competitors launching new or restaged brands. Another reason is some deficiency in the competitive functional performance of the advertised brand itself, which becomes apparent only after the campaign has got under way.

But by far the greatest problem faced by advertising is the consequence of an idea introduced in Chapter 1: buying inertia.

The Role of Habit

In stable markets—which is the normal pattern, because of the rarity of successful new brands that would upset the shares of existing brands—the purchasing of individual brands is driven more by habit than by anything else. Many consumers have bought the same brands for decades, so that habit understandably becomes deeply etched in many people's psyche. Purchasing everyday products is not an important matter to consumers. As mentioned earlier, it is known as a low-involvement process. A purchaser in a supermarket does not agonize about whether he or she will buy brand A, B, or C (as long as all these are on the buyer's normal list of alternatives: something described as his or her brand repertoire).

Habitual buying—what I have referred to as "buying inertia"—has been studied in much detail by experienced researchers, notably the British academic Andrew Ehrenberg, with the result that we know a surprising amount about it.

Consumer purchasing is governed mainly by two variables that can be measured: (1) penetration (the percentage of households that buy a brand at least once in a defined period); and (2) purchase frequency (how often they buy it on average during that period).

In the very short term—in one day or one week—sales of brands are very volatile. A brand's penetration will go up and down in response to sales stimuli for the brand itself and for competitive brands. But as the period is extended—to one month, three months, twelve months—the ups and downs cancel out, and the average sales level, and with it the brand's underlying penetration and purchase frequency, all become astonishingly stable.

Here are three of many common and repeated patterns:

• In any period of a month or more, a brand's penetration is normally the same as in every similar period. But this number does not describe the same people each time, because some people who buy in the first period drop out in the second. However, those who drop out are balanced by the new buyers who did not buy in the first period. This goes on with the passage of time, at least for the majority of brands that do not have pronounced seasonal sales peaks and troughs.

• Strongly seasonal brands show a slightly higher penetration during sales peaks (and slightly lower during troughs), and these levels are constantly repeated year after year.

• Net penetration builds over the course of a single year. But the rate of increase slows down, because in each month the number of genuinely new buyers diminishes, most having been counted already some months before. This growth in a brand's penetration, but at a declining rate, repeats itself fairly precisely year after year.

Purchase frequency can be analyzed in the same way as penetration, and we again see regular patterns. In fact, the measurements of penetration and purchase frequency are so uniform that they can be modeled mathematically, and from these models we can predict a number of things: not only the future course of penetration and purchase frequency themselves, but also the number of people who will repeat their buying from the first period to the second, and also what *other* brands will be bought by purchasers of any individual brand in a category.

These discoveries were derived from massive quantities of information from many product categories and a number of different countries. The facts are not seriously in dispute.

These facts, however, raise an obvious question: If habit plays such a large role in buying behavior, *what does advertising do?* The answer is: Three things, one of which may not be at all obvious either to the amateurs who think about advertising or to the other members of the public who do not.

First, in the rare cases in which new brands succeed in entering a product category—and this may happen only once in five years or even more rarely in some cases—a successful launch is impossible without advertising. But this has to be run at such a high rate that a new brand is rarely profitable within its first three years. Because the majority of new brands are failures, their advertising is of course wasted.

Second, in the less rare cases of successful restages of existing brands, with functional improvements and new or amended advertising campaigns, the advertising does a special job. It reminds existing users of a brand to reappraise it, and it gives a prod to some potential new buyers. If these people like the new version, they are encouraged to go on buying it.

However, advertising's third role is the one that has the greatest *general* importance. This is to address existing users of a brand, to encourage them to go on using it. By this means, advertising actually underscores and strengthens the patterns of repeat buying that have just been described. Much if not most successful advertising is therefore defensive; it protects a manufacturer's existing business. In some cases it also makes this business slightly more profitable because it helps to open up economies of scale. Defensive advertising is more appropriate for large brands than for small ones, and large brands account for most of the volume in nearly all categories. Because users of brands pay more attention to the advertising for them than do non-users—a result of perceptual screening—large brands have an advantage in generating effective advertising. Because they have more users than small brands do, large brands have more people who will look at the advertising. This is a genuine scale economy related to the advertising alone.

We can now appreciate the point made at the beginning of this chapter. At one level—when advertising is aimed totally at change in behavior—people are not much influenced by it. But at another level—if advertising is aimed at *continuity* of behavior—advertising is often effective. If members of the public automatically assume that advertising is carried out to make them change their minds, they are quite correct in saying that it has little effect on them. At the same time, they may not realize that a large amount of advertising is actually run to encourage people to continue doing what they are doing at the moment. They will not, therefore, realize how well it may be working because of their inability to diagnose what the advertising is really trying to do.

Continuous, defensive advertising—advertising that is harmonious with the psychological attitudes of regular buyers toward the brands they use—makes a key contribution to strengthening the position of these brands. And by doing this, it also makes it increasingly difficult for competitive manufacturers to introduce new brands, unless these are significantly better in functional terms than others on the market. As a general rule, advertising is a force for continuity and reinforcement, not change and volatility. And this is something that will become even more important in the future, as purchasing habits become yet more unvarying and existing large brands yet more indispensable.

The myth that appears at the beginning of this chapter—which is centered on the idea of advertising as a force for change—is wildly untrue. It leads to a gross misunderstanding of what advertising can accomplish and an often devastating waste of scarce resources.

3

Added Values

Myth:

"Most products, today, are almost identical. Many clients throw two newly minted half-dollars on the table and ask us to persuade the public that one is better."

Products and Brands

A talented young graduate from a prestigious university recently joined Procter & Gamble (P&G) as a brand assistant. At a meeting with more senior colleagues soon after she joined, she expressed her opinion that "all competitive brands are alike and are only differentiated by their advertising." She was soon disabused. P&G has built its formidable success on the basis of functional superiority for its brands. Nevertheless, the curious notion of "product parity," like the views of the amateur experts discussed in Chapter 2, represents a widely held belief. It is, however, an almost total fallacy, and the small amount of truth it contains is highly dangerous.

Before consumer-goods markets began to take their present form more than a century ago, people bought undifferentiated commodities, most of which were produced locally. Brands developed for a number of reasons. One was to give legal protection to a manufacturer's trademarks and patents. Another was to identify products manufactured in factories geographically distant from most consumers: products that were not, therefore, known at first hand.

Brands became established quite quickly, and this was largely because they were functionally better—and certainly more uniform in

19

quality—than the unbranded commodities that people had bought before. Ivory was better soap; Royal baking powder made better textured cakes; Quaker Oats made a more delicious type of cooked breakfast cereal; Gillette safety razors provided a far better way of getting a close and comfortable shave. The manufacturers of these and other pioneer branded goods soon realized the value of advertising in carrying out at least four important jobs: (1) To give information to consumers; (2) to compensate for the weakness of wholesalers, which was a source of great frustration to manufacturers; (3) to boost the sales efforts of the retail trade (which was at that time fragmented and small in scale); and (4), at the same time to attack competitive brands and keep aggressive rivals at bay.

Before many decades had passed, however, manufacturers began to discover that continuous and consistent advertising was adding something of its own: an *extrinsic* quality to add to the intrinsic (i.e., functional) qualities of their brands. The person who first noted this phenomenon was James Webb Young, a highly experienced copywriter who worked for the advertising agency J. Walter Thompson. He coined the term *added values* to describe these extrinsic qualities. The description is precise. The values are added to a brand's functional performance and they do not substitute. Following Young's discovery, only a small leap was necessary to define a brand accurately as *a product that offers functional benefits plus added values that some consumers value enough to buy.* In contrast, unbranded products offer only functional performance—and a generally weaker performance than that provided by brands.

A brand's functionality is what is provided by the contents of the box or, in the case of a service, by the bare bones of that service, such as travel, credit, or communication. Added values, whether they relate to goods or services, are in the buyer's mind, working to reinforce his or her preference for the brand. Both functionality and added values are important and there is synergy between them. But of the two, functionality always was and continues to be the *more* important.

Functionality

Two methods are used to measure the functional performance of a brand. The first is by properly conducted product tests among samples of the consumers to whom the brand is targeted. Most such tests are comparative, to examine the brand alongside its competitors. The brands to be tested, the manufacturer's plus one or two competitors, are given to a scientifically selected sample of about 200 consumers. The testing is generally *blind*, which means that the containers are unidentified and the brands are coded to distinguish one from the others. After a period during which the research panel tests the brands in use, the members are questioned carefully about their reactions.

The second method is by scientific analysis, which can provide precise data on such things as the quantity of certain ingredients and the measured end-result of the brand in use, for example, the amount of hair (measured by a microscope) that is cut by a brand of razor blade.

A totally unsatisfactory method of evaluating the functional performance of brands is for a person who wants to make generalizations to examine and use a collection of brands and to conclude subjectively that one does this and another does that. Very commonly, such a person will conclude that they all appear to do the same job equally well.

A good deal of evidence is available to demonstrate the importance of a brand's functional performance. Here are four pieces of such evidence, which mostly come from the largest market research company in the world, ACNielsen:

- The biggest brands in every category are generally preferred to others in blind product tests. This does not mean that they are preferred for every attribute, but only for the attributes that are the most important ones in influencing brand choice. Listerine's power to kill germs was originally signaled by its strong medicinal taste, and this belief has really sunk in. It is now also associated with Listerine's mint version, although Scope's mint flavor is also liked. But Scope's taste is still not liked enough to give the brand as large a market share as Listerine. Existing brands that lose share over time suffer in most cases because they do not keep up with the functional superiority of new competitors. The greatest mistake a manufacturer can make is to fail to maintain a strong brand's functional lead. A sad story can be told about Ivory soap, which lost a third of its business following the successful introduction of Lever 2000.

- Although most new brands fail, the successes are normally associated with demonstrable functional superiority over the competition. This superiority is often accompanied by a higher-than-average price, which shows that consumers are quite willing to pay more for something better.

• If a new brand is to have any chance of success in the marketplace, it must be preferred over its major competition in blind product tests in a ratio of 60:40; it has a better chance if the ratio is 65:35. Such superiority is essential for a new brand because it must compensate for the functionality *plus the added values* of existing brands. A new brand comes into the world naked and must devote much of its initial advertising to building added values for defensive reasons, if nothing else. If existing brands lose share, they will be reformulated urgently. But despite manufacturers' efforts, this process will take time, and it could be six months or even a year before a reformulated product with revised packaging is in full retail distribution. This provides a grace period for the successful new brand. During this time, it has to build added values if its success—which was based originally only on its functional superiority—is to be maintained.

In view of these facts, we can now appreciate the reason why the statement at the beginning of this chapter is so dangerous. It encourages manufacturers to embark enthusiastically on new brand ventures without the necessary functional superiority for their new brands. The almost inevitable result of marketing a "me too" brand is costly failure.

Added Values—The Result of Planning or Coincidence?

One thing must be emphasized immediately: The concept of added values is neither fanciful nor merely optimistic. It is possible to *prove* that added values exist, by a simple but ingenious type of market research.

This chapter has explained how blind product tests are carried out. It is equally simple to carry out *named* product tests, that is, tests with brands this time in their identified containers. When we compare the results of product tests with matched samples of consumers—one sample evaluating unidentified brands and the other sample comparing those same brands in their normal boxes—we see interesting differences. The large brands test more strongly when they are identified; and the small brands test more weakly.

A typical strong brand, such as a packaged food, which is preferred by 48 percent of the sample overall in a blind test, will typically achieve a 60 percent overall preference in a named test. The difference—a one-fourth greater preference—comes from the qualities embodied in the name and packaging; in other words, the brand's added values. Remember that the functional preference has already been established in the blind test, and the difference between the two is therefore a measure of the brand's extrinsic rather than intrinsic qualities. In this particular example, the overall preference for the brand in question can be broken down into its two parts: If total preference is expressed as 100 percent, 80 percent is due to its functionality and 20 to its added values. With a packaged food, the proportion of added values is only about 20 percent, but this proportion is likely to be higher in fields such as toiletries and proprietary drugs.

I have already suggested that the main source of added values is the long-term legacy of a brand's advertising. This statement must now be slightly qualified.

The bedrock of added values is the consumer's personal experience of the brand. He or she is guaranteed the same benefits from the next purchase as from the last. There is no risk involved in paying money to buy the brand. The consumer's experience of brands is influenced by advertising, but in an indirect way. The most important influence is from advertising that reinforces habitual buying patterns.

Three other sources of added values are more directly related to the advertising. The first is the type of people who are associated with the brand and are therefore featured in its advertising. Brands, especially those consumed publicly like beer and soft drinks, can form a bond uniting their users. This is sometimes called a brand's "club" or "necktie" quality, in the same way that there is a bond between members of the same club or wearers of the club necktie. These user-associations are not always a literal description of a brand's buyers. They are specifically planned in a brand's advertising strategy as a means of influencing perceptions of the brand, some of which encourage buyers' aspirations. Lux, the largest selling bar soap in the world (despite its decline in the United States), is supported by advertising featuring Hollywood stars. This does not, of course, mean that the brand is used only by such people; merely that some of the glamour of Hollywood rubs off in a small way on large numbers of users. (This conclusion is based on research, not guesswork.) In the United States, Pepsi-Cola is presented as a drink for the urban young, although it is actually sold to a broad cross section of the population. The manufacturer is anxious that the brand should be differentiated from

Coca-Cola as being associated with youth rather than age, and with city streets rather than the countryside.

The second source of added values that is strongly and directly related to the advertising is a (perhaps unconscious) belief in a brand's effectiveness. How much are the effects of cosmetics on a woman's beauty derived from her belief that they will make her more beautiful? How much does the efficacy of a headache remedy come from the user's faith that it will cure the pain? There is reliable evidence from carefully conducted product tests that the actual efficacy of branded over-the-counter drugs is due to their brand names as well as their chemical ingredients. Continuous advertising, again encouraging habitual use of a brand, reinforces users' trust in its effectiveness.

The third source of advertising-related added values is the brand's packaging, which is normally featured in all its advertising. The packaging must in fact perform three different tasks. It must be robust enough to keep the brand tidily on the supermarket shelf. It must display the brand name in the competitive environment of the retail store. And it must provide an external expression of the brand's added values: this last task is generally its most important function.

The added values of brands are to a large degree planned by their manufacturers. But there are some things that manufacturers cannot control because consumers respond to *all* signals from brands, from both planned and unplanned sources. It is difficult for advertising to portray a bank successfully as a warm and helpful organization when some people's personal experience of it may have been totally different. Gasoline companies are often perceived as money-grubbing despoilers of the environment. Even a brand enriched with very positive added values is sometimes handicapped by some negative associations. Campbell's is a greatly respected—even loved—brand, yet when consumers are asked to visualize "Mrs. Campbell" she is often seen as an old lady "with a ration of liver spots on the back of her hands." Added values cannot be changed much, and manufacturers are wise to roll with the punches and not try to correct weaknesses. It is more important to reinforce strengths. This is probably the most important role that advertising can accomplish.

This discussion has been confined to manufacturers' brands, particularly those that are well established. As a general rule, "price" brands and generics have no added values at all, and this is also true for the majority of store brands. In a growing minority of cases, however, store brands are acquiring added values connected with the name and reputation of the store that markets them. This trend represents a significant potential threat to manufacturers' labels.

A Lesson From Economics

Every brand is unique in the sense that its name and packaging are different from every other brand. Advertising deepens this uniqueness, *to the financial benefit of the brand.*

It works in this way. One of the most important measurements of a brand is its *price elasticity,* a technical word used by economists to describe the response of the brand's sales to a change in price. If the price goes up and the brand loses little sales volume, then the elasticity is low. This is obviously what manufacturers want. Elasticity is a measure of how easily brands can be substituted for one another. Low elasticity—signaling a small loss of sales to a price increase—means that consumers will be reluctant to substitute a competitor for the now more expensive brand. Again, this is what manufacturers want.

It is not difficult to understand how advertising aims to impede such substitution. The added values built by advertising are intended to make the brand totally unique. And there is good evidence that advertising does this job effectively. It can be shown to reduce a brand's price elasticity.

We should not be surprised, therefore, that large, successful brands have prices at least 10 percent higher than their category average. These are *effective* prices, that is, what the consumer actually pays, and they are higher because brands that have been advertised successfully for long periods rely less than weaker brands do on sales promotions, which in general have only a temporary effect and are also unprofitable to the manufacturers that are compelled to run them.

In a supermarket in upstate New York, Cheerios, manufactured by General Mills and the leading brand in the cold breakfast cereals category, has a "unit price" (i.e., price per pound) of $5.10. This compares with $2.66 for a similar store brand. The taste of the store brand is quite satisfactory, although most people would slightly prefer the taste of Cheerios. But Cheerios is 92 percent more expensive. Consumers are perfectly aware of the prices of the two brands because the cereals are displayed alongside one another, yet Cheerios outsells the store brand by about four to one. This practical demonstration of the added values built into the Cheerios name illustrates succinctly what consistent advertising over a long period can accomplish for a brand.

Readers might wonder how a pack of good quality oat cereal can be sold for as little as $2.66 per pound, while Cheerios is so much more expensive. Two reasons exist for this. First, major expenses are saved in manufacture and marketing: a lower cost of goods (because the store brand is not a top-quality product); and a *zero* cost for trade promotions, consumer promotions, and consumer advertising.

However, I believe that a second reason is also very important. The store brand is almost certainly made by a brand-name manufacturer, and large retail groups compel such manufacturers to supply store brands at a very low wholesale price as a condition for the retailers giving shelf space to the manufacturers' brands. Manufacturers of branded goods have (as explained) lower selling costs for the store brands they make. But, in addition, they will be compelled to reduce their wholesale prices so much that they may make little or no profit themselves. This is yet another example of the unceasing warfare between manufacturers and the more concentrated parts of the retail trade.

The points made here have not exhausted the very important topic of added values. The subject will be picked up again in Chapter 13.

Longevity

Added values are an investment in the long term. Even if advertising support is removed from a brand and before too long its sales begin to fall, it will probably provide its manufacturer with a few more years of profitable life because the money saved from the advertising budget will now be added to the bottom line. The previous investment in added values will slow the decline in sales and will carry the brand along for perhaps a few years.

In happier circumstances, if the manufacturer continues to support the brand with effective advertising and—most important—if the brand's functional performance is kept up to date compared with its competitors, its profitable life can be prolonged virtually indefinitely, with no loss of sales volume. It is not difficult to think of brands that have maintained their market leadership for decades. Here are a dozen examples, all household names: Budweiser, Campbell's, Cheerios, Coca-Cola, Crest, Dial, Listerine, Marlboro, McDonald's, Tide, Tylenol, and Visa.

Yet despite both the logic and the evidence, one negative idea—one that was first hypothesized during the 1950s—is still widely believed both in the business world and in academia. This is the theory of the life cycle, which claims that the life of a brand goes through four stages: introduction, growth, maturity, and decline. In parallel with the flora and fauna of the natural world, the last phase of the life cycle is irreversible.

The fallacy of the concept is that brands are *not* like flora and fauna: They are not organisms with a life and death determined by nature. Brands are the product of human enterprise and are created and controlled by businesspeople. If a brand is managed continuously with brains, imagination, and vigor, it is likely to prosper continuously.

Nevertheless, the theory has for a long time been believed by university professors, and it appears in every textbook devoted to marketing and advertising (although the more recent works at least admit the possibility of staving off decline, bucking what is still seen as a normal trend).

If the life cycle remained merely a theory to describe a pattern of sales that sometimes take place, it would be relatively innocuous. But it can have dangerous consequences if marketing people actually believe it and allow it to affect their policies.

Its influence is felt in the following way (as I personally discovered when working with at least six different clients during my professional career). Consider a specific successful brand that is judged to have reached its maturity. Decline is now considered to be inevitable. Having foreseen this, the manufacturer, for some time, will have been developing a new brand, often called a "long-term reinforcement" (although "replacement" would be a better word). It is easy to understand that this long-term reinforcement will receive the first call on resources: first preference for management time, product development, and marketing and advertising investment. Before long, the original brand will be starved, and very gradually its sales will begin to slip, although for a time it will still be profitable, for the reason given earlier. The forecast of decline proves to be totally accurate. But the real reason for the decline is never talked about too much.

If the new brand is unsuccessful (as 90 percent of new brands are), the manufacturer will now have two losers on its hands. This describes the experience of the Dial Corporation when support for its leading brand, Dial, was pruned to provide heavy support for the launch of a new brand, Tone (which turned out to be not very successful). But the Dial Corporation sensed the danger of its actions and reinstated support for Dial, with beneficial results. This brand is still the leader by volume in the bar soap category. (This should be more precisely described as the "toilet bar" category, since not all toilet bars are soaps.)

As can be inferred from the number of brands that maintain a leading position over long periods, the life cycle theory is not accepted by many—perhaps the majority—of *major* manufacturers (those which take the lead in marketing thinking). Three quotations will bear on this point: The first two come from major marketing companies, which are also direct competitors to one another, and the third quotation comes from a widely used marketing textbook.

First, from Procter & Gamble:

The first thing they tell you is, "Forget product life cycles and cash cows!" One of the soaps has been reformulated over eighty times and is thriving.

Second, from Unilever:

The decline, or "milking" phase of the life cycle exists only as a self-fulfilling prophecy. Provided that a brand is kept up-to-date as a product, by technical innovation and updating, and that its communication is kept relevant, it can be sustained for decades or more.

And third, a different story—actually, a myth—taken from a textbook:

"Products have a limited life. . . . Most discussions of product life cycle portray the sales history of a typical brand as following an S-shaped curve. This curve is typically divided into four stages, known as introduction, growth, maturity, and decline."

Part II

*Advertising Strategy
and the Difficulty of Locating
Target Consumers, the
Development of Creative Ideas,
and Facts About How Much
Advertising Produces an Effect*

Five Myths:

"There are some major benefits to maintaining a strict communications perspective in setting advertising objectives."

"Target audiences are described in terms of their demographic categories. . . . Each time you add a descriptor, the targeted audience gets smaller because the group is more tightly defined."

"If written properly, the creative work plan will tell you what the message should be in the ad."

"The success of advertising depends not on its logical propositions but on the kinds of fantasies it offers. The world of ads is a dreamworld where people and objects are taken out of their material context and given new, symbolic meanings, placed on hoardings or on the screen where they become signs."

"One exposure of an ad to a target group within a purchase cycle has little or no effect in most circumstances."

ll five statements are almost total fallacies, although the first three give the appearance of common sense.

4

"Why Exactly Am I Spending All This Money?"

Myth:

"There are some major benefits to maintaining a strict communications perspective in setting advertising objectives."

Ends and Means

If asked about the objectives of their advertising campaigns, all advertising agencies—and even some advertisers—will talk in such terms as "dominating the competition," "building brand awareness," "raising advertising awareness," "boosting competitive preference," and "strengthening brand image."

These statements sound like common sense, but there are three serious things wrong with them. First, all five statements are imprecise, or "soft." Does dominating the competition mean spending more money, or running a better campaign, or both? If it is running a better campaign, how do we do this? The statement does not help us. The second point is that these are not objectives at all but means of achieving objectives. This point is connected with the third problem, which is the most telling one. These statements are much too remote from the brand *as a business.* They mostly focus on advertising as if it were a self-contained activity, which it is not. Advertising's sole value is in its ability to help brands meet specific commercial objectives. Advertising does this by influencing consumer behavior (which can be measured). Consumers spend money, and the advertiser sells the brand.

Reinforcement of awareness and attitudes is more the result of buying than the cause of it.

Advertising is an expensive pursuit. If the expenditure on it is boosted without having much effect on a brand's sales, the profit on that brand will go down by almost the same amount. This is obviously true when the sums are measured in dollars, but it can also be true in percentage terms. A brand's advertising spending and its earnings are often similar sums of money. For example, if both sums are $100 million, then a 10 percent advertising increase (from $100 to $110 million) could mean a 10 percent profit reduction (from $100 to $90 million), *if sales are not boosted by the advertising increase*—quite a common situation.

If advertising builds or maintains sales—and, even more important, profit from those sales, if this can be quantified—it is justified no matter how high the advertising expenditure. But if it does not do these things, then it is not justified no matter how low the expenditure. In the latter case, advertising is a drag on the business, and it is better to convert the advertising spending into profit. The advertiser must then, of course, take urgent steps to develop an effective campaign and run it with little delay.

Advertising's influence on sales does not always, or even often, mean *increasing* sales. With the majority of large brands, advertising is working if it helps to hold volume in the face of tough competition. In some circumstances, advertising can even be working if it succeeds in decelerating the pace of an inevitable decline. These are perfectly sensible jobs that advertising can help carry out. But there are a variety of ways in which it can contribute. They all demand that the objective (or objectives) of the advertising should be set out in such a way that they relate to these strictly business-oriented tasks.

Sources of Business

An advertising strategy is a management plan that sets out two things: the objectives of the campaign, and the ways that advertising will work to achieve these. The objective must be stated in "hard," robust, terms. These do not necessarily need to be quantified. For instance, if the objective is to bring in new users from a different market segment by increasing the brand's penetration (i.e., its net number of buyers), we do not need to specify that the penetration should rise from, say, 25 to 30 percent. When we evaluate the effect of the campaign after the event, however, it is valuable to measure precisely the penetration increase, if any.

The objective of the advertising must be defined in terms of where the brand's business is going to come from. We must specify the numbers and types of consumers who are likely to buy our brand, identifying them by *what they are buying already.* For instance, if we are advertising Kellogg's Corn Flakes (KCF) aggressively, our source of business will be buyers of its most direct competitor, Cheerios, and these people have certain demographic characteristics. The strategy should then go on to describe the main means by which—it is hoped—advertising will get to users of Cheerios. These means might include building awareness of KCF, increasing consumer preference, and so forth. But these things are only relevant to the extent that they contribute to a specific business task.

A brand has only five sources of business, and its sales will come from one of these or from a combination of more than one. Before listing these sources, the reader must understand some simple definitions. A *category* is a product group broadly defined (e.g., beer, breakfast cereals, credit cards). A *segment* is a product group narrowly defined (e.g., domestic beer/imported beer; standard breakfast cereals/sweetened cereals/high fiber cereals; cards for extended credit/charge cards/debit cards). Penetration and purchase frequency were described in Chapter 2. To recapitulate, *penetration* describes the number of households that buy a brand at least once in a defined period; and *purchase frequency* describes the average number of times they buy it during that time.

The *first source* of business for a brand comes from new buyers entering a category. This is not an enormously important source in the United States, where 90 percent of consumer purchasing takes place in categories that are not growing, because the high level of consumption has led to saturation. (The situation is different in developing countries.) In the United States, new categories are created extremely rarely, and planning for such an eventuality is not a serious possibility for most manufacturers. The only important examples during the past two decades have been sophisticated electronic devices whose prices have been dramatically reduced as a result of massive economies of scale, for example, personal computers, cellular telephones, CDs, DVDs, and digital cameras.

But it is true even in the United States that in many categories of everyday products, different age-groups—sometimes called "cohorts"—welcome new users continuously as these people become ready to join the user group. In their teens, girls are introduced to cosmetics and boys to shaving. In their twenties, people buy automobiles. In their thirties, they are in the market for various types of insurance. And so on, cohort by cohort, until in old age people begin buying hearing aids and incontinence products. In most categories, however, the total number of buyers does not change much because the new buyers in any single age-group are balanced at the other end by people who drop out, summoned by the Grim Reaper. And in most cases, by far the greatest quantity of goods and services is bought by people who are already purchasing, since first- and second-time buyers account for relatively small volumes.

The *second source* of business for a brand is from growing segments. This happens quite often because most categories are composed of segments, some of which are growing and some declining, leaving the total size of the category unchanged.

Segments generally grow for reasons connected with society and not because of brands *per se*. In fact, the opposite is usually the case: Successful brands succeed because they *respond* to changes in society. Healthier lifestyles result in an increasing consumption of low-calorie food and light beverages. The watches on people's wrists have over time become perceived in different ways: as devices to tell the time (Timex), or as jewelry (Patek Philippe), or as fashion statements (Swatch). Personal travel increases the demand for imported beer and foreign cuisine, and overseas brewers and the American prepared-food industry cater to this demand with imagination and enthusiasm. An above-average number of new births at any time will be followed a few years later by increased sales of sweetened breakfast cereals.

The *third source* of business is to steal sales from directly competing brands within the same segment. The commonsense view of advertising is that this is advertising's sole purpose. This is not true, but this source of business is nevertheless very important in a market where segments are as stable as the total category from which they splintered. Business must therefore come from changes in share within the segment. The most public statement of the strategy of taking business from specific competitors is through the use of comparative (or comparison) advertising, in which competitive brands are named. This accounts for an estimated 15 percent of all national campaigns.

These three sources of business are all concerned with bringing new users to a brand; in other words, to increase its penetration. The fourth and fifth sources do not address new users at all. They are focused exclusively on existing buyers, with the intention of increasing or maintaining the business that comes from them. This can often result in a lift in the brand's profitability beyond what comes from any modest increases in volume. In fact, increasing purchase frequency is important for *all* brands, but, in the cases of the first three sources of business, penetration is comparatively more important.

The *fourth source* of business is to increase the purchase frequency of existing buyers. This is the most important strategy for most large brands, because such brands find it very difficult to attract new users. Most people who do not already buy a big brand know about it perfectly well but are simply not attracted by it. On the other hand, purchase frequency from existing users can most certainly be increased. In virtually all categories, the largest brands (normally representing the top one-fifth of the total) have a measured purchase frequency much above the category average.

The penetration of many large brands overlaps with that of their competitors. Most McDonald's users also buy Burger King, and vice versa. The advertising for these two competitors cannot effectively increase their already very high penetration. But some McDonald's customers can be nudged to go to McDonald's more often and to Burger King less. And some Burger King customers can be nudged to go to Burger King more often and to McDonald's less. Note the word "nudged," a favorite expression of Andrew Ehrenberg, the British researcher mentioned in Chapter 2. The word nicely describes how advertising operates. Advertising is normally an evocation of past brand experience rather than explicit persuasion. As I also argued in Chapter 2, persuasion—sometimes known as hard selling—is very rarely effective as an advertising device, because viewers and readers switch off their attention.

The *fifth source* of business is strictly defensive. In the not uncommon cases when a category is declining, such as cigarettes, hard liquor, dairy products, and coffee, manufacturers are wise to batten down the hatches and concentrate on maintaining their existing business. If they succeed in holding the levels of both penetration and purchase frequency, a brand's market share will actually go up if the category is in decline.

Knitting Together a Brand's Strategy

Once an advertiser and its agency have determined the source or sources of business for their brand, some additional research data and a good deal of thought can be knitted together to produce the advertising strategy. Different advertising agencies have their own methods for doing this, but there is a large overlap between what they all cover. The following four points are all included in most advertising strategies.

Demographics. It is not difficult to define the demographic characteristics of the people identified as the source of business. With the first and second sources, we can easily define demographically the people coming fresh into the category or segment. With the third source of business, the demographics of the users of identified competitive brands are easily located; similarly the users of the advertised brand itself if we are pursuing the fourth or fifth sources of business. Detailed up-to-date demographic information on the usage of brands by different demographic groups is published by the well-known research organizations Mediamark Research Inc. (MRI) and the Simmons Market Research Bureau (SMRB). The annual reports from these organizations are syndicated, that is, widely disseminated to subscribers, and they are used by all advertising agencies.

Hard demographic information to describe the target group—the people at whom the advertising is directed—is extremely important because it is needed to select the most suitable media vehicles for the brand from among the vast range of available options. But demographic information alone is not very helpful to guide creative people when they are writing a campaign. This is because the demographic analyses themselves are crude. The income groups, age-groups, and other simple classifications do not help us understand very much about *why* members of any such group buy any particular brand.

Why should younger consumers favor Dial soap and also Caress?

The two brands are functionally quite different from one another. The demographics of one brand are often quite similar to those of even its direct competitors. With large brands, there is little demographic selectivity at all: no subgroups of above-average importance. Creative planning calls for a deeper level of understanding of consumers. This can only come from insights gained from qualitative research.

Psychographics, or the Study of Lifestyles. Psychographics provide much more helpful information to help discriminate between brands with the aim of developing a unique appeal for our own brand. Once we have defined the relevant population groups as sources of business, the psychographic characteristics of these groups can be studied with the help of qualitative research. (This is discussed in more detail in Chapter 14.)

Many helpful and well-known techniques have been developed over the years during which qualitative research has been practiced. An imaginative extrapolation of demographic data can also provide some insights. With psychographic information, creative people can focus on the lives, habits, tastes, and hobbies of their target consumers, so that the campaign can reflect these things. The target consumer can see himself or herself in the advertising, as if in a mirror.

The Proposition. The qualities of the brand in the round—its amalgam of functional properties and added values—are projected by successful advertising. The best way to plan how to do this is to work out the ways in which target consumers are likely to *respond* to the brand and its advertising. This depends on our understanding the psyche of our consumers. Advertising is much better at reinforcing, or sometimes modifying, existing attitudes than when it attempts radical change. The proposition should therefore be presented against a background of what the target consumers already know, believe, and feel about the brand. Again, we are very much in the world of qualitative insights.

The relative emphasis given in the advertising to functional properties and added values varies brand by brand. In general, newer and smaller brands weight their advertising more toward functionality, while older and larger brands depend more on added values. The specific functional characteristics of the brand that are shown in the advertising are decided by the strength of those features in comparison with competitive brands. This comes back to the brand's source of business, in particular the important third source: stealing sales from directly competitive brands within the same segment. Our advertising has to show *superiority* over these other brands.

It is not, incidentally, a good idea to concentrate the proposition on a single point of functional difference between the advertised brand and its competitors. This was once a fashionable doctrine derived from the fable of the Unique Selling Proposition (USP), an idea that stemmed from flawed research, known as Usage-Pull. The USP is much less effective than this research suggests. But the ultimate problem is that a USP is easily copied, which means that the advertising on which it is based soon loses its cutting edge. When I worked on the Gillette advertising account, and when my colleagues and I were tempted to base the advertising for a new razor blade on its ability to provide seven good shaves, the client quite correctly asked us what we would do if a competitor introduced a blade that gave eight shaves.

The Role of the Advertising. We should avoid leaving questions in consumers' minds as a result of the advertising. It is difficult enough to induce the public to look at an advertisement anyway, and it is a gratuitous impediment to leave behind unanswered questions. The question that should be answered in the strategy is: How *directly* should the advertising be expected to work? What are people to *do* as a result of noticing the advertising? Call a 1-800 number? Visit a showroom to find out more information? Or should the advertising influence the consumer when she or he next goes to the supermarket to shop for toothpaste or anything else because the household supplies are low? In this case, is the purpose of the advertising to nudge someone to take our brand down from the shelf in preference to a competitor's, through reinforcing existing favorable feelings toward the brand?

Between these two extremes—total directness and total indirectness—there is a continuum of specific steps. These include relating to the consumer's special needs, recalling satisfactions, and modifying attitudes. These are quite specific roles, and research after the event can assess how well advertising carries out the task.

An effective advertising strategy is a product of judgment applied to facts derived from quantitative investigations and insights from qualitative research. Writing a strategy is a logical (sometimes described as a vertical) process, which means that the thinking follows a straight line without any diversion into byways. The people who write a brand's strategy are generally the account executives and account planners in an advertising agency, but the proposal must have the client's full endorsement before it becomes an action plan. But sometimes the client organization itself writes the strategy and gets the agency to agree to it.

One final ingredient in a strategy is a spark of optimism, even when the objective of the advertising is maintenance rather than growth. With large brands in mature categories, volume growth is exceptionally difficult. But it is never impossible. If there is will and resolution behind the objectives and strategy, the brand has a chance of exploiting rare opportunities for growth. But this is most unlikely if the objectives are set in totally neutral, albeit realistic, terms.

The strategy should describe the residual impression of the brand in the minds of consumers after they have been exposed to the advertising. But the tactics—the advertising ideas themselves—are quite separate. The campaign ideas are required to carry out the exceptionally difficult task of establishing some engagement between the advertising and the consumer.

A good strategy is succinct and totally relevant to the brand with no superfluity, and it must be regarded by creative people as helpful to them rather than a rigid set of rules. To do these jobs, the strategy must be written with skill and sensitivity. To a large extent it is a creative endeavor, because it is the trigger for the most important constituent of an advertising campaign, the creative idea embodied in it. A centrally important element in a brand's strategy—the size and location of the target group—is the subject of the next chapter. This leads naturally into Chapter 6, which examines the creative process itself.

5

How Many Fish Are There in the Pool? And Where Are They?

Myth:

"Target audiences are described in terms of their demo-graphic categories. . . . Each time you add a descriptor, the targeted audience gets smaller because the group is more tightly defined."

Mass Marketing—and the Search for Precision

The quotation given at the beginning of this chapter contains a very appealing idea. Many manufacturers, perplexed by the difficulties of selling to an untidy mass of end-consumers, have been only too grateful to receive and to implement such neat, scientific advice. But there are two problems with it. First, it contradicts the important principle established when consumer goods markets were first developed—and something that remains extremely relevant today—that large volumes generate scale economies. The second difficulty is that pinpoint accuracy can never be realized in terms of either a brand's users or the media vehicles that we must employ to reach them. In practical terms, the statement is a myth.

Mass production; *mass* market; *mass* consumption; *mass* media. These are popular phrases used to illustrate what mass marketing is about. The phrases are appropriate enough. The mass marketing of consumer goods grew in scale and sophistication over a period of more than a century, starting in about 1880. The meaning of "mass marketing" is simple: producing huge volumes of merchandise and selling it to similarly huge numbers of consumers with the help of media that can carry advertising into virtually all the homes in the country. This system differs from narrowly focused marketing based on personal selling and various types of direct response advertising. These are often important activities, but they are dwarfed in sheer sales volume by the type of mass marketing just described.

Mass production can be highly efficient because the very size of the output reduces the cost per unit, sometimes dramatically. When ballpoint pens were first introduced after World War II, they sold for about $100 (in today's dollars); the equivalent price today is a few cents. Electronic products of all types—computers, calculators, television sets, videotape players, automatic cameras—are all dramatically cheaper than they once were. The price of air travel, in real terms corrected for inflation, is a fraction of what it was in the 1950s. Even in the various fields of low-cost packaged goods sold in food and drug stores, prices have come down and product quality has greatly improved over the years.

Mass marketing means large volume and low cost, and these things are good for manufacturers. But relentless competition among manufacturers, not to speak of the bargaining power of the retail trade—which is getting stronger and more concentrated every year—forces manufacturers to pass the low cost of their goods to consumers in the form of low prices. This means that mass marketing is good for consumers, too.

The growth in mass marketing has, however, led to a reduction in the gross margin earned by manufacturers on each unit produced, although this has been more than outweighed by the manyfold increase in the quantities sold. Nevertheless, manufacturers have to scrutinize their costs continuously in an effort to make small savings, and one of their largest items of expense is consumer advertising. In many cases, this represents a manufacturer's largest payment to outside suppliers, except that for raw materials. As early as the 1920s, manufacturers tried to make the best use of their advertising investment by targeting each campaign, to concentrate it on a group of people much smaller than the total population: a group of users or potential users thought to be of above-average importance to the brand advertised.

Starting in about 1930, manufacturers went further and applied the principle of targeting to their brands themselves. This meant that each manufacturer started to produce a portfolio of brands in each category, each rather different from the others, so that they would not cannibalize one another. During the latter part of the twentieth century, this process went further. Manufacturers began to splinter their brands themselves in a redoubled effort to reach clearly defined (and ever-smaller) subgroups of consumers. This meant the production of multiple varieties, each appropriate for defined groups of people who (it was thought) could be reached economically by consumer advertising. The result was six functionally different varieties of Tide laundry detergent, eight versions of Coca-Cola, six types of American Express card. This trend was carried into all types of goods and services; the most extravagant example of all was Crest toothpaste, which at one time was sold in fifty—yes, fifty—totally separate variations.

Manufacturers splintered their brands in this fashion because they thought they could cover their total market in the most efficient and comprehensive way and at the same time make the best use of their advertising dollars. And when categories stopped growing in overall terms, manufacturers could also search out small pockets of growth among certain demographic groups. But when the process had begun, another force became even more important: the force of competition. Brand fragmentation feeds on itself. Once a single competitor in an oligopolistic market begins to fragment its brands, all competitive manufacturers immediately follow suit, for defensive reasons. Fragmentation becomes a standard feature of the market, and something that cannot be reversed without the greatest difficulty.

This description of markets reveals a strange dissonance. On the one hand, manufacturers aim for sales volume and cost reduction; on the other hand, they narrow their focus in the search for precision and the elimination of waste. Unfortunately, this second endeavor contradicts the first one, and not surprisingly it has been less successful.

The Reality of the Marketplace

In the real world, unfortunately, a large difference exists between defining a target and hitting it even moderately efficiently. Very few substantial brands—or even subvarieties of such brands—have ended up being used by narrow but strong concentrations of consumers. People are described most precisely in demographic terms, and the facts are readily available (and will shortly be presented) to demonstrate the point I am making. What makes for even greater difficulty is that the mass advertising media are also imprecise in their coverage of any group, and the largest media are the most imprecise of all.

This means that the theoretical notion of targeting brands and brand variations to meet the needs of specific groups of consumers—and reaching these consumers with media that are equally tightly targeted—is utopian if not fanciful. The reality of marketing is that groups of consumers with little homogeneity are reached (in a very approximate fashion) with the use of advertising media whose audience is also not very homogeneous. The targets aimed at and the means of reaching them are both extremely fuzzy. I write these words on the day after returning from a large academic conference on "Marketing Science," a phrase that carries a delightful implication of polished precision. Marketing Science is certainly not a happy description of the method used to sell most mass market goods with the support of advertising in the major media.

What, then, is the reality? Here are some facts about three major American brands—Budweiser, Cheerios, and Crest—the market leaders in the beer, breakfast cereals, and toothpaste categories respectively. Each brand is sold in multiple varieties, and I shall concentrate on the most important ones: the varieties covered by the leading syndicated research services.

Six points are reasonably clear from the following figures:

1. The number of varieties differs brand by brand: Budweiser (market share 34.4 percent), three varieties; Cheerios (market share 14.0 percent), five varieties; Crest (market share 26.5 percent), six varieties.

2. With every brand, one variety has a larger market share—with two of the brands, much larger—than the others: Budweiser (Regular), 30.0 out of 34.4 percent; Cheerios (Regular), 7.5 out of 14.0 percent; Crest Tartar Control paste, 8.3 out of 26.5 percent.

3. The purchase frequency of the large varieties is invariably high. That for the smaller varieties is mostly low and sometimes very low.

4. Regarding how much the users are concentrated in particular demographic groups, there is an important difference between the degree of such concentration in different-sized *brands* and different-sized *varieties* of a single brand. Large brands tend not to have pockets of demographic concentration but are used more or less uniformly by all parts of the population. But minor

brands are sometimes polarized demographically, with small groups of users being much more important than others. However, as a brand grows, it always loses its demographic skew. This pattern is much less true of large and small varieties of individual brands. Large varieties (like large brands as a whole) are fairly uniformly spread across the population. *Not only do the small varieties of a large brand not become polarized*, but they are also spread across the population in a way that is not much different from the large variety that gave them birth.

5. The last two points suggest strongly that the smaller varieties of a brand are mostly used by the users of the large variety, *but not so often*. They are all part of the overall brand franchise (i.e., user group), but the large variety is a regular purchase and the small varieties are bought only infrequently.

6. Minor varieties are not economically attractive for manufacturers. This is because small production runs do not provide the same economies of scale as are available for the much larger-selling major varieties. However, it is difficult for manufacturers to cut back their number of minor varieties because this might cause them to lose business to competitors, which may still be marketing matching minor lines. Nevertheless, during the 1990s, Procter & Gamble made a major effort to simplify its range both of varieties and of brands, and this certainly benefited the company's profitability. The company reduced its total number of lines from 3,400 in 1991 to 2,300 in 1996. During this period, unit sales increased significantly in total, with great benefit to P&G's profitability.

Where Are the Fish Swimming in the Pool?

The advertising for large brands is normally addressed to the users of those brands. It needs to speak to heavy users for defensive reasons—to make sure they remain heavy users and are not lured away by competitive brands. And it should address light users in order to boost their frequency of purchase. Non-users are generally not very important to large brands, because these brands' penetration rarely increases despite the impetus provided by heavy advertising and sales promotions. Non-users know about the brand and are simply not interested.

The first matter to address is the numbers. Syndicated research does not give estimates of total brand franchises. But the number of surveyed adults who had bought Budweiser (Regular) during the previous six months was 23.2 million. The number of homemakers who had bought Cheerios (Regular) was 27.6 million. And the number of adults who had bought Crest Tartar Control paste was 22.7 million. Note the similarity in the size of these figures. They are typical of large brands. For simplicity, the analysis that follows will be based on one brand, Budweiser, although the same conclusions could be drawn from Cheerios or Crest or any other comparably large brand in any category.

Budweiser is a massive brand by any standard. With relatively few sales outside the United States, its American sales volume makes it the largest-selling beer in the world: bigger even than Heineken, which is brewed in twenty countries.

As we have seen, Budweiser (Regular) was drunk by 23.2 million adults in a six-month span. However, we must qualify this large figure in two ways. First, it must be divided into two, to separate heavy users from light ones. We can do this quite easily by following the "80:20 rule," which applies at least approximately to all products and services. The 20 percent of heavy users account for half of total volume, and the 80 percent of light users account for the other half. Applying this rule to Budweiser produces an estimate of heavy users—the most important group—of 4.6 million adults. The second point to be made about the total number of users is that when it is calculated in percentage terms, based on the total number of adults, the figure becomes much smaller: users of the brand represent 11.9 percent, and the figure for the heavy users is 2.4 percent.

These numbers, although large, do not quite convey *mass* in the way the concept was described at the beginning of this chapter. In practical terms, we are going to be looking for slightly more than one in ten of all adults. The pond is anything but densely crowded with fish. How do we locate them?

The most concentrated demographic group for Budweiser is adults aged between 25 and 34. About 6 and a half million users of the brand (6.4 million, to be precise) are in this age-group. But a much larger number—16.8 million—are outside that group. In other words, for every 100 fish swimming in the most concentrated shoal, there are 260 swimming in other parts of the pool.

To reach Budweiser users, we select the media to be used for our advertising campaign by employing readily available information to match the demographic coverage of the media to the demographic characteristics of the brand's users. As discussed already, however, this is a rough-and-ready process. All we can hope to do is to match media, whose coverage of specific demographic groups is very loose, to the users of the brand, whose clustering in demographic groups is equally loose. On its own, media selection is not a good method of reaching for and attracting the fish in the pool.

However, a strikingly obvious point about the media used for an advertising campaign is that—irrespective of where we choose to give above-average weight—we should cover at least minimally all parts of the population. Many users of the advertised brand lie hidden away, and we must therefore—as a first priority—extend the reach of the advertising schedule to cover everybody possible.

If media planning is an insufficiently effective way of locating a brand's users, we must find another system of getting to them. There is fortunately another method available to do the job, although it does not pretend to operate scientifically, that is, in a statistically based, analytical, or even totally rational fashion.

The tool to do the job is the advertisement itself. It must be planned to reach out unmistakably to a brand's users, and it is often able to do this. Viewers and readers who use the brand must be able to see themselves reflected in the advertising as if they were looking at themselves in a mirror.

Writing advertising is an artistic activity: the product of the genius of the people who do the job. The word *genius* is hyperbole, perhaps, but we must never forget that effective advertisements are in the minority, so there must be something very special about the imagination that creates the relatively few successful ones.

There are no rules to follow. Successful advertisements tend to be unexpected and slightly incomplete—which means that the communication of the message, although initiated by the advertisement itself, must be completed by the audience. If communication is to work, both parties must participate in it. Successful advertisements often use techniques directly focused on the users of the advertised brand. These include how users are pictured (the Pepsi-Cola campaign is a good example); how the voice-overs are often friendly and encourage people to listen (as in the Lever 2000 commercials); and, most of all, how the advertisements project the added values of the brand, gently underscored by a reminder of its functional properties (techniques well exemplified by much advertising from General Mills and Procter & Gamble).

Remember that the users of a brand are more inclined to pay attention to its advertising than nonusers are, as a result of perceptual screening. This eases the task of the advertising in locating them. The advertising does not have to be strident; indeed, stridency is likely to be counterproductive by turning people off. The advertising will talk to the user of the brand as a friend. There is a real quality of friendship in the brand-user relationship, particularly with heavy users.

Advertising will not work unless the audience gives its full attention to it. We know from research into the readership of press advertisements that only about 5 percent of readers get fully engaged. (There are no comparable figures for television, although judgment suggests that the figure is higher.) If we are trying to locate 10 percent of the population, we should try to ensure that these 10 percent should include the 5 percent who will fully absorb our advertisements. Not much business is generated by "glance readers."

As I argued in Chapter 2, writing effective advertisements is a daunting task: so daunting that it is indeed surprising that it is so often carried out successfully. As stated in that earlier chapter, writing advertisements is not a job for optimistic amateurs. However, it is a subject of the greatest importance and of the most compelling interest to everybody involved in advertising. It is the topic of the next chapter.

6

The Advertising Imagination

Myth:

"If written properly, the creative work plan will tell you what the message should be in the ad."

Advertising's Patchy Performance

The idea embodied in the quotation given at the start of this chapter is attractively simple. If an agency spends its time on developing the strategy ("the creative work plan"), this will provide a blueprint for the creative people to use to construct the advertising. The authors of this quotation seem to be saying that the strategic and creative processes are connected seamlessly. However, as anyone who has every worked in an advertising agency will confirm, if strategy dominates the creative in this way, the result will be dull and ineffective advertising. For productive advertising—which calls for a high degree of originality—the connection between strategy and execution must be a good deal more sensitive and subtle.

Approximately 20 percent of advertisements cause sales to spike upward within seven days of their appearance and sustain some of this effect. These are mostly advertisements for small brands, because they are more volatile than large ones, and successful advertising for small brands is more easily measured. Advertising can also work for large brands, but its effect can be teased out only with some difficulty. When we do this, we find that a further 20 percent of advertisements are successful in protecting and adding buoyancy to the sales of large brands. In all cases, we can identify the effective campaigns, and this knowledge provides the background to many of the things I say in this chapter about the sort of advertising that seems to work.

A success rate of 40 percent is not a woefully inadequate performance. With the 40 percent of effective campaigns, the advertising can be having a powerful influence on the manufacturer's business, and it can even be producing a net return from the large amount of money spent. For large companies, the advertising expenditure is usually considerable whether or not it turns out to be an investment or—with 60 percent of campaigns—a drag on profit.

But the advertising industry does not have too much to be proud of in the *overall* effectiveness of what it does. Specifically, what are the reasons that 60 percent of advertisements do nothing for the brand advertised? Although some people still believe the strange myth that imperceptible effects can accumulate in some hidden way into an effect that is eventually perceptible, there are no facts to support such a belief. The best available evidence shows that advertisements that do not work immediately are unlikely to be doing much good below the surface. The money is spent; there is no effect; profit is reduced by the money wasted on the advertising; and that is the end of the matter.

The Causes of the Trouble

In some cases—I believe a minority—managerial problems connected with the performance and distribution of the brand and with the advertising budget and the strategy are the cause of trouble. Rules exist to help businesspeople make good decisions about these things. But rules are not helpful in writing advertisements, a point that will shortly be discussed. Writing a potentially productive advertising strategy is not an especially difficult job. But writing an effective advertisement based on that strategy is a different matter altogether; this is why the quotation at the beginning of this chapter is a dangerous myth. Most of the problems causing ineffective advertising are deficiencies in the creative work, and this is where we should look to diagnose what is going wrong.

The most obvious creative deficiency is that there is simply not enough creative talent. The result is a good deal of unoriginal and rather stale advertising. Nobody recognizes this more than advertising agencies, which devote their greatest recruitment efforts to finding talent, particularly among young people whose promise is as yet unfulfilled. Agencies do not necessarily use the best methods of finding people who can produce work that is both original and effective. But recruitment is not a topic immediately relevant to this chapter. It is a delicate and highly important matter that deserves to be discussed at length in another place (although, alas, not in this book). A second reason for the ineffectiveness of creative work is that much advertising is written to a formula. There is no shortage of formulas, because they are encouraged—and sometimes required—by certain clients and agencies. Clients find that formulas make the difficult job of judging advertising proposals much easier; and agencies find that they help to sell the creative work to clients.

A good example is the Unique Selling Proposition, discussed rather unfavorably in Chapter 4; this is a method of writing advertising based on finding a point of functional differentiation between the advertised brand and its competitors. It is still occasionally employed, despite its widely recognized flaws. Another formula widely followed during the 1960s was the Slice of Life, a style of commercial in the form of a minia-ture sitcom in which the brand played a starring role in solving a prob-lem troubling one of the members of the cast. This became an especially stale and repetitive technique, but it had the merit of producing high scores in Day-After-Recall tests. When, during the 1980s, this research technique was found to show nothing of value, the Slice of Life was at last abandoned by many advertisers—although it was not totally laid to rest.

A different type of formula was developed in Britain and is still popular there. I call it "Small Steps." This requires the advertising to communicate little more than warm feelings about the brand, in the belief that there is "a gradual build up of 'effects' perhaps over the whole duration of a campaign (or even spanning a series of campaigns with similar themes)." Such a doctrine makes sense only if there is a measur-able effect to start with, and few agencies try and find this out.

Other types of formula, followed in many countries, lay down how to construct television advertisements (e.g., dictating the number of times the brand is mentioned in a commercial); still others provide detailed rules about the best types of copy and layout to use in press advertisements.

David Ogilvy, an advertising practitioner with the highest reputa-tion, was one of the strongest protagonists of formulaic advertising. Some of his rules are followed even today in his agency, Ogilvy & Mather. But his guiding principles were fresher when he followed them himself forty years ago, before he set them in concrete.

The problem with formulas is not that the individual precepts are invariably wrong (although they sometimes are). The insuperable handicap from which formulas suffer is that they lead to predictable advertising—the sort of advertising to which consumers are already only too well accustomed. This totally negates the quality of unexpectedness that many analysts—including myself—deem to be a very important ingredient of an effective advertisement.

There is a third problem that stems from creative deficiencies. Many advertisements do not have a weak idea. They have no idea at all, as if this were deliberate policy (which perhaps it is). The advertisement presents the proposition (as it is described in the strategy and often sensible enough) with a minimum of adornment and with little concession to the person who, it is hoped, will buy the brand—and in particular to what the potential buyer really wants from this or any brand in the category. An evening spent watching television and an hour or two reading typical magazine and newspaper advertisements will provide plentiful examples of what I mean.

The real problem here is that too many professionals in the business—both in client companies and advertising agencies—believe that an advertisement is a simple extension of a brand strategy, as described in the quotation at the beginning of this chapter. They should know better. It is quite common for a sound strategy to lead to a deplorably ineffective campaign. Advertisers and agencies should ask themselves: "Why *should* a consumer be interested in my strategy?"

More than a barely developed statement of a strategy is necessary in order to pop into the consumer's mind (perhaps barely perceptibly) the thought that he or she will probably buy the brand next time. The process of doing this is usually indirect and more often than not a reminder of an occasion when the consumer previously used the brand. It needs ingenuity, because the average viewer's or reader's response to what an advertiser is saying is to switch off attention—generally quite unconsciously, but usually instantaneously. There is no doubt at all that effective advertising communicates with some subtlety. Buyers are experienced and are mostly intelligent. How many advertisers and agencies even think about this, let alone recognize it and do their work accordingly?

For many years, theorists believed that advertising communication followed a logical pattern (known as the Hierarchy of Effects), which takes the consumer from awareness of a brand to preference for it and finally to purchase. This theory was exploded many years ago, as a result of two rather obvious objections to it. First, the buying of brands (especially low-priced ones) is governed more by habit than a conscious weighing of the pros and cons. Second, the effects can work in reverse, since buying can influence both awareness, through selective perception, and attitudes, through the way in which buyers justify their purchases to themselves (a process known as "the reduction of cognitive dissonance"). Of course, the use of the brand itself also has a strong influence on buyers' feelings toward it.

We can draw some conclusions about the types of advertising that work from the styles of advertising that appear not to work. In most large categories of consumer goods, advertising usually cannot be effective by being strident. It cannot work by relying exclusively on logical arguments, no matter how persuasive they appear to be. Nor can it produce results by concentrating exclusively on intensive emotional imagery. And it is rarely a matter of "big ideas," although "big ideas" are the verbal currency of advertising agencies, especially when they are pursuing new business.

The acknowledged masters of the advertising business—Bernbach, Burnett, Ogilvy—produced much more successful than unsuccessful advertising; otherwise their businesses would not have grown as large as they did. These men were first and foremost writers of advertisements, and their advertisements are well worth studying. The main feature of all their work has always seemed to me to be its simplicity. This does not mean that the advertisements are commonplace or impressionistic or unidimensional, nor that they talk down to the audience. The headlines in their press advertisements are always intriguing without suffering the besetting sin of most contemporary advertising: obscurity. The simplicity of the advertising is the end result of superb focus.

I have already suggested that advertising can communicate in a subtle way, and Bill Bernbach in particular shared this view. The element in an advertisement that causes a spark cannot be forecast and it is sometimes serendipitous. A single word can make a difference between success or failure. It is exceedingly difficult to predict the effect on an audience of one word rather than another.

The people who have the greatest sensitivity to audience reactions are comedians. One of the most famous, Groucho Marx, tested his wisecracks on audiences. When he was making the film *A Day at the Races,* he experimented with slightly different versions of a joke in front of different live audiences. He tested alternatives for one important word. He tried *obnoxious, revolting, disgusting, offensive, repulsive, disagreeable,* and *distasteful.* The last two words raised a titter. The other words got a more positive reaction. Finally, a new alternative, the word *nauseating,* drew roars of laughter. The resulting line became a comic legend: "That's the most nauseating proposition I ever had."

Small differences are, if anything, more important in the visual of a commercial—a point made succinctly by Bill Bernbach: "How do you storyboard a smile? Yet the quality of that smile may make the difference between a commercial that works and one that doesn't work."

"Bisociation"

The most *important* thing about advertising is its role in the economy: how it contributes to the prosperity of many individual companies. But its most *interesting* feature to practitioners is that it depends totally on original thinking. It is the only major business activity that is art, if we define this word broadly. It is not invariably good art (although it sometimes is), but, when it works, it always does so by applying the human imagination to commercial opportunities or problems.

I now come to the forbidding job of describing what an advertising idea actually is. This is so difficult to do because good creative people work instinctively and are usually more interested in the future than in the past. With very few exceptions, they cannot be persuaded to make the attempt to analyze how they do what they do, especially how they actually came to write specific campaigns, even well-known ones.

One of the rare exceptions was James Webb Young, who had five decades' experience of writing successful advertising and became an avuncular figure. He once made the remarkable statement that an original idea is *nothing more than a rearrangement of existing ideas.* As I hope to show, this is a seminal concept.

All successful advertisements contain certain ingredients; in most cases, they contain three. I shall try to describe these, but the purpose of what I am doing is analysis strictly defined. I have absolutely no ambition to produce a formula for how to write effective advertising, because any such formula would suffer from the handicaps already discussed.

The first and most obvious element of a successful advertisement is that there must be some mention of the properties of the brand. By this I mean all the most relevant signals—both the functional and the nonfunctional ones—and I shall name these the "brand-related properties/signals/ideas." These are identified in the strategy, which also proposes what is most important and what is less so. For unfamiliar brands, the advertising spells out the brand-related properties, although this is normally done very economically. For familiar brands, only the smallest hint is necessary. A very good illustration is provided by the long-lasting advertising campaign for diamonds run by De Beers.

Although diamonds are an unbranded commodity, the De Beers campaign has been highly effective in the marketplace and has succeeded in clothing diamonds with all the qualities needed to make them one of the most select *brands* in the world. The brand-related properties of diamonds are that they are beautiful and durable and valuable and say something very special about the person who wears them. In the advertising campaign, these properties are brought to mind by the simplest visual means. The stones are shown dramatically, and nothing else needs to be said about them.

We now come to an ingredient in successful advertising that is much less obvious. A new idea also has to be introduced, but this time it is one that must come from "left field." It is something totally unrelated to the brand itself.

With the De Beers campaign, the "left-field" idea is the love of a man for a woman. This is a very powerful thought, and it is totally unrelated to diamonds. The De Beers campaign works because it brings the brand-related and the "left-field" ideas together and causes them to fuse. The new idea that is created—the rearrangement of existing ideas—is that the durability of the diamond expresses the durability of the love; and that the beauty and value of the stones echo the way in which the giver regards the recipient.

Such fusion is at the heart of all successful advertising. The most perceptive student of the genesis of creative ideas, Arthur Koestler, coined the word "Bisociation" to describe the process of thinking up and selecting the two separate and initially unconnected ideas. When they are brought together, he called the process "Bisociative Fusion": an awkward phrase but one whose meaning is totally clear.

It is an interesting exercise to look at advertising campaigns with the idea of Bisociative Fusion in mind. I can think of large numbers of examples from my own professional experience, and I can see them on the contemporary advertising scene. An arresting example is the Marlboro cowboy; another is the frogs who croak the word *Bud-wei-ser*. The high-profile magazine campaign for Absolut vodka provides myriad examples of "left-field" thinking around the shape of the bottle. Other colorful examples are the mountain climbers in the Ford

Explorer commercial; the cat trying to jump through the plate glass window that has been cleaned with Windex Wipes; the swimming elephant in the Coca-Cola commercial; and the green gecko in the advertising for Geico Insurance. The most delightful example I can think of appeared during a Super Bowl break: an advertisement for a specialist technical organization based in Dallas, Texas—Electronic Data Systems (EDS). The commercial, a *tour de force,* demonstrates the complex and constantly changing process of handling large volumes of statistical data by featuring a crew of ranch hands herding a vast swarm of cats.

The brand-related and "left-field" ideas are the first two ingredients of a successful advertisement, and its degree of success depends largely on how powerful a fusion can actually be made to take place.

But a third ingredient is also needed. This is something much simpler to describe: what people in the advertising business call *production values.* These embrace every part of a television commercial—the camera work, the lighting, the voice-over, the sound effects, the music—and every element of a print advertisement—the writing of the body copy, the typography, the quality of the illustrations, the placing of the elements, the use of white space. With much advertising, these things are the product of polished craftsmanship. Although the content of advertisements is almost always ephemeral, the creative people in agencies, and the filmmakers and other talented people who take advertising ideas and express them in their finished form, work with painstaking care and often possess the highest degree of sensibility. They frequently manage to transform an advertisement—which is, after all, a piece of communication with a simple commercial purpose—into something that can be compared, in form if not in substance, with many exhibits in respectable art museums.

Production values provide another, rather subtle benefit. In the vast majority of cases, they provide depth and enrichment to a creative idea. However, in a small minority of cases—when the creative idea is actually weaker than was originally thought—the expensively acquired production values will expose the idea's inadequacy absolutely relentlessly. The advertising will communicate production values and little else. The client and the agency will therefore have to make a tough choice about whether or not to abandon the campaign, despite the money that has been spent on film production. (They will, however, be protecting the much larger expenditure on screen time, which might have been wasted.) I have come across this situation four times in my professional career, and in all cases the decision to abandon the creative idea was painful. It is important to remember that production values can *never* serve as a substitute for a creative idea.

Two Grab Bags

Bisociative Fusion is a subtle and important concept. The problem is how to put it into practice. What makes a bisociative relationship so difficult to find is that logic will not help us find "left-field" ideas. We use logic to isolate our brand-related signals, but, if we continue to follow a logical path in the hope of also finding an appropriate "left-field" idea, we very soon come to a full stop.

Interestingly enough, there is a well-known technique to solve the problem. This was most clearly set out by James Webb Young, whose concept of the fusion of ideas predated Koestler's, and is described by Young rather differently. He recommends working through a five-step process. The first step calls for a study of all aspects of the strategy, and this must be carried out thoughtfully and in great detail. After a break, the process is then repeated; the second digestion of the data must be as thorough and conscientious as the first. The third step is to lie fallow—to do nothing while the unconscious mind churns over everything that has been fed into it. The fourth stage is the magical one—the arrival of the idea itself, sometimes suddenly but sometimes quietly. The fifth stage is devoted to working out the idea into detailed advertisements.

I personally find this system effective and have used it for many years. However, it is important to follow Young's five steps meticulously, with no shortcuts. Young's system relies on the way the subconscious mind will roam around the problem and make connections. It is not, however, the only way that people write advertisements—or solve other types of intellectual problems for that matter—and a number of other systems have been published, all of which have been found useful by some people. What all the systems have in common is that the creative step is quite separate from the strategic step. There is a distinctly different mental process, in which the logic of the strategy gives way to the imagination and intuition of the creative leap. The myth that appears at the beginning of this chapter totally fails to detect this crucial change of mental gears.

Young talks a good deal about the personality and qualifications of the best creative people. He constantly reiterates the importance of a cultivated and wide-ranging mind. This is a point that can be illustrated with a metaphor of two grab bags (i.e., sacks filled with gifts into which children put their hands to select an unidentified parcel).

Consider the creative process as using two grab bags: one small and one very large. The small bag represents the accumulated information we have learned about the brand we are advertising, including everything we know about the strategy and why it was formulated in the way it was. The first two steps in Young's method describe the filling of this small bag. The brand-related idea is going to come out of it.

The large grab bag contains everything in the mind, memory, and experience of the person who is writing the advertisement. Obviously a person with a broad general education, wide experience, and a thoughtful mind set that stores things away will have much more material in his or her grab bag than a person with a thinner background and a less contemplative mind. This is where the "left-field" idea is going to come from.

Young's process of generating ideas—rearrangements of existing ideas—is like picking something out of the small bag and something out of the large one, and with luck finding a startling connection between the two things we take out. The fuller the two bags, the better the chance of finding something rather special to say about the brand.

The Locked Strongbox

One important final point about the creative process must still be made. For an advertisement to work, the first requirement is originality: an arrestingly unusual idea. This is the outcome of the processes discussed in this chapter. But although originality on its own is necessary, it is an *insufficient* criterion for deciding whether or not to spend money in exposing an advertising campaign. What matters even more is whether it will produce a behavioral effect; although originality is often associated with effectiveness, this is not always the case. Forecasting results is a much more problematic endeavor than judging originality. We have good evidence that advertising professionals (although not the amateur experts referred to in previous chapters) generally have the skill to evaluate originality, but they are much less good at forecasting whether an advertisement will actually produce the right sort of effect in the marketplace.

Many students of advertising would agree that we have a fair knowledge of one part of the creative process—idea generation. But some original ideas have to be thrown away, not because they are not original enough but because *an important extra is missing*. We need to know which ideas to keep and which to reject. Assuming that we judge correctly that our advertisement has originality, it is much more difficult to divine whether our advertising idea will actually sell soap (or whatever).

Because effectiveness cannot be ignored, subjective judgment is simply not good enough. The experts need some help. Market research can provide useful guidance, as we shall see in Chapter 14. That chapter has a good deal of ground to cover, and the journey must progress over a minefield of controversy. The best research technique can forecast reliably the likely effect of an advertisement on sales.

This research has been carried out into many thousands of advertisements. The conclusion that emerges fairly clearly is that successful advertising (i.e., advertising that tested well and also produced sales) contains a nugget—often no more than a hint or a reminder—of some of the functional properties of the advertised brand. Advertising can—and often is—substantially emotional, but a rational message is contained, as it were, within an emotional envelope. If there is an emotional envelope with nothing in it, however, the advertising will not work. This brings to mind another myth, one widely believed by the more vocal consumerists who believe in advertising's supposedly hidden power and perhaps by many members of the general public as well.

"The success of advertising depends not on its logical propositions but on the kinds of fantasies it offers. The world of ads is a dream world where people and objects are taken out of their material context and given new, symbolic meanings, placed on hoardings or on the screen where they become signs."

At the heart of the advertising enterprise—a $130 billion business in the United States alone—there is a locked strongbox that contains the most important secrets but that no one has been able to open. Perhaps we have not tried very hard. Researchers tend to shy away from the toughest problems because they think instinctively that the most important questions are those that are easiest to answer, and that if we have a lot of information this must *ipso facto* be valuable. We can make a good start at doing better by eliminating our prejudices against potentially useful research methods, such as the quantitative techniques discussed in Chapter 14.

7

Bursting the Dam Wall

Myth:

"One exposure of an ad to a target group within a purchase cycle has little or no effect in most circumstances."

The Imaginary Dam

Until recently, many advertising practitioners and academics believed the idea given in the quotation at the beginning of this chapter. Some still do. They visualize an advertising threshold or tipping point. If one exposure does not work, how many are needed: two? three? four?

Think of a large dam. The lake behind it holds millions of gallons of water. But the dam wall, the work of prudent engineers, is much higher than the water level. Then there are some totally unprecedented periods of rain, and the water level rises higher than it has ever done before. The water pressure builds up, and a fissure appears. Very dramatically, the dam bursts, releasing a mighty flood.

As the metaphor applies to advertising, advertisements for a brand run over a long period. The people receiving them supposedly store them in their heads but do not act on them. But eventually these people, having received so many vivid impressions about the brand from the advertising, are forced by the cumulative force of these impressions to rush out to buy it.

It is a fanciful but undeniably vivid theory, and it goes some way to explain the optimism—and perhaps even to pacify the latent doubts—of practitioners if they see nothing happening when they run their campaigns. The theory is, however, a myth. And it is a dangerous myth because it encourages advertisers and agencies to believe that no immediate effect is to be expected, and that they should go on spending money until the dam bursts. The best evidence shows that if a campaign is ineffective as soon as it begins to run, extra money spent on it will be totally wasted. A campaign that does not generate immediate sales does not build up pressure. The metaphor of the dam (like the dam wall itself) does not hold.

Because the theory is potentially so wasteful, we need to scrutinize it very carefully to find out whether it contains even the smallest grain of truth. In technical terms, we need to examine meticulously the *incremental effect of additional doses of advertising*. According to the bursting dam theory, the doses have to accumulate to a critical volume and pass a threshold before they produce an effect. True or false? It is false. And I shall show why.

Measuring How Advertising Produces Sales

Advertising specialists have always found it difficult to measure in any precise way the effect of advertising on sales; it was once considered an impossibly difficult task. Admittedly, for many years we have been able to measure some important things. For seventy years we have tracked accurately the sales of large numbers of brands in retail stores. For sixty years we have measured the purchasing of similarly large numbers of brands by consumers, with good information on the demographics of those consumers. For a multitude of brands, we have tracked sales and market shares going up and down, over short periods and long periods. The problem has been that we have not been able to calculate reliably and accurately how many of the "ups" in any brand's sales are due to consumer advertising; nor have we been able to estimate how many of the "downs" are because of other brands' advertising.

There are simply too many factors influencing sales in addition to the advertising. There are price offers, sampling programs, contests, buying incentives, media publicity, word of mouth, in-store displays, and retail distribution. As far as any individual brand is concerned, competitive activity plays a very important negative role. Finally, overall factors affecting all brands in the category influence the individual brands in it: seasonality, consumer incomes, fashions. For convenience, all these factors will be referred to as "sales stimuli." A group of advertising professionals once counted a total of thirty-six different sales stimuli. Advertising was also a factor, albeit a rather important one.

The problem, then, is to untangle the influence of advertising from everything else. This calls for a very special and rigorous type of research. However, if we *do* manage to discover a technique to measure accurately the effect on a brand's sales of any quantity of advertising within a particular period, we should be able to use simple arithmetic to subtract the effect of one advertisement, two advertisements, three advertisements, and more. In other words, we will have a method of measuring the incremental effects of advertising pressure. But the problem we are left with is the basic measurement of advertising and advertising alone. We have to find a way of eliminating the effects of all other influences on sales and calculating what is left.

The way natural scientists tackle such a problem is to use a controlled experiment. If they are measuring the properties of a chemical compound, they choose two identical combinations of chemicals but add a particular substance—one in which they are particularly interested—to one mixture but not the other. In the way in which the chemicals react against one another, there is likely to be a difference between the two compounds. This can be reliably attributed to the extra ingredient in one and not the other.

If we apply this principle to the advertising problem, the controlled experiment can be carried out by selecting two groups of consumers who are identical in demographics and purchasing habits. We monitor their buying of the brands in the product category we are interested in. Both groups receive the sales stimuli listed earlier. But one group receives advertising for a specific brand and the other does not. The buyers who do not receive advertising are responding to the sales stimuli, although much buying also follows habit. The extra sales by the group who receive the advertising are a result of the advertising on its own, because the sales stimuli and normal buying habits are the same for both groups.

This is the method used to measure the effect of advertising—and advertising alone—on the sales of a brand. The method is not unduly complicated, but it is extremely expensive to operate because we need to monitor continuously the buying and media viewing of a large sample of consumers. The technique is called "Pure Single-Source research," and the descriptive words need to be explained.

Single-Source means that there is a single place from which we get the information about the two most important things—the purchasing of each specific brand and the advertising received for that brand. For comparison, we also measure the purchasing without the advertising. This single place is each individual household—and every household is measured separately. The households that buy the brand are logged and grouped into *ad households* and *adless households*. *Pure* means that we take very great care to identify the specific brand bought and to relate this to the reception into the household of advertising for that specific brand during the previous seven days.

The way in which the research is carried out is to extract all the information from a single panel of 2,000 households, properly balanced demographically and covering all parts of the country. Because these households are statistically representative, their buying habits in each product category are typical of the country as a whole. And, of course, every household is like every other household in the way they receive sales stimuli for any brand.

For each brand in turn, we pick out, from the 2,000 homes, the buyers over the course of the whole year. We are interested in their numbers of purchases, because most buying homes buy twice or three times at least. All the analyses are based on the separate purchases in the individual homes. With most brands, the research provides at least 1,000 examples to work with. We isolate and count the buying occasions that were preceded by advertising for the brand that had entered the home during the previous week. We then put these *ad households* back with the other buyers of the brand. (This is because some buyers, stimulated by advertising, may have also bought without it.) We then carry out the same process for the buying occasions not connected with advertising. These are made by the *adless households*.

We then compare the average number of purchase occasions for the brand in the *ad households* and the *adless households*. This provides an estimate of the average short-term effect of advertising on sales. This has a name, STAS, which stands for Short-Term Advertising Strength. It is calculated as a percentage: the specific percentage by which the buying stimulated by advertising is above (or sometimes below!) the buying not stimulated.

The research is extremely laborious, and I shall give some additional details of how it is carried out in Chapters 10 and 12, which contain some more thoughts on the things discussed in this chapter. But for the time being, I have described all we need to know.

The Effect of Increased Pressure

As just described, we can measure the immediate effect of advertising—and advertising alone—on a brand's sales. Having done this, we can now subtract the sales associated with different amounts of advertising. We start by isolating the sales in households that have received one advertisement up to seven days before they buy the brand.

Here are some rounded figures that have come from six different investigations in five different countries. If the total sales driven by advertising are counted as 100 percent, 70 percent of sales are made in homes that have received only one advertisement; 20 percent are made following two advertisements; and 10 percent come from households receiving three or more.

These figures are derived from research studies based on large statistical samples, and they cannot seriously be disputed. Their meaning is quite clear.

- A single advertisement *can* have a very strong effect on sales. The degree of effect varies a great deal according to the campaign, but with effective campaigns the proportion of sales coming from a single advertisement is very high. Of course, with ineffective campaigns nothing happens at all.
- In comparison with the effect of a single advertisement, the extra effect of additional advertising pressure falls rapidly. This is clear evidence of diminishing returns—an important concept in the field of advertising measurement—which points dramatically to the wastefulness of high advertising pressure.
- Little extra effect is felt from more than three advertisements during a seven-day period. It is also true that very little effect is felt over a longer period than seven days.
- *Very importantly,* an advertisement must be written as a complete stimulus. It must be based on the assumption that, if it is going to be effective at all, it will work with a single exposure.

Where does all this leave the bursting dam? It of course shows that the theory is invalid. The first advertising exposure has far more effect on sales than subsequent ones, and after the limit of three advertisements there is very little effect at all. The time scale for advertising's immediate effect is also very short. Advertising *can* have a long-term cumulative influence on brands, but this is a totally different concept from the bursting dam. Advertising works in the long term to strengthen a brand, by increasing the rate of buying, and at the same time helping the manufacturer increase the brand's profitability.

If any theory is to be taken seriously, it should be propped up with at least some statistical evidence: evidence that will illuminate as well as provide some confidence in the theory's validity. One of the most striking features of the bursting dam is that no one has ever shown factually that it has ever operated with any real brand. It is, therefore, in a class of its own in unreality, even by the standards of other advertising myths.

Are Diminishing Returns Universal?

As explained, diminishing returns are the standard pattern when we measure the sales produced by increments of advertising. Sales grow but at a falling—usually sharply falling—rate. The reason for this, in terms of consumer psychology, is that successful advertising trips a small switch in the viewer's mind, normally prompting a fleeting recall of a favorable experience of the advertised brand. The advertisement does not have to be repeated.

But what of the (admittedly rare) cases of successful new brands? A new brand's name and attributes are by definition unfamiliar to consumers. Therefore, some advertising repetition is necessary for consumers to get the point. Whether they will actually look at the advertisement two or three times depends solely on how interesting they find the creative message. But if viewers *are* sufficiently intrigued by the message, what is needed is a maximum of three exposures over the period of a week; this pattern should be repeated over a relatively short period, normally no more than three months.

In the case of successful new brands, the short-term effect of advertising does not produce diminishing returns. It is more likely to show increasing returns up to the level of maximum effect—normally three advertisements—when viewers understand what the campaign is all about. This situation is rare and applies to no more than 5 percent of all national brands. And in no way does it resemble the bursting dam. It is, however, an important consideration for developing the media strategy for a new brand and is an example of a rather *recherché* piece of research that has direct operational value.

Diminishing returns rule, with rare exceptions. Diminishing returns mean that advertising should be written with the objective of producing an effect from a single exposure. Consumers must not be asked to store incomplete messages from a series of advertisements in the hope that a complete message will be composed from all the separate bits. Consumers will never take the trouble to do this, and the advertising budget will be wasted.

Part III

Advertising Investments, Promotional Expenditures, Media Strategy, and Media Tactics

Six Myths:

"In theory, the total promotional budget should be established where the marginal profit from the last promotional dollar just equals the marginal profit from the last dollar in the best nonpromotional use. Implementing this principle, however, is not easy."

"Consumer-goods companies normally devote most of their funds to advertising, followed by sales promotion, personal selling, and finally publicity."

"Sales promotion can be more effective than advertising in motivating customers to select a specific brand—particularly when all brands appear to be equal. . . . And certain promotions generate a more immediate, measurable payoff than traditional advertising campaigns."

"Contemporary broadcast television offers advertisers a variety of advantages over competing media—mass coverage, low cost, some selectivity, impact, creativity, prestige, social dominance."

"Although advertising has a greater ability to reach a larger number of people simultaneously than do sales promotions, it has less ability to prompt an immediate behavioral change."

"Continuity should match consumer-use cycles (the time between purchase and repurchase)."

A lthough the first statement appears to be sensible, it bears no rela- tion to how budgets are actually drawn up. The others are fallacies.

8

Overspending and Underspending

Myth:

"In theory, the total promotional budget should be established where the marginal profit from the last promotional dollar just equals the marginal profit from the last dollar in the best non-promotional use. Implementing this principle, however, is not easy."

"Gut" Feel, Opportunism, Extravagance

The quotation presented at the start of this chapter, as it clearly states, describes theory and not practice. It should not, therefore, be criticized because it is impossible to implement. ("Not easy" greatly underestimates the difficulty.) The major problem with it, however, is that it ignores the element that plays the most important part in determining real advertising and promotional budgets: entrepreneurial judgment.

This chapter is concerned mainly with advertising budgets, and the best way to study how manufacturers arrive at these is to look at some examples. Consider four different brands and how they responded to specific but different market conditions.

The first is Anheuser-Busch's Budweiser, longtime market leader in the American beer category (and the largest-selling beer in the world). Budweiser has always spent heavily on media advertising, and it has done this to keep the competition at bay. It has been very successful in doing this. Yet there are excellent reasons for thinking that the advertising could have done its work with much less money spent on it. A series of meticulously conducted market experiments made this precise point. They showed even more. Reduced advertising not only increased profit because of the money saved, but it also resulted in an increase in volume sales, boosting profit even more. But the reductions in expenditure did not last long, and Anheuser-Busch is today an extravagant spender. The company maintains what an informed observer has described as its reputation for "pouring money into advertising."

The second example is Lux toilet soap, once a leading brand in the American bar soap category. Lux was first marketed in the 1920s, but more than forty years later its market share had been forced down by the success of a number of strong competitors. When Lux's share had fallen to 5 percent—much less than its former share but still a respectable figure, putting the brand halfway down the list of the top twelve in the market—the manufacturer, Unilever, removed all advertising support. This decision was made on judgment. A choice was made between which brands deserved to receive support and which existing brands should be "milked," which means stopping advertising and taking the maximum profit (albeit at a falling rate because of the inevitable decline in sales resulting from the removal of advertising). The judgment was a narrow one and could very well have come down in favor of continued support for Lux. Such support would have led to at least a few more years of profitable life, while finding alternative uses for the funds meant taking a substantial risk, because much of the money was swallowed by new brands, most of which failed (as usually happens). Lux is still profitable today in most countries and continues to be advertised in many of them. In the United States, however, it has all but disappeared.

The third example is Warner-Lambert's Listerine, a very old brand that has always been the market leader in the mouthwash category. Listerine had things its own way for more than eighty years until it was confronted with a serious competitor, Procter & Gamble's Scope. With Scope's arrival on the national scene, Warner-Lambert immediately doubled Listerine's advertising budget. It is an open question as to whether such a huge increase was necessary. What made the greatest contribution to dampening the growth of Scope (whose market share has always remained below Listerine's) was a radical change in Listerine's advertising campaign to incorporate an extremely strong selling message. Because it was the campaign that really did the job, the new creative idea would have made much more effective use of Listerine's earlier and lower advertising expenditure. This would probably have made the large increase in the budget quite unnecessary.

The fourth brand is British: Oxo, a bouillon and soup concentrate in cube form that has been a household name for more than one hundred years. As in the case of Listerine, the strength of Oxo in the market kept out potential rivals. But eventually a dangerous competitor was discovered to be selling in a test region. This was a cube version of a familiar and well-liked brand of meat extract called Bovril. The new Bovril cubes were directly competitive with Oxo. The manufacturer of Oxo acted quickly to counter Bovril before the latter was rolled out into national distribution. Oxo's advertising budget was boosted and the content of the campaign was strengthened. The result was that Bovril was stopped in its tracks. Because the manufacturer of Oxo had reacted to potential competition even more swiftly than the manufacturer of Listerine had, Oxo's performance in protecting its position was even more decisive. But—also as in the case of Listerine—the change in Oxo's campaign was the decisive factor and the budget increase was probably unnecessary.

These four examples—which, from my experience of the advertising business, I find more typical than atypical—throw light on how manufacturers *really* address the important matter of setting an advertising budget. They rely on their "gut" feel: unsupported judgment (occasionally used with flair). They are invariably aggressive, impulsive, reactive, and sometimes more emotional than rational. As described in Chapter 1, budgeting is only too often a display of a manufacturer's *machismo* in the presence of its competitors and the retail trade. This is not a description of the budgeting process as it is pictured in the myth that appears at the beginning of this chapter.

Does the success of these four brands justify the present methods of budgeting? Should these policies be immune from criticism? The answer is "no." To make the best use of the statistical tools at our disposal, budget setting must be a process of maximizing the effect on the brand's profit of marginal increases and decreases in the money spent on advertising. It is excessively wasteful to depart from this process of careful measurement and to use an advertising budget like a sledgehammer (Budweiser, Listerine, Oxo), or like a gambling chip (Lux).

Although a budget should be the product of some process of calculation, the mathematical calculation that plays a part in most budgeting is unfortunately the most inappropriate one possible.

Spending What a Firm Can Afford

In any single year, a firm's total advertising and promotional (A&P) budget will always be fixed in advance. The principle used to decide it is the amount of money the manufacturer thinks it can afford to spend, while at the same time maintaining planned profit. If A&P spending goes up and sales remain only at the original target level (sometimes known as the "datum sales level"), profit will drop. If A&P spending is maintained as planned but sales fall below datum, profit will also drop. The biggest trade-off of all is between A&P and profit. After this there is a subsidiary trade-off within the A&P budget, between consumer advertising (known as "above the line") and sales promotions (known as "below the line").

Consumer advertising and sales promotions are inevitably competing for the same dollars. During the past twenty years, promotions have done better than advertising and have mopped up most increases in the total A&P expenditure. This trend has not been at all good for manufacturers' earnings, although it has benefited consumers because of lower prices and also retailers because their profits have gone up.

The division between advertising and promotions can move between one and the other during the course of a year, as well as in following years. In addition, the total amount does not necessarily remain the same every year, even if sales remain more or less unchanged. (We would expect the A&P budget to go up if sales increase and to go down if they fall.) As suggested in the last paragraph, there is a tendency for overall A&P expenditure to grow. Between 1997 and 2001, Procter & Gamble's total expenditure on everything except direct costs increased from 28 percent to 32 percent of the firm's revenue. Very large sums of money were involved here, and the largest part of this total of nondirect expenditure is represented by A&P. The example of Procter & Gamble is typical of most major consumer goods companies.

As a shorthand description of the process they follow to decide advertising expenditure, manufacturers generally use the "case rate" system, which means a certain number of cents or dollars of advertising for each case of the brand sold. The actually number of cents or dollars can go up and down year by year. It is a cheap and cheerful method, although there are some slightly more complicated variations, such as basing the arithmetic on this year's anticipated sales rather than last year's actual sales; or on this year's anticipated profit rather than last year's actual profit. These all more or less come to the same thing, in that they address the same question: "How much can I *afford* to spend?" Advertising is the only purchase that a manufacturer makes that is governed by the principle of what it can afford rather than what it needs to spend to do the job.

More than 90 percent of advertisers worldwide use this method. A small number of them use additional and more sophisticated procedures, but the majority of the 90 percent use the "case rate" and nothing else. Although the system appears to represent the most obvious type of common sense, it is based on an extremely serious flaw: one that is so obvious that it is astonishing that so few manufacturers and their agencies are conscious of what they are doing.

The defect in the system is that it is based on the internal cost structure of the brand. This is most certainly *not* the place where sales are determined. Advertising's sole justification is its ability to influence buying, which means that consumers should be the focus of attention. A brand's sales depend totally on the marketplace, and a budgetary system that looks inward into the brand and is totally disconnected from the marketplace cannot possibly provide a sound basis for estimating the amount of money needed to boost or even maintain the sales of any brand by influencing the behavior of its consumers. The result of the "case rate" is either overspending or underspending. Rarely is it the greatly more attractive alternative in between: spending the right amount.

Fact-Based Judgment

Deciding a brand's above-the-line budget would be much easier than it actually is if there were a *system* to help us do the job effectively. (One of the features of the "case rate" that makes it so popular is that it provides a simple routine.) Such systems, which are alluringly easy to follow, are normally a preferred alternative to using the brain, which is a very much more onerous procedure. Determining a brand's budget in the most reliable way possible calls for the use of judgment based on facts, to weigh the competing importance of a number of inputs from the marketplace, and eventually to reconcile these with what the brand can afford to spend if it is not to go into the red. The brand *must* eventually spend what it can afford, but affordability has a time dimension. We should accept the possibility of making less profit in the short term in exchange for making more profit in the long term.

Although budgeting can and should be a rational process rather than a matter of emotion and "gut" feel, one of the most important influences on it should be the competition, which is so often a source of irrational responses. But there is a method of measuring the influence of competition in a dispassionate and objective way.

Such an analysis of the competition is the first of three factors that advertisers should balance against each other when they calculate, using their best judgment, what should be spent above the line on any brand. The second factor is the brand's history, in particular how brands in the market have in the past responded to given amounts of advertising; the information here is usually incomplete and anecdotal, but it is always valuable. The third factor is a more difficult matter altogether: the use of hard data on the response of sales to specific levels of advertising expenditure in the past. This is done using techniques labeled, rather forbiddingly, "econometrics." Not many advertisers have the skill and resources to carry out the complicated mathematics needed for econometric analysis. But many major marketing companies in the United States do this routinely. Those that repeat their analyses year after year and that check forecast against reality are building a hidden *cache* of information of enormous present and future value.

As I write this, I have on my desk a series of econometric reports that each describes a year's performance of an important brand marketed by one of the largest consumer goods companies in the United States. These annual reports analyze in full detail the sources of sales (advertising, coupons, trade promotions, brand equity) for the brand. Such information makes a major contribution to determining efficiently the overall A&P budget, its division above and below the line, and the distribution of advertising among different media.

A Rational View of the Competition. It is not at all difficult to establish reliable facts about competitive advertising. Data on media expenditures by brands in most categories are published every quarter, and figures for even shorter periods can be provided. This information can be studied dispassionately, and important conclusions can be drawn.

To start with, however, we must find a method of comparing how important advertising is to brands of different sizes. Measured in dollars, large brands nearly always spend more money than small ones do, but this obvious piece of knowledge does not get us very far. We need a yardstick to examine *relative* expenditure. What is normal for a brand of a given size? What is normal for a larger one? And for a smaller one?

One can calculate this in one of two ways. The first is to work out a brand's spending above the line as a percentage of its net sales value. This gives a crude but realistic estimate of how important advertising is for the brand. But although we can do this easily for our own brand, it is much more difficult to do it for competitors because we can only guess their net sales value. The second, and more practical, method also involves comparing two separate things. The first is the brand's share of market (SOM), which is based on consumer sales and percentages of the brand's share of the total category. The second is the brand's share of voice (SOV), which is its share of total category advertising.

As a general rule, a brand's SOM should be approximately in line with its SOV, because of the similarity in cost structure between different brands in any market. If a brand of given size can afford to spend a given amount on advertising, we would expect a brand twice as large to spend twice as much.

Important exceptions exist, however, and because we have been studying these relationships for a long time we know quite a lot about these exceptions. And there are consistent patterns. Small brands invariably overspend (with SOV *higher* than SOM). Large brands invariably underspend (with SOV *lower* than SOM). A brand with an SOM of 3 percent will spend an average of 8 percent SOV. A brand with a market share of 24 percent will spend an average of 21 percent SOV. This comparison shows how the advertising for large brands is much more productive (i.e., in sales per dollar invested) than advertising for small ones. This is an important point that will be discussed in Chapter 13.

A table giving a range of SOV:SOM relationships as they apply to different-sized brands has been widely published, the information being based on hundreds of brands in many different countries. Using this table, it is an easy matter to start with a brand's market share and to calculate exactly what its share of voice should be: how much higher—or lower—than its share of market. This produces a reasonably exact dollar figure, representing an expenditure level sufficient to maintain stable sales, assuming of course that the brand does not have any abnormal features and that the campaign is effective. The differences in share of voice between brands of various sizes are fairly precise; if a large brand reduces its spending by even a point or two below the underspending that is normal for brands of its size, this will cut into the muscle and the brand will lose sales. There are dramatic examples to demonstrate this.

Each percentage point of SOV accounts for a good deal more than $1 million in most American product categories, and this represents many millions of individual advertising impressions on consumers. It is therefore not a surprise that small differences in SOV can have large consequences in terms of SOM.

As mentioned, the average relationship between share of voice and share of market is generally what is needed to maintain sales at a stable level. However, if a manufacturer is ambitious to use advertising to drive a major increase in market share, the brand's SOV must be set significantly above the normal level. Again, a certain amount is known about the levels needed to reach specific objectives. But there is no way in which these high expenditures can be economic in the short term, and their payout must be calculated on the basis of how much they can boost a brand's market share and how long the share can be maintained at this higher level.

A Brand's History. Brand managers change jobs regularly. Some of the changes stem from the restlessness of their personal ambitions; some are because of the constant desire of top managers of companies to inject new energy into their marketing operations. Irrespective of the advantages (or disadvantages) of such rapid change to the efficiency with which brands are managed, it is a fact that at regular intervals the past is forgotten. In choosing between two alternatives—being influenced by the past (and perhaps being subject to its tyranny), and making a new beginning with a clean slate—most companies will opt for the latter rather than the former. Forgetting the past may be common but it is very unwise.

In the 1980s, I wrote a book of nineteen real-world case studies. These were all based on full proprietary information I had received from the clients and agencies involved with these nineteen brands. One of the cases I remember most vividly was Listerine, discussed at the beginning of this chapter. As a means of collecting comprehensive information that was also easy to use, I went to the agency, J. Walter Thompson, New York, and was taken to a large gray metal cabinet that had two doors and that stood six feet high. Inside were the contents of a treasure trove.

I spent a hard-working but enlightening month eating my way through a formidable battery of research reports. What I found most directly valuable to my study were the agency's annual Review Board documents, which stretched back for almost twenty years. These provided a remarkably cogent and lucid account of Listerine's progress each year, detailing the reasons for its ups and downs, all based on good research.

Readers can judge for themselves the use I made of all this material in the study of Listerine that I published in 1989. The reliable and comprehensive data on the history of the brand told me precisely why particular advertising campaigns had succeeded (or failed) and what role the budget and media had played in that success or failure.

I drew an important general lesson from this experience, and this has been confirmed by many additional cases I have subsequently studied. Mature and prudent managers can learn really important lessons from the past without being dominated by it. This is the reason I have put the brand's history as the second factor that should influence the size of a brand's advertising budget. If the people responsible for the budget digest the lessons of the past, they will learn that previously successful experience is able to guide future policy. And not too many mistakes from the past need be repeated.

Econometrics. Econometrics is a word borrowed from macroeconomics. In the sense that it is used in advertising, it means calculating what contribution to a brand's sales is made by the various causes of these sales (known technically as independent variables):

1. advertising;
2. each of the other sales stimuli: coupons, trade promotions, and so forth;
3. the brand's equity, which represents its base sales that would be made without any help from advertising and promotions.

In making the estimates, econometrics zeroes in on the contribution of each independent variable on its own.

The process is laborious. It uses statistical information—separate quantities of data relating to each of the independent variables—and these are compared with the final outcome, that is, the brand's sales. Each separate mass of figures is run through computer programs using a technique known as "Multivariate Regression." This shows at least approximately the contribution of each stimulus. If total sales are expressed as 100 percent, the contributions of all the separate stimuli add up (or should add up) to 100. This process is described as "sales deconstruction."

There are many real difficulties with the technique, not least because very few nonspecialists can understand it. Most advertising decision makers are nonspecialists. The use of econometrics for advertising has not yet fulfilled its great promise. Nevertheless, econometrics, together with new methods of measuring advertising effects directly, has opened up a new world. Before these tools came into use during the 1960s, we knew virtually nothing about how advertising works.

It is possible, although difficult, to extend sales deconstruction to provide the most valuable of all tools to plan increases and decreases in a brand's advertising budget. This tool is a brand's advertising elasticity: the percentage rise in sales that will follow a 1 percent increase in advertising expenditure (independently of all other stimuli).

The average advertising elasticity tends to be low, with a 5:1 relationship between percentage increases in advertising and sales. In other words, a 1 percent advertising boost will cause sales to rise by 0.2 percent, and a 10 percent increase will lift sales by 2 percent. These are, as stated, average figures; in individual cases—depending on the effectiveness of the advertising campaign—the sales increase can be higher or lower (or zero).

The advertising elasticity is normally used to estimate the value of the extra sales to be expected from a decent-sized increase—say $1 million—in the annual advertising budget. It is not difficult to calculate the profit from these extra sales, after deducting the increase in production costs. Most important, this additional profit can be compared with the $1 million additional investment. This will tell us quite reliably whether or not the extra advertising pays its way. It rarely does; if we factor in long-term effects, however, the extra advertising can be seen to be profitable in many cases. The higher the advertising elasticity, the better the chance that increased advertising weight will be profitable. Andrex, an important British brand and market leader in the bathroom tissue category, provides an instructive example of how to use advertising elasticity to help with the advertising budget. This is described in Chapter 11; advertising elasticity is also discussed in some detail in Chapter 13.

A Balancing Act

The balancing act we must now carry out is to arrive at our budget by some compromise between two alternatives: the money called for by the market and the money that the manufacturer can afford to spend while maintaining the brand's planned profit. Once again, fact-based judgment must be our guide.

The place to start is the market, and in particular the three sources of information derived from it: information from the competition, the brand's history, and econometrics. Each will provide an approximate dollar figure for the budget. These must now be reconciled. When I have tried to carry out this process, I have found that the figures have not differed too widely, although any differences at all should be taken seriously. It is the best policy to start with—and give the greatest weight to—the competition, bearing in mind our objective for the brand: maintenance or sharp growth. The latter requires a large upward ratchet in the expenditure. The figure suggested from the competitive analysis can now be adjusted up and down with the help of the sales estimates that come from the brand's advertising elasticity. Finally, the whole thing can be checked for "reasonability" using the historical records.

When we have weighted these factors—competitive expenditures, the objective for the brand, elasticity estimates, and a check of the historical records—we will arrive at a round figure: ideally an exact amount but less ideally a top and bottom limit with a range in between. I will call this figure or these figures the external estimate, because it is derived from the market. The brand's budget has probably been based traditionally on the "case rate" system. If we apply this to the projected sales for the year ahead, we get a new figure—the internal estimate—because it is derived from the cost structure of the brand. We must now do our balancing, by reconciling the external and the internal estimates. We shall have to consider three possibilities.

The first is that the two figures coincide. This is rare, but it can happen. If we are fortunate enough to arrive at such a single figure, there is no difficulty in setting our budget.

The second possibility is if the internal estimate is larger than the external one, which means that we can actually afford to spend more than we need. This sounds like a delightful possibility. But implementing it is not entirely straightforward, because if the external were to be put into effect immediately, the spending on the brand would perceptibly drop. When this happens, we must be careful that there are no concealed dangers: ones that we were unable to detect despite the care we have taken to evaluate the data.

The best policy in this case is to downweight the advertising in a few substantial regions of the country for a period of at least a year. This downweighting must be done in regional media (and not network television or most national magazines, which can be used only on a nationwide basis). The performance in these regions should be carefully monitored, not only by measuring sales but also by tracking consumers' perceptions of the advertised brand and its competitors. The results of these measures can be compared with the rest of the country (where the traditional weight of advertising continues); if there is no weakening in the downweighted areas, the policy can be applied nationally, to the benefit of the brand's profit. If there is a marked weakening, however, we must go back to the drawing board, although we will have avoided the worst penalties of poor judgment, because the business in most of the country will be intact.

The third possibility is the most difficult one to handle. What do we do if the external estimate is larger than the internal one? In other words, we cannot afford to spend enough money to do an effective job. This suggests that the traditional level of advertising has been below the threshold of effectiveness, which inevitably raises doubts about whether the advertising has ever contributed much to the brand.

In these rather difficult circumstances, the best thing to do is to make what is effectively a new start and plan the progress of the brand over an extended future period: three years at the very least of higher advertising. During each year, sales can be assumed to take an upward path: a realistic outcome of the boost in advertising investment. In this plan, we must accept a reduction of profit in year one, but profit can perhaps be lifted up again in year two. And in year three, as a result of increased sales, profit could be quite a lot higher because of the scale economies of greater production, and this extra profit can go some way to compensate for the shortfall in year one. In year three, the brand will become stable at a higher level of sales, advertising, and profit than in the period before the first increase in spending. We can also be reassured by the strong likelihood that advertising is contributing to the brand's higher sales and generally healthier position in the market.

The processes described here are judgmental and frankly difficult. They are, however, a generally effective way of handling the complexity of the marketplace. Mechanistic systems like the "case rate" require much less effort, but I hope I have demonstrated that they are also very much less efficient.

9

Margins and How to Slice Into Them

Myth:

"Consumer-goods companies normally devote most of their funds to advertising, followed by sales promotion, personal selling, and finally publicity."

The Pipeline

The quotation given at the start of the chapter was published in 1984. It was even then seriously out of date. Today it is hopelessly so.

The best way to compare advertising and promotions is to use the metaphor of the pipeline, which describes how goods find their way from factory to consumers. It is of course a means of illustrating how merchandise flows through the distributive trade: either through wholesalers and small retail stores, or else through large stores that buy direct from manufacturers and where the majority of consumers do their shopping.

Trade promotions, which describe the different types of buying incentives directed at wholesalers and retailers, load goods into the pipeline at the manufacturer's end. Media advertising influences consumers and induces them to pull the goods out from the opposite end of the pipeline. Consumer promotions—temporary incentives of various types to stimulate consumers to buy—also have a "pulling" job to do. But they also "push," because they persuade retailers to increase their inventories in anticipation of the extra demand that is about to be created.

To discuss these activities, we need another pair of technical terms (ones that have already been used in this book). These terms are borrowed from the world of accounting: above the line (to describe media advertising) and below the line (to describe sales promotions of all types). Serious sums of money are involved both above and below the line. Total advertising and promotional (A&P) expenditure has been discussed in earlier chapters. Here I am going to concentrate in more detail on one part of the total: below-the-line spending. But before doing this, we must look briefly at what has happened to media advertising above the line so that we can make a comparison.

Over the past twenty years, the money spent on media advertising in the United States has more than tripled, from $41 billion in 1982 to $133 billion in 2001. This seems on the surface to be a huge increase. The period saw cyclical trends in advertising expenditure: upward from 1982 to 1988, downward from 1988 to 1993, upward from 1993 to 2000, then downward again in 2001 and 2002. Trends, because they go both ways, can come out in the wash if we choose a long period, like twenty years, for our period of measurement.

During the years between 1982 and 2001, advertising grew on average at a compound rate of 7 percent per annum: a reasonably high rate of increase. But a great deal of this is accounted for by inflation, which normally runs at an annual rate of 3 percent, which brings down the average increase in advertising to about 4 percent in "real" terms. The total amount of advertising is really determined by the size of the Gross National Product (GNP), which is helped by the normal population increase of about 1 percent per year. If the GNP goes up, advertising goes up; if the GNP goes down, the opposite happens. Because the GNP has climbed a lot since 1982, advertising has grown more or less in step. This means that advertising's contribution to business (which can be measured as a percentage of GNP) has not changed very greatly over the period. Media advertising accounts for about 1.35 percent of the GNP as a broad average, although in some years it is a little higher and in others a little lower.

Media advertising in real terms and calculated as a share of the GNP has not grown particularly strongly when viewed over the long term, despite what appear to be large dollar increases. But what has happened to sales promotions during these same twenty years? The story is quite different.

Pull Gives Way to Push

The figures of media expenditure just quoted are based on measuring the advertising in the different media: a laborious procedure that has produced reliable estimates for every year since 1948. The most authoritative statistics, and all the figures used here, come from Robert Coen, a respected specialist in the field who works for the Interpublic advertising agency group.

Making estimates of money spent on sales promotions is a much more difficult procedure. The largest item—trade promotional expenditure—is virtually invisible to statisticians because it takes the form of deals negotiated between manufacturers and retailers. We therefore have to find a different way of doing the sums. Incidentally, it is more accurate to use the words "promotional money" or "promotional expenditure" in preference to investment, because promotions do not often take the form of money paid out as part of a careful plan to build business and generate a return. Rebates and incentives to move goods quickly are really reductions in a manufacturer's income. They represent substantial money, but they are negative items in the accounts and not genuine investments.

Estimates of promotional spending have been made for every year since 1976, using a technique quite different from Coen's. They are based on surveys carried out every year among a representative sample of large advertisers. These advertisers are asked to quantify the proportions of their total A&P budgets that go into trade promotions, consumer promotions, and media advertising. Large advertisers account for a substantial but not overwhelming share of total advertising, so that the figures describing how they divide their A&P cannot be compared precisely with the advertising figures in the previous section, which were based on all media advertising by every advertiser in the United States. We can, however, compare the two sets of figures in a general way.

The first and most striking thing that has happened, according to the A&P figures, is that the share accounted for by media advertising above the line has gone down from 40 percent in 1982 to 24 percent in 2001. Because advertising has not fallen in absolute terms and has actually grown slightly, the only way we can explain advertising's loss of share is because spending below the line has gone up substantially. It is little short of amazing that three times as much money is now spent below the line as above the line (the exact ratio is 76:24). This trend is the most important thing that has happened in the marketing field during the past two decades and more.

The second change is that, although the share accounted for by consumer promotions has remained virtually the same, the money saved by holding back advertising increases has gone into trade promotions (mainly financial incentives to the retail trade), which have been boosted from 36 percent of the total in 1982 to 51 percent in 2001. More than half of all A&P now goes on direct rebates to the retail trade. Remember that the total A&P is now much larger than it was twenty years ago, so that the increase in funds allocated to trade promotions is now even more pronounced when measured in dollars.

We now come to another remarkable phenomenon. If we are to rely on what is written—in general media, professional journals, the trade press, teaching texts, business handbooks, the memoirs of distinguished practitioners, or anything of any sort written about advertising—advertising is presented as the only thing that matters. (A single small exception is a *cri de coeur* from David Ogilvy, which strikes a chord although his message is very brief and is emotional rather than empirical.) Even in the better books on the important subject of Integrated Marketing Communications, the things that are talked about are basic strategy, database marketing (i.e., stimulating repeat business from specific consumer groups), public relations, and consumer and trade advertising. It is quite impossible to discover from any of these sources that, in the world of A&P, it is sales promotions that have grown to a position of dominant importance. The myth at the beginning of this chapter—that manufacturers favor advertising over promotions—is indeed a myth. We have left the world of pull and entered the world of push. The question is why.

The Balance Tips Below the Line

It will be no surprise to readers to learn that the strength of the retail trade has had a great deal to do with the growth of promotional spending. Manufacturers do not like to be dragooned in this way and would much prefer to take more profit from their brands so that they can put some of this into media advertising to try to take business from their competitors. But the pressure from strong retailers is unrelenting, and most manufacturers regard it as painful but inevitable.

Strangely enough and despite the fact that manufacturers are uncomfortable with the power of their retail customers, very few are troubled by the influence of growing promotional expenditure on the health of their brands. The Association of National Advertisers (ANA) is the powerful professional organization representing all major advertisers in the United States: an organization that should obviously be interested in the topics I have just discussed. In 1996, I gave a speech at a major ANA conference in New York City in which I pointed out as strongly as I could the long-term dangers of overpromotion, and specifically how it will lead to a weakening of brand franchises. I was extremely surprised with the response to my words of warning. People in the audience showed much more politeness than alarm. My tocsin had sounded a cracked note.

As if to counter the negative effect of retail buying power, many manufacturers have convinced themselves that promotions are devices that can produce positive effects. (I should add that this attitude is strongest among manufacturing organizations that have not done their homework very thoroughly.)

What promotions *can* do is to shift volume: to lift sales dramatically (albeit temporarily). But to look at this point in more detail, we must compare two separate objectives of A&P activity: franchise building and sales generation. Franchise building means acquiring more end-users of the brand and encouraging them to buy repeatedly. It looks at today and, more important, tomorrow. On the other hand, sales generation drives purchasing at both the retail level and among consumers. Today matters; tomorrow matters hardly at all.

Media advertising is substantially franchise building. Trade promotions are totally sales generating. Consumer promotions do a limited amount of franchise building, but they are more concerned with sales. For franchise building, the best types of consumer promotions are premium offers. Unilever's Lux toilet soap (still an enormous brand outside the United States) for decades ran a series of highly creative promotions. Among the many interesting ideas Unilever used during the years I was associated with the brand, the one that sticks in my memory was a lottery for an elegant and extremely expensive sports car. The winner was chosen by a simple method. One single bar of Lux had the car key secretly embedded in it: something that produced an unimaginably delighted surprise for a single buyer. Collecting schemes also have some franchise-building effect. So does the extremely expensive process of house-to-house sampling of innovative new brands. All such ideas—ideas that have strong thematic values—offer great possibilities for in-store displays.

The majority of consumer promotions are price related, however: coupons, price-offs, banded packs (e.g., four for the price of three), plus other price reductions disguised with varying degrees of subtlety.

Of the total of A&P spending, about 33 percent is devoted to franchise building (24 percentage points accounted for by media advertising, plus a "guesstimated" 9 points from franchise-building consumer promotions). Sixty-seven percent goes to straightforward sales generation (fifty-one percentage points accounted for by trade promotions, plus a "guesstimated" sixteen points from consumer promotions). Another way of making this same point is that *two-thirds of all A&P is spent on price cutting or variations on the theme of price cutting.*

Sales promotions evoke no interest at all from advertising agencies, whose attention is confined to their media budgets. Consumer promotions that are genuinely franchise building offer considerable opportunities for the talents of creative people in agencies. Unfortunately, these people are as uninterested in "creative" promotions as they are in price-offs. In the eyes of agencies, all promotions are tarred with a brush figuratively labeled with the motto "Price cutting degrades the brand image and causes the business to go downhill." Agencies are not always wrong.

Why Many Manufacturers Like Promotions—and Why They Are Usually Misled

Sales promotions move goods from retailers' shelves into buyers' homes. More precisely, they move goods from retailers' shelves into buyers' store cupboards, because much buying on promotion results in a loading of household inventories: something almost certain to depress future purchasing.

One of the things that makes promotions attractive is that we can fairly easily measure their effect on sales, certainly in the cases of promotions that are really price reductions. These represent, as explained, 67 percent of all A&P expenditure—a sum that equals almost 90 percent of all promotional spending.

The effect of price reduction on sales can be measured with a method and name, price elasticity, first employed in microeconomics. The responsiveness, or elasticity, of sales to price changes is normally very high. A sample of more than 300 cases has produced an average elasticity of −1.8, which means that a 1 percent reduction in price will lead to a 1.8 percent increase in sales. All studies of price elasticity have been based on consumer prices and therefore apply to price-related consumer promotions. At the retail level, however, demand is also very sensitive to price changes. Therefore, there is no reason to doubt that there is as much price elasticity in the demand by retailers for goods from manufacturers, as there is in the demand by consumers for goods they buy in stores.

To explain the arithmetic in the simple way, on average a 10 percent price reduction will boost sales by 18 percent. The fact that price reductions have such an enormous effect makes them highly attractive to manufacturers, particularly to brand managers who hope to advance their careers on the back of stunning sales increases for the brands they manage. They are lured by the realistic possibility of making their sales shoot up by almost a fifth. But is this the end of the story? The answer is "no."

Promotions may boost volume, but they affect both receipts and costs. First, receipts: A brand's net sales value is slashed by the amount of the price reduction. A dime-on-the-dollar price cut means a 10 percent reduction in receipts for all the merchandise sold on promotion. Second, costs: Promotions sell many more goods, but the manufacturer must pay the direct costs involved in producing these. Direct costs include raw material, packaging, and piece-work labor, and together these can account for as much as 60 percent of total costs for certain types of product, food in particular.

Manufacturers are therefore hit in two ways. The increased volume is accompanied, for every unit sold, by less money coming in and more money going out. As a result, promotions always slice deeply into a brand's margin. A substantial proportion—perhaps as many as three-quarters—of all price-related promotions *reduce profits significantly.* The manufacturer earns less from the larger volume of goods sold on promotion than on the much smaller volume he or she would have sold without the promotion. A cynic once described promotional activity as a demonstration of the death wish.

I have not talked at all about the long-term dangers of promotions because the immediate effects are bad enough. But the additional long-term problems are very real. First, the effect of promotions on sales is always temporary: Sales come down again as soon as the promotion comes to an end, sometimes to below-average levels (as explained earlier) because consumers will have bought ahead. Second, promotions fuel the flames of competition. Promotion is met by retaliatory promotion, and the stakes are raised at each stage. The third point is that agencies are usually correct in thinking that promotions devalue the image of the brand in the eyes of consumers. The brand begins to lose the esteem of its users, a generally irreversible process.

Readers must be wondering why manufacturers go on promoting their goods in such an unthinking and irresponsible fashion. Part of the answer is that they are forced to do so by the retail trade and also of course by their competitors. But—perhaps more important—there is a self-destructive force within the management ranks of many companies. This drives decision makers to concentrate attention on share of market at the expense of the profitability of their brands. The poetic (and tragic) outcome of this is that if one manufacturer leads the way along the promotional route to boost its market share, all other manufacturers will follow and the first manufacturer's share will soon go down again.

This is precisely what happened during a stage in my career when I handled the advertising for a leading brand of laundry detergent in Denmark. Over a period of three years, all the major manufacturers in the category followed the course charted in the previous paragraph and rapidly went down the route of funneling money below the line. By the end of this period, all shares of market had settled back to their previous levels. The only difference was that all three manufacturers in the category had by now lost all profit from their detergent brands.

Finally, it must not be thought that orgies of promotion are confined to manufacturers that sell their goods in food and drug stores. Sales of new cars in 2001 and 2002 were driven by the incentive of zero percent interest on car loans: the equivalent of a rebate of some thousands of dollars depending on the car model. Because the competing manufacturers have followed one another, none has gained any permanent advantage and all have seen their profit eroded. Detroit's share of the American car market, having slipped from 73 percent in 1996 to 63 percent in 2002, is "on course to fall below 50 percent within a decade."

This chapter began with a myth. It will conclude with another:

"Sales promotion can be more effective than advertising in motivating customers to select a specific brand—particularly when all brands appear to be equal. . . . And certain promotions generate a more immediate, measurable payoff than traditional advertising campaigns."

The first problem with this statement is that established brands in any category are never seen as equal, because they are differentiated both in functional terms and by their added values. The second problem stems from the word "payoff." If the authors of the quotation mean the relative profitability of advertising and promotions, their statement is unambiguously wrong.

10

Fishing in Different Parts of the Pool

Myth:

"Contemporary broadcast television offers advertisers a variety of advantages over competing media—mass coverage, low cost, some selectivity, impact, creativity, prestige, social dominance."

A Branch of Show Business

The quotation at the start of this chapter is a good example of received wisdom that is accepted by large numbers of people in the advertising world. Yet it has a fault line running through it. By claiming television's overall superiority to competing media, the statement conceals the fact that, in some respects, alternative media provide greater benefits to advertisers than television does. Television has nevertheless developed a powerful mystique among advertisers and agencies, and it has established a special position for reasons that transcend its objective merits. This is the main concern of this chapter.

Major national brands in the United States weight their advertising media heavily toward television (with the sole exception of the "sin" products, cigarettes and hard liquor, whose advertising is kept away from television because of legal restrictions and agreements within the advertising industry). Seventy percent of advertising for the largest marques of automobile is devoted to television; 80 percent of that for the largest brands of repeat-purchase package goods; 93 percent of that for the leading fast foods. Individual brands have proportions even higher than their category averages. The figure for Volkswagen is 81 percent; for General Mills breakfast foods, 90 percent; for KFC, 98 percent.

Although television's share of all media advertising in America is only 41 percent, these very much larger figures should not surprise us too much, because we are so accustomed to seeing advertisements for the largest firms in all product categories when we watch television. However, the reasons for this degree of concentration are worth exploring. Is it because large national brands naturally choose the largest national medium, which is considered by many advertising people to be television? This assumption is not totally correct, and anyway this argument cannot provide a complete explanation; because all these advertisers use massive amounts of spot (i.e., local) as well as network (i.e., national) television, this means that regional advertising must be very important to them all. Newspapers and radio both offer excellent regional coverage yet are used relatively sparingly by large advertisers.

The real reason for such a heavy use of television must simply be because there is some underlying philosophy that all large advertisers share. I have myself observed for years a powerful—and surprisingly uniform—belief that television is the strongest advertising medium for contributing to the sales and profits of these large but variegated organizations. Television has a very special magic that attracts large amounts of business from rich advertisers. Advertising is conventionally regarded as the best medium for brand building. This view is partially true, but not totally so. This is because advertisers reach this conclusion from their use of television alone, and the relative merits of alternative media have rarely been explored.

One of the most striking characteristics of advertisers' media plans is that they change very little from year to year. This means that large advertisers' experience has for a long time been largely confined to television, so that many of them have no recent knowledge of the selling ability of alternative media. Pre-tests of advertisements are almost totally confined to television. And there has historically been very little work on how advertising in other media actually performed in the marketplace (although much interest has been taken in this subject since the mid-1990s).

Decades ago, General Foods—always an enlightened advertiser—required every year that its brand managers examine the whole range of media alternatives for its brands. No advertisers do this today. The general attitude seems to be that "television has done well for us in the past and we shall go on using it in the future without asking any questions."

A range of quantitative and qualitative arguments are made in favor of television. The audience numbers persuade advertisers that it offers complete national coverage (a notion that will shortly be examined). It is considered to be unequaled in its ability to deliver a mass audience quickly if not instantaneously. The Super Bowl has a special place in the life of the American public and has a magical attraction to advertisers that can pay the price. Other arguments are subjectively evaluative. Television is widely believed to provide a captive audience and an absence of distractions, so that viewers sit transfixed by the advertisers' messages. Television is judged to attract more than one of the senses by offering the combined advantages of picture, movement, and sound. It can demonstrate products in action. It can communicate mood.

Above all, television is a glamorous medium. Advertisers like to have their advertisements talked about by their colleagues and competitors (and also by the public, although this is more rare). Large advertising agencies have clients that can afford the sometimes astronomical production costs for commercials; they relish the process of making high-profile films and going to award shows to receive prizes: rather *kitsch* plaques and statuettes with which to adorn their offices. Creative people in agencies get better jobs on the strength of their personal show reels. (In Britain, account executives are sometimes also recruited in this way.)

It is not surprising that all large advertising agencies devote at least two-thirds of their clients' advertising budgets to television. The perceptive advertising journalist Randall Rothenberg once called the advertising agency profession a branch of show business. People who know how advertising agencies operate can readily appreciate what he meant. Television may in reality be nothing more than a commercial device for delivering advertising messages (and an overloaded one at that), but creative people in agencies take a different view of it. They relish all the show business trappings: the location shootings in exotic places, the close relationships with prominent actors and actresses, the glittering film productions often under the control of world-famous directors.

There is, however, another, more rational, explanation for agencies' love of television. The medium is more profitable to them than other media are. A single film can be exposed a large number of times to support a sometimes massive screentime expenditure. By contrast, newspaper and magazine advertising demands the labor-intensive production of multiple variations of a single advertisement to cover relatively modest expenditures on advertising space. Note how this argument favors the agencies and not the clients.

The points made in the previous four paragraphs about the advantages of television have floated around the advertising industry for so long that they have become accepted without any question at all. We need to take a hard look at them. The nonrational arguments and the importance accorded to them demonstrate the fallacy of the myth that appears at the beginning of this chapter: that selecting advertising media is a rational process based on measures of audience and cost.

Do Media That Attract the Most Advertising Dollars Have the Greatest Horsepower to Produce Sales?

It would be logical to expect the distribution of clients' budgets between different advertising media to be approximately in line with the relative ability of those media to produce sales. Surprisingly, the real world shows a very different picture. This is a matter about which we are fairly well informed.

Because major advertisers spend so much of their total expenditure on television, television also attracts the largest quantity of research funds. These are devoted to many different aspects of media measurement; (1) the size and characteristics of the audience; (2) comparisons of the cost of reaching different groups of people, sometimes using calculations of considerable sophistication; and (3) the medium's sales-generating efficiency. The money to fund this research comes mainly from the media themselves, but advertisers also spend a great deal, and market research companies and advertising agencies have (at least in the past) funded some important studies.

The cost of monitoring continuously the size of the television audience is extremely high, but this is accepted because the information forms the basis for all advertising rates and thereby controls the expenditure of more than $50 billion per annum in the United States alone. This type of measurement is not our concern here, however. Our focus is on how efficiently the advertising on television (and for comparison the advertising in other important media) positively influences sales. More accurately, we are going to examine how much advertising in these different media increases the sales of small brands and protects or marginally boosts the sales of large ones. No attention will be paid to the influence of campaigns on consumers' knowledge of brands and their attitudes to their various features and characteristics. The concentration will be on hard measures of sales volume: measures that can be related tentatively to profit and loss.

Many large advertisers carry out research to estimate the sales directly attributable to their television advertising. In doing this, the research attempts to exclude the effect of all other influences: advertising media other than television, promotions of various types, and overall market forces, such as consumption trends, competition, and seasonality. Many advertisers look at print and radio advertising as well, but these media are normally lower on the totem pole. The research is carried out brand by brand; and the results are never published, because they are bought at great expense for the contribution they make to marketing plans, which are of course confidential.

This type of research normally uses Multivariate Regression, a technique derived from macroeconomics. It is a complicated statistical method that compares figures from different independent influences on sales with a dependent output, the sales themselves. The aim is to measure the relative importance of each independent input. This is information that should be—and often is—of considerable help in deciding how to allocate a brand's advertising budget between different media.

However, the most familiar research into the effect of advertising over a broad range of brands was not based on regression analysis. It was derived from the Pure Single-Source method, outlined in Chapter 7. It was possible to publish the information only because the individual brands were not identified. The investigation provided a good general picture of the packaged-goods field because it covered a total of 142 brands.

This study was based on fieldwork done in the United States in 1991 and 1992 by the ACNielsen Company. As described briefly in Chapter 7, it was confined to the influence of television on sales, and it did the job by dividing into two groups the households making every purchase of every brand on a list: (Group A) those that had received identified advertising for it during the seven days before purchase (the *ad households*), and (Group B) those that had not (the *adless households*). In all other respects, including their exposure to promotions, the households were identical. We could therefore easily calculate the sales driven by advertising (and advertising alone) by deducting B from A.

The research revealed for the first time some important truths, two in particular. First, *there is an effect* from television advertising. Thirty percent of campaigns produced a powerful and immediate sales jolt. Another 10 percent contributed to maintaining the sales of large brands. This meant that the overall effectiveness rate was 40 percent. The average sales increase across all the brands in the sample was 18 percent, a remarkable figure considering that 60 percent of campaigns had a weak or even negative effect. By the end of the year this 18 percent had gone down to 6 percent, however, and only 20 percent of brands remained well ahead.

The second point about television advertising is that *a single exposure produces nearly all the effect.* High levels of frequency are unnecessary. Because of diminishing returns they are also very wasteful.

It was clear from this research that television advertising *can* work very well: a point that was encouraging to media owners as well as advertisers and advertising agencies. However—and this is a very important qualification—it works in a highly selective way. Effectiveness is a matter of the right campaign.

This research has been replicated, producing substantially similar results, in the United States and a number of foreign countries. The general conclusions are no longer a matter of dispute, although there was enough dispute at the beginning, among media specialists in particular. This research told a very positive story about television, but it said nothing about any other media. This became a gradually growing concern, and during the course of the 1990s at least three series of research studies addressed the sales effectiveness of advertising in other media, especially magazines, and how this compares with television.

The first investigations were in Europe: in Germany, Denmark, and Norway. Pure Single-Source research was used to cover magazines, and it was discovered—to many people's surprise—that a single magazine advertisement could have an immediate effect not much different from a single television advertisement. Again, the effect was highly selective. As with television, the productivity of magazine advertising depended on the campaign.

The second study took place in the United States and was made possible through the discovery of a way of simulating Pure Single-Source research by making a special analysis of a massive quantity of historical information on specific magazines received in homes and the buying of brands advertised in those magazines. Again it was found that there was much variation among campaigns. But from a large sample of campaigns, the average sales effect of a single magazine advertisement was found to be a sales increase of 19 percent: a strictly temporary effect, as had been found with television. The reader will note the startling similarity between the magazine figure of 19 percent and the television figure of 18 percent, discussed earlier.

The sharp effect of a single print advertisement should have caused no surprise to researchers. A remarkable work, published in the United States as long ago as 1972, had demonstrated quite clearly that newspaper advertising can produce just such an effect. The paper describing this research had been entitled, appropriately enough, "What One Little Ad Can Do."

The third investigation (or series of investigations) of the capacity of different media to produce sales was made with the use of regression analysis. The example I shall give is typical of many others, most of which remain unpublished.

In the late 1990s, the prominent econometric analysts Marketing Management Analytics (MMA) made a detailed study of 35 prominent American brands of repeat-purchase packaged goods. This was an exceptionally rigorous work because the econometric model was applied to each brand every year for a number of years. This made it possible to check forecasts against reality. Not many models do this.

The aim of the studies was to break up—deconstruct—each brand's sales in order to estimate the proportion in any year that could be attributed to (1) three advertising media, analyzed separately; (2) two promotional activities, again treated separately; and (3) the brand's equity, that is, the sales that would be made in the absence of any media or promotional support. The results were computed in two ways.

Payback: Dollar Input/Dollar Output. Payback means the financial return from a dollar spent on each activity; it is calculated by deducting the direct and indirect production costs of the extra sales from the value of these sales. This is a neat and accurate method of measuring the intrinsic horsepower of each advertising medium (and each promotion) to produce sales, because it demonstrates the return per dollar and therefore factors out the varying amounts of money spent on each medium.

The findings of this analysis were remarkable. On average, television was found to return 49 cents on the dollar; print (i.e., magazines and newspapers), 91 cents; and radio, 114 cents. The high figures for print and radio are quite striking, but they should be interpreted with some care (for reasons to be examined later in this chapter). A separate and recent series of figures relating to products other than packaged goods also shows other media performing better than television.

The point I make here is a simple one. Nothing in these figures helps explain why advertisers spend so much more money on television than they do on other media advertising. In terms of sheer horsepower, television in fact seems to perform comparatively badly. This refutes with great emphasis the myth at the beginning of this chapter.

Deconstruction: Sources of Sales. When the sales in any year were broken down into their various individual sources, 4.6 percent were due, on average, to television; 1.7 percent to print; and 1.2 percent to radio. The reason for the superior productivity of television should now be obvious to the reader. The difference is certainly not the result of any intrinsic superiority of television to produce sales. It is a straightforward effect of the larger number of dollars spent on it.

This skew of expenditure continues year after year with most large advertisers, and television's effectiveness—or perceived effectiveness—has perpetuated it. But this bias has concealed the advertising opportunities available from alternative media: media whose latent strength is certainly no less than television and which in some circumstances can be greater.

There is also a special influence that perpetuates and even exaggerates the strong balance of media money in favor of television. In two circumstances—when advertising is reduced overall (as happened in 2001), or when the cost of using television rises out of line with other media—the proportion of advertising budgets going to television can actually *increase*. Advertisers refuse to sacrifice their television schedules although they will give up much of their advertising in other media, because they believe instinctively that the latter form of advertising is less valuable. Thus the other media suffer disproportionately (again as happened in 2001). They become financially weaker, with fewer pages and probably lower circulations. This makes them less effective for advertising purposes and thus less attractive to advertisers. Economists have a name for this unexpected consequence. It is called the Giffen Paradox. (This paradox was named after a nineteenth-century economist who discovered that, if the price of bread went up, poor people bought more of it. They could not afford meat, and the bread was the cheapest "filler.")

Does Television Reach All the Fish in the Pool?

In Chapter 5, we looked at the size and spread of target groups for major brands of consumer goods. Users of big brands represent large although not dominant numbers of people, and they are always distributed over the population as a whole. Even with brands bought by a greatly above-average percentage of people in small demographic pockets, there are many more buyers outside the pockets than within them. The fish are swimming all over the pool, and the individual shoals are anything but densely crowded.

Because of this wide spread of users, the advertising for large brands really needs to cover the whole population. One of television's greatest strengths is its supposed ability to reach the total population, because virtually every home in the United States owns a television set. It is dangerously misleading to rely on this simple fact, however, because it is not true that everybody can be *reached* by television advertising, despite the universal presence of television sets in American homes. The facts are quite clear.

Viewers vary a great deal in the amount of television they watch. The population can be ranked on a continuum from the heaviest users (who spend all their waking hours in front of a screen) to the lightest (who do not watch at all). The 60 percent of heaviest viewers represent the real television audience. The 40 percent of lightest viewers watch the screen for a relatively small number of hours, and they choose programs selectively. As might be expected, lighter-viewing homes tend to be above average in both incomes and education. And these are people who are important to most advertisers because of their purchasing power. If an advertiser increases its advertising budget to try to reach a greater number of light viewers, it will not succeed. The result will be that heavy viewers will view the campaign even more often, so that the productivity of the overall television expenditure will decline because of diminishing returns.

This is an accurate general picture and the lessons apply to all brands. But there are refinements. Recent developments in market research have begun to identify the television programs viewed most, not just by the population as a whole or by specific demographic groups, but by *actual and potential users of a brand,* for example, sufferers from a common ailment who are therefore in the market for branded remedies to treat it. This research adds precision to the way in which we deploy a media budget among specific television programs. In the pharmaceutical field, some of the advertising schedules based on this research reduce the expenditure on television, but in other cases they increase it slightly.

These are, however, only changes at the margin. In no circumstances can television be regarded as ubiquitous. Belief that it reaches everybody has led too many large advertisers into the trap of missing large numbers of people. Advertisers whose brands are used by the population as a whole spend most of their budgets reaching only 60 percent of it.

In addition to this disturbing fact, there is a second limitation to television's value: one that stems from its very popularity among advertisers. The advertising for the majority of brands produces diminishing returns: more expenditure, smaller increments of sales (i.e., lower selling effectiveness). This process also works in a general way with media: more expenditure on each medium, lower selling effectiveness. Because large advertisers concentrate their budgets to such an extreme degree on television, it should not surprise us that the sales results are weakening. The average payback has been brought down by the dwindling effect of less productive increments of expenditure.

Diminishing returns to advertising on television are driven by the fact that most viewers are saturated by the number of hours their sets are switched on. Television viewing is low involvement, with decreasing amounts of attention paid to both programs and advertisements. The commercial difficulties being encountered by the TiVo system, which makes it possible for viewers to "cherry-pick" programs and exclude advertisements, provide persuasive evidence that most viewers do not feel strongly enough about the programs and advertisements to be selective about the former and switch off the latter.

In contrast, magazines and radio have much smaller volumes of advertising money spent on them, with the important result that their productivity has not begun to decline. This is the explanation for the difference in the sizes of the payback figures for print media (91 cents) and radio (114 cents) in comparison with television (49 cents). The figures for print and radio are based on relatively small samples, and I believe that they slightly overstate the superiority of radio and print media over television. However, the *general* relationship among the productivity of the three media is certainly valid. Television is the weakest of the three.

A very large increase in total expenditure on magazines and radio would certainly lead to diminishing returns there as well, so that these media would eventually be unable to hold their present high levels of payback. But the present expenditures on these media are so much smaller than those on television that there is a good deal of leeway to be made up before their productivity begins to fall.

Where Does This All Leave the Perplexed Advertiser?

Television has always offered and continues to offer great benefits to advertisers, and it has an impressive track record of success. But it is also difficult to dispute the incompleteness of television's coverage, or that the horsepower—productivity per dollar—of television advertising is no greater than that of other media.

Because large advertisers see the fish they are trying to catch swimming in all parts of the pool, their most sensible path is to scale down their total expenditure on television to a percentage of the total budget in line with television's coverage of the population: nearer 60 percent than the 80 percent or more that is so common at present. Other media should be used to fill the gap, and these should be planned to reach the demographics of light television viewers, because these are the people whom the additional media must reach. One of these extra media could well be the Internet, which has an as-yet unrealized potential, and this use for it could become important.

Because media coverage of target groups is so imprecise, many people who see a brand's television advertising will also be exposed to its advertising in other media (and vice versa). This crossover effect is an advantage because there is synergy between advertising in multiple media. People get hit from different directions with different versions of the same message.

The recommendation to increase the use of other media makes sense only on the assumption that the people who create the advertising will bring as much talent and enthusiasm to the job of writing for print and radio as they do to television. More than twenty years ago, David Ogilvy was seriously critical of advertising agencies' loss of skills in handling print advertising, but there is no evidence at all that practitioners have heeded his words, even within his agency, Ogilvy & Mather.

The advertising agency business is changing rapidly and it will be some years before its position on the marketing landscape becomes firmly settled. One way in which agencies can stake out a place for themselves is by extending their range of professional interests and activity to a broader advertising world than that of the small screen, and they will thereby become a less important branch of show business. They will do this by expanding their range of creative skills and developing a greater degree of scientific objectivity than they possess at present. The real difficulty will be for them to do all these things without also losing their magic touch with television. Television will continue to be an important medium for large advertisers, but it will be to advertisers' advantage if its share of the total pie were to be reduced. Even if it continues to be the number one medium for major advertisers, it is more appropriate that it should be more *primus inter pares* than it is at present. (The people in J. Walter Thompson, where I worked for more than two decades, were uniformly well educated. *Primus inter pares* was a favorite phrase, and we considered it rather *déclassé* to use the simpler English expression, "first among equals.")

11

Regularity and Frequency

Myths:

"Although advertising has a greater ability to reach a larger number of people simultaneously than do sales promotions, it has less ability to prompt an immediate behavioral change."

"Continuity should match consumer-use cycles (the time between purchase and repurchase)."

Media Planning: Fashions and Anachronisms

The two statements at the beginning of this chapter are seriously flawed. They both directly concern media tactics, that is, the most appropriate way to distribute advertising budgets over time, and they should be discussed together. Media tactics are generally considered to be related to consumers' buying habits. However, this relationship is rather more subtle than is usually realized.

Most people buy everyday goods with great regularity. But we differ a great deal in the frequency with which we buy those things we purchase regularly. Although we do our shopping every week, we do not buy everything every week. Some of our purchases are high frequency; others low frequency. Perishables and goods we consume fast—breakfast cereals, cat food, salad dressing—are weekly purchases. But we buy other things at less frequent although still regular intervals; an example is toothpaste, which most of us buy every three weeks. Three weeks is looked on as a very common purchase interval in the field of repeat-purchase packaged goods. In the United States we are increasingly going to warehouse-type retailers (such as BJs and Sam's Club) for shopping in bulk for goods that can be easily stored. Nevertheless, the supermarket remains our main point of contact with most brands.

With all regularly purchased goods, advertising has little or no influence on whether or not we buy a product on our weekly shopping trip. (By product, I mean one brand or another in a category.) We decide which product to buy according to whether our last pack has been used up. Sales promotions can have some effect on product buying, encouraging us to build up household stocks at low promotional prices, which means that we will not be buying after the next regular three-week interval, nor perhaps three weeks after that. But advertising rarely if ever has such an effect.

Although advertising does not influence *product* purchase, it is quite capable of influencing the consumer's selection of a brand if the product is already on the shopping list. This is actually how most advertising works. This simple fact means that frequency of advertising messages has always been an important consideration in planning advertising campaigns. Most professionals believe, with good reason, that they should advertise their brands shortly before people make their product purchases.

During the 1970s, the idea emerged that the consumer had to see three advertisements for a brand if this advertising were to influence purchase of it, and, as discussed in Chapter 7, these advertisements had to appear shortly before the actual buying. This idea was supported by psychological theory but only the most fragmentary evidence on actual purchasing. Nevertheless, the idea took hold and became the basic strategy for most media planning in the United States and in other countries. It was invariably referred to by a well-known name: the Effective Frequency doctrine. A book was written about it.

There is, however, a large hurdle between the theory and its implementation. It is impossible to buy television time in such a way as to provide three exposures and no more, because the television audience is strongly biased toward heavy viewers. The more we increase our media weight to achieve three exposures (described technically as Opportunities-to-See, or OTS), the more we reach heavy viewers rather than light ones. By the time we have achieved the planned repetition among light viewers, vast numbers of homes will be receiving many more than three OTS. The situation was even worse in the cases in which advertisers followed a temporarily fashionable doctrine called "impact scheduling," which was based on a blind and unsupported belief in the cumulative effect of multiple exposures. The policy led for a time to an unproductive and expensive degree of repetition and as a result a spectacular waste of resources.

In all circumstances, frequency builds astonishingly quickly when we try to boost the *average* number of exposures even modestly. We calculate media weight by Gross Rating Points (GRPs), one GRP representing 1 percent of all homes with a television set switched to the channel at the time the advertising for the brand is running. Twenty GRPs can mean 20 percent of homes exposed once, or 10 percent of homes exposed twice, or other variations (e.g., 5 percent viewing once, 3 percent twice, and 3 percent three times). If we are planning a 35 percent coverage of women aged 25 to 54, getting them *once* means sixty GRPs. Getting them *twice* means 180 GRPs. Thereafter, the weight climbs fast. Concentrations of GRPs, known as "flights" (and in Europe as "bursts"), often built up to 400 or more in a three-week period, as media planners tried to achieve an average of three exposures. We sometimes even see this weight in schedules today.

For more than two decades, the standard pattern of media planning was heavy flights run over three-week periods; the three weeks represent the average purchase interval for large numbers of products. Such heavy clustering of weight into relatively short flights meant that advertising budgets were soon exhausted, and large gaps were opened up over the course of a year. For the vast majority of brands, there were many more weeks without advertising than weeks with it. Gaps do not matter too much in periods of low seasonal sales, but the gaps also covered periods of high sales. Naturally, when a brand is unadvertised it will lose sales to competitive brands that are being advertised effectively during these gaps.

In summary, therefore, two principles were at work in this type of media planning based on concentration into short flights: (1) Effective Frequency, and (2) advertising to cover the purchase cycle. We shall now look at how valid these principles are.

Two Traps for the Unwary

Since the mid-1990s, it has been perfectly clear that the Effective Frequency theory has no basis in fact. As we saw in Chapter 7, reliable evidence has now proven that a single advertisement is capable of a large effect on sales; when we add further advertising, this causes sales to grow at a rapidly diminishing rate. Concentration of media weight means waste of scarce resources. This evidence was a great surprise to the advertising industry, although, when the research was first published, a small number of influential thinkers in manufacturing companies and advertising agencies immediately accepted the point that three exposures were not only unnecessary but also extremely wasteful. These people soon got the message and adjusted their policies accordingly.

But although the research had removed the (very thin) empirical support from the Effective Frequency doctrine, many people continued to believe in it on emotional or commonsense grounds. In the words of a prominent advertising agency media director when Effective Frequency was first seriously questioned, a policy of lowering media weight was counterintuitive. What this individual was really saying to the research community was "my prejudices are more valuable than your facts," an attitude that was for a while quite common.

At one time I worked on the advertising for a major cosmetics client. The head of this company, who was a man with a powerful personality, had a favorite saying: "I love the word *concentration*." Such an attitude is not easily changed, and it is not confined to the advertising business. In the social sciences and even in the natural sciences, people who have believed for long periods in particular theories find it virtually impossible to alter their views even in the face of strong evidence.

This is an almost perfect description of academic controversy. Many people believe that scientists, when their hypotheses are subjected to empirical examination, quietly bow to "superior" evidence. This belief demonstrates nothing beyond the fact that those people who accept this idea have remarkably little acquaintance with scientists. In reality, scientists of all types (not to speak of professors of the humanities) cling to their beliefs like barnacles to a ship's bottom. Their beliefs normally die with them, although on very, very rare occasions they have been proven right after all. The history of science is littered with theories that were eventually discarded: "the earth is the center of the universe," "the atom is a small solid particle of organic or inorganic matter," "the leech is an effective therapeutic device," "astrology has considerable predictive properties." Perhaps Effective Frequency is joining this distinguished collection of doctrines.

It was five years before the Effective Frequency policy was finally abandoned by large numbers of advertisers. As the leading professional organization, the Advertising Research Foundation (ARF), said at the time: "The three-exposure rule of thumb has been amputated. And like all amputations, it was painful."

One of the two reasons to concentrate advertising expenditure into flights was therefore removed during the mid-1990s, and most practitioners had accepted this by the end of the decade. But there remained the second argument: the relationship between the length of the advertising flight and the consumer's purchase cycle. Consumers are still buying their toothpaste (or whatever) at unchanging intervals of three weeks. What is the relevance of this three-week purchase cycle to the three-week advertising cycle? The answer is: none at all. The connection between the two cycles can be disproved by the use of simple logic, and it is remarkable—even astonishing—that no one grasped this logic during the long years when flighted plans were used so universally.

The unstated assumption of planning media to coincide with the buying cycles is that everybody buys on the same day. The advertising is therefore concentrated over the preceding three weeks in order to influence sales at the end of the period. The media buying is often "end-loaded," to give extra weight to the last days. This policy is only appropriate for those buyers who are in the market at the *end* of the three weeks. As explained, the extra frequency is wasteful. But there is an even more important point: these people represent only a small proportion of all buyers of the brand.

Every individual follows his or her purchase frequency in buying any particular product, and most people's purchase interval is the same as everybody else's. But their purchases do not take place on the same day. I buy toothpaste today and three weeks from today; my sister buys yesterday and three weeks from yesterday; my daughter tomorrow and three weeks from tomorrow.

Buying therefore takes place every day; indeed every minute of every day. This is true of all goods and services no matter how high or low their purchase frequency. When products have strong seasonal sales patterns, the daily purchasing is heavier during the peak period than during the troughs. Nevertheless the principle is the same: some buying takes place every day and at all times right through the day.

This pattern of buying—which is absolutely universal—means that we need to advertise a brand all the time in order to influence the buying that is taking place all the time.

The State of the Media Art

Media planning is a business of trade-offs. It is based on the use of judgment to balance conflicting claims on our resources, with the aim of finding the optimum combination. Four separate factors are involved: (1) coverage: the proportion of our target audience we should reach at least once in a defined period (e.g., a week); (2) OTS: how often we should reach them; (3) continuity: how many weeks we should be on air; and (4) cost-efficiency: the dollar cost of reaching 1,000 homes, a sum described technically as CPM (cost per mil; this phrase is unique to the media world, where "mil" is used to mean a thousand).

The most logical way of carrying out media planning is in the following six steps:

1. Advertise weekly, because people are buying all the time and most of them do their main shopping once a week.

2. Advertise toward the end of the week, when most shopping actually takes place.

3. Plan the weekly coverage of the schedule. This is a marketing decision that depends on the brand, especially on its size and that of its main competitors. A typical coverage figure is the example given earlier in this chapter: 35 percent of a large demographic target group. There must always be enough weight of advertising to produce an effect large enough to move sales (but not so large that it is wasteful).

4. Estimate the number of weekly GRPs needed to reach our target of homes *at least once*. Reducing audience duplication involves many practical difficulties, but the best way to do it is by choosing spots individually to build unduplicated coverage. In our example, the planned target was the (quite common) level of 60 GRPs. Because this provides a 35 percent reach, we can calculate the average OTS by dividing this number into the 60 GRPs. The answer is about 1.7. Putting this in commonsense language, we are covering 35 percent of our target group a little less often than twice a week on average. (Because we were aiming for once a week, this calculation illustrates how imprecise media buying really is.)

5. In purchasing the spots, balance different times and different days. We should use relatively few high-rating (and high CPM) spots but larger numbers of low-rating (and low CPM) spots. The latter help to increase the cost-efficiency of the schedule as a whole.

6. Run the schedule for as many weeks as the budget will allow. There will still be gaps, but these should be arranged in periods of low-season sales.

Note the importance of determining the minimum level of weekly weight *before* increasing the number of weeks on the air. If these priorities are reversed—in the most extreme circumstance by dividing the budget by 52—then the result will almost certainly be an ineffective campaign because the weekly weight will be too low.

Advertising can be effective only if it covers a reasonably large proportion of a brand's target group. Too low a weekly weight might mean that a huge proportion—perhaps as much as 90 percent—will not be reached at all. Even if we attempt to cover some different people each week, the aggregate coverage over quite a long period will remain fairly small.

Assuming that the television dayparts are planned to give good coverage of the demography of the target group, we must now estimate what level of coverage will be provided by given numbers of GRPs. Typical figures for a large brand with a broad target group are as follows:

80 GRPs 47 percent reach of the target group

70 GRPs 42 percent reach of the target group

60 GRPs 35 percent reach of the target group.

The most important judgment call is for the minimum level of weekly reach that is acceptable for the campaign. This is unlikely to be less than 35 percent. Some advertisers might aim to boost this figure, perhaps to as much as 50 percent.

The method just described is based on the use of good audience research. The underlying principles are soundly based and are also derived from reliable research: the best information available on how advertising actually works. Like all advertising planning, however, the process depends entirely on the soundness of the judgment of the individual drawing up the plan. With media, as with all other advertising planning, formulas should never be used to replace the human brain.

The method of planning media just described has been given the name of Continuity Planning (a title coined by a prominent media guru, Erwin Ephron). The advertisers who began to follow this principle during the mid-1990s have continued to do so, from which we can presume that they are satisfied with its performance.

Continuity Planning is an eminently practical method. But putting it into effect calls for both a clear focus on what we should be doing and also a hands-on knowledge of the media market, because we need to select specific television programs with the aim of boosting reach rather than repetition. The actual buying process is opportunistic and involves bargaining over rates.

Here are two examples of this relatively simple policy in action. The first relates to a brand, the second to an entire company.

The first example is British, and the brand is a very large one, Andrex, the market leader in the bathroom tissue category. I personally worked on the brand's advertising campaign during the 1970s, when it was decided to change the brand's media policy. Andrex is a rigorously researched brand, and one thing we investigated was the shape of its advertising response function (i.e., the sales response to step-by-step increases in advertising weight during the period just before purchase). This type of research was an innovation in the 1970s. We were all surprised to discover a sharp pattern of diminishing returns. The first advertisement had a very strong effect, but the sales produced by additional advertisements rapidly tailed away.

Because agencies during the 1970s believed strongly in Effective Frequency, Andrex's response function stopped us in our tracks. We therefore resolved to experiment. We selected a number of areas in the United Kingdom and distributed media in a pattern of Continuity Planning at relatively low weight, while in the rest of the country the standard pattern of Effective Frequency continued.

I am understating our reaction to the eventual results when I say that we were surprised. Sales in the Continuity Planning areas were much higher than in the Effective Frequency regions. The lesson was clear, and we did not hesitate to reverse our previous policy. The national media planning for the brand was immediately changed to Continuity Planning, and it has brought great prosperity to Andrex for more than twenty years. Its progress has been described in two well-documented published case studies.

The second example concerns a whole company whose identity must be veiled for reasons of confidentiality. I shall call it Ubiquity, Inc. It is a massive international consumer goods company whose base business is in the United States, where it is one of the largest advertisers.

Decision makers in the company showed an early interest in Continuity Planning, and they decided to carry out a series of marketplace experiments in different areas of the United States. These experiments covered more ground than Continuity Planning versus Effective Frequency. The company explored the use of untraditional media to stretch the coverage of the advertising, and it also experimented with a variety of tracking systems to evaluate the various media alternatives.

Ubiquity, Inc. has nine separate operating divisions, and the brands in these divisions are household names. As a result of fourteen separate, rather expensive marketplace experiments carried out during 1995, the media scheduling moved to the Continuity Planning pattern in eight of these divisions. (Effective Frequency was found to work better in the ninth.) The average number of weeks on air in all nine operating divisions was sixteen on average in 1994, which meant that thirty-six weeks were uncovered. The average GRP level was ninety-seven. In 1996, the number of weeks on air had increased to twenty-two, at an average GRP level of eighty-four. The policy continues, and it continues to pay dividends.

The prominent econometric organization Marketing Management Analytics (MMA) carried out a large study in 1999 to examine the productivity of the advertising of 800 American brands. MMA found that the advertising for the brands that followed a policy of Continuity Planning was decisively more productive than that for the (relatively small) number that still applied the policy of Effective Frequency.

Precisely the same finding emerged from a totally different type of analysis carried out in 2003 by the research company that specializes in pre-testing television commercials using the Advertising Research Systems (ARS) technique (which is discussed in Chapter 14). This organization demonstrates the accuracy of its system by comparing the advertising pre-test scores for individual brands with the marketplace performance of each brand shortly after the tested advertising had been run. They applied the same technique to brands that were running Continuity schedules, and compared the results with those running flighted schedules. It was found that Continuity produced strikingly higher sales than flighting.

This chapter has been based on the evaluation of advertising effects. Evaluation will also be the theme of Chapters 12 and 13.

Part IV

How Advertising Works

Four Myths:

"Advertising works over a period of time as a part of the gradual evolution of the individual's perceptions of a brand and its relations to other brands."

"The effect of a single isolated advertising exposure is likely to be minimal in most markets."

"Peace and happiness result from a willingness to admit error, from an accepted fallibility."

"The lower the price the greater the likelihood that the world will accept standardized modernity."

The first statement is wrong as far as short- and medium-term effects are concerned, although it provides some (although an incomplete) explanation of long-term effects. The other statements are all complete fallacies.

12

The Gatekeeper

Myths:

"Advertising works over a period of time as a part of the gradual evolution of the individual's perceptions of a brand and its relations to other brands."

"The effect of a single isolated advertising exposure is likely to be minimal in most markets."

Market Research: Transparency and Opacity

Theories about how advertising works are just that—theories—and at best they are supported by "soft" research into consumers' awareness and attitudes. Chapters 12 and 13 try to do better, because they are underpinned by substantial amounts of "hard" data measuring the influence of advertising on consumer behavior.

These chapters cover three separate orders of effect. This chapter describes advertising's immediate short-term influence, felt within seven days of an advertisement's appearance. This effect comes through either boosting or protecting a brand's sales. It also acts as a gatekeeper to all further effects. If there is no short-term effect, nothing else with happen. This chapter then examines the repetition of short-term effects across the course of a year, which can add up to a measurable medium-term effect. Chapter 13 moves on to advertising's long-term effects, which come through the continuous and prolonged process of strengthening the advertised brand. A successful brand is (as stated in the title to that chapter) the main source of a manufacturer's profit.

This chapter is focused on repeat-purchase packaged goods, a group of categories that has provided most of our knowledge about advertising's effects. Over the years, however, other categories have overtaken packaged goods when measured by volume of advertising, although expenditures on packaged goods remain large. But the important thing to remember is that the key lessons from packaged goods—particularly that a single advertising exposure can be effective—apply to advertising in virtually all other fields.

One of the most interesting professional activities of young agency account executives used to be to attend Nielsen presentations, to learn about the progress in the marketplace of the brands they were working on. These presentations took place every two months for each client. Account executives sometimes attend similar meetings today, although agencies are so short staffed that there is very little time to devote to improving the agency's knowledge in this way.

The research method, which was invented by a man called Bev Murphy (who went on to become a very successful head of the Campbell Soup Company), was pioneered by the ACNielsen company. It was brilliantly simple although quite expensive to implement. It was called a "retail audit" because it was based on statistically representative samples of food and drug stores. The Nielsen field workers (known as "checkers") called on these stores every two months to count the physical inventories—on the shelves and in the stockrooms—of all the brands in many product categories. The checkers also collected the manufacturers' invoices for the new deliveries of those same brands over the two-month period since they were last in the store.

By simple arithmetic, Nielsen could calculate the sales of every brand in each store over the two-month period. They did this by taking the inventories at the beginning, adding the two-month deliveries, and deducting the inventories at the end. The data for all the stores were aggregated and then projected to give an estimate of national sales. These were generally also analyzed in different regions, since the overall samples of stores were large enough to make this possible.

By adding together all sales in the category and percentaging each brand, Nielsen invented the most important measure ever used in the marketing field: a brand's share of market, which is its share of sales to consumers during a specific period, calculated either from volume or from dollars. As well as sales, Nielsen was able to produce useful information on each brand's stocks, deliveries, distribution, display, and the proportion of stores out of stock.

The real value of these figures was in their ability to reveal bimonthly and long-term sales movements. One year's information made it possible to measure seasonality, and over longer periods manufacturers could track trends in category sales, segment sales, and sales of individual brands.

Most manufacturers also supplemented Nielsen figures with information from consumer panels, which measured the same brands from the viewpoint of the buyer. The information was collected from pencil-and-paper diaries completed by homemakers in a representative sample of households, and the data were collected monthly and then aggregated and projected to represent the population as a whole. Consumer panel information estimated the penetration (i.e., the user base) of each brand and analyzed the demographic characteristics of its buyers. Most important, it also revealed their buying habits, that is, purchase frequency, repeat purchase, and multibrand buying.

Retail audits and consumer panels produced a formidable battery of information that was totally transparent. The data were easy to interpret, and they hid nothing. However, the infrequent data collection caused a great problem when manufacturers tried to measure the effects of advertising campaigns.

Retail audit and consumer panel figures did not change a great deal from period to period, except for the regularly recurring seasonal ups and downs. In the long term, however, the figures (especially the annual estimates) often revealed trends. When these moved up, manufacturers drew indirect inferences about the effectiveness of their advertising campaigns. And when the trends moved down, they drew tentative conclusions about the effectiveness of their competitors' campaigns and the relative ineffectiveness of their own.

But in nearly all cases, it was impossible to detect any immediate effect of advertising on sales, and this led to a conviction that became accepted almost universally in the marketing field—that there *was* no immediate effect from advertising on sales. Hence the two myths that appear at the beginning of this chapter (which are direct quotations from a prominent market researcher).

During the 1980s, we began to learn something quite different about markets, as a result of an important development in the way in which we collected sales data. Instead of the accurate but laborious processes of store auditing and diary keeping, scanners were introduced to record sales, one at a time. This was not only an accurate system but also a far simpler and speedier process than the ones that had been used before.

One thing was discovered very quickly from scanner research: sales in the real world are highly volatile. Sales of individual brands dart up and down week by week, and sales volume in every week is different from every other. This was quite unexpected after the stability we had observed over so many years in the figures produced by retail audits and consumer panels. It did not take researchers long to discover that the reason for the difference was because of how often the data were collected. Under the old system, the figures were accumulated over a number of weeks: eight or nine weeks for retail audits and four weeks for consumer panels. Some of these weeks showed high sales and some showed the opposite. The weekly ups and downs canceled one another out, and the final result showed very little change from one period to the next.

The old types of retail audits and consumer panels, despite their enormous value for their main purpose of tracking sales and market shares, were totally opaque in revealing short-term sales movements. It was, therefore, impossible to detect any short-term effect from advertising, even if there had been such an effect, and a large one at that. In addition, data collected in stores gave no information at all about consumers. Because media advertising is directed at consumers and not at the shelves of retail stores, the information needed to measure advertising has to come from actual buyers.

Good Cooks Make Biryani

In the 1980s, ACNielsen established a household panel statistically representative of the U.S. population. This still operates today, with 60,000 homes signed up. Each homemaker has a hand-held scanner to record all the everyday goods he or she buys. The homemaker only has to point the laser of the scanner to the Universal Product Code (usually known as the bar code) on each pack bought, and the details of the brand, size, and variety are automatically recorded. The homemaker then punches in the date and time of the purchase and the identity of the buyer. The information is sent to Nielsen every week over the telephone, and the scanner transmits the coded information automatically. It is the state of the art in data collection. The research tells us what packs were bought and precisely when they were bought.

In order to examine advertising effects, however, we now had to do something more complicated. What was needed was to relate this buying to the television advertising for the brands purchased. (The original research was restricted to television, as the main advertising medium used for everyday consumer goods.)

Two thousand representative families in the Household Panel were selected to have meters fixed to all the television sets in their homes (up to eight sets per household). These meters made a log of the exact period when each set was switched to a channel (also identified). Yet another data source was set up to monitor all the commercials that appeared on air on all the stations. This identification of the commercials made it possible to flag the specific advertisements entering each household, because we already knew when each set was switched to any channel. As a result of all this, we could relate the date and time at which a brand was bought to the date and time an advertisement for it had entered the home. For comparison, we could also measure the purchasing in the households that had not received any advertising. It was all done in the following way:

The first stage was to decide the product categories to be measured. We selected on judgment twelve different categories with the aim of covering as wide and typical a range as possible.

When the research was set in motion, we recorded every purchase occasion in every product category, and we noted the name of the brand bought. The sample of 2,000 homes was grouped into buyers and non-buyers, and in the buying homes each brand's market share was calculated. The buying homes were then put into two groups and market shares separately calculated. These groups were the homes that had received advertising during the previous seven days for the brand bought (the *ad households*), and those that had not (the *adless households*). The difference between these two figures became the measure of Short-Term Advertising Strength (STAS).

After the sorting of the 2,000 homes in the way described and after the calculations were made, all these homes were put back "into the pot." The sample was differently grouped when the next product purchase took place. Note that the same sample of 2,000 was used throughout. This guaranteed that there were no differences between the *ad households* and *adless households,* with the single exception of the presence—or absence—of advertising for the brand that was bought. The research, therefore, gave us a pure measure of advertising effect.

This describes the method used to carry out Pure Single-Source research, an important subject that has already been touched upon in Chapters 7 and 10. The technique is immensely cumbrous. The original research, published in 1995, collected more than 111,000 separate statistical readings, each arrived at by a separate analysis. But the result justified the effort, because we were able to make the crucial connection between the *ad households* and *adless households,* thus calculating STAS.

This research demonstrated much variation among campaigns. However, the most successful ones had a most remarkable effect. Twenty percent of brands (mostly small ones) showed advertising working very aggressively to generate sales, with the advertising campaign *doubling* sales on average immediately after exposure. A single advertisement produced most of this effect. A further 20 percent of campaigns produced a noticeable sales increase; the advertising showed less effect than with the top 20 percent, but it certainly helped to maintain the (already high) sales levels of the larger brands.

In 30 percent of cases, the advertising did not have much effect at all. And, surprisingly, in 30 percent of the cases the campaigns were associated with sales reductions, the reason being that stronger advertising for competitive brands was being shown during the same week and consumers were responding to this.

The average immediate (STAS) increase, taking the successful and unsuccessful campaigns together, was 18 percent. Although this figure was generated by a relatively small number of purchase occasions, the number was so large that the analysts who carried out the research could not at first comprehend the reasons for it. We were even more astonished at the sales increases at the top end, those relating to the most successful campaigns. Such figures had never been seen before for established brands.

When manufacturers look at the progress of their brands, they normally examine annual sales data, what I shall refer to as "medium-term figures." At the end of a year, the 40 percent of campaigns that were working strongly in the short term were now working much less well, and the average sales increase (covering all brands) had come down from 18 to 6 percent. This is rather a high number when compared with the normal sales increase for a national brand, but the two figures are at least in the same "ballpark." Among the Single-Source figures, the odd man out was the short-term sales increase, an average of 18 percent.

The research showed that sales increases from the advertising *moved a step downward over time* (from 18 percent in a week to 6 percent at the end of the year), and this appeared to contradict common sense. Another complicating factor was that all brands that moved up at the end of a year showed a short-term increase first. In other words, a short-term effect was a precondition—acting as a gatekeeper—to further sales progress. It took much thought to work out the reasons for these complications.

Consumer goods are bought on multiple occasions over the course of a year. Any annual increase in sales attributable to advertising is the aggregate effect of all the advertising that appears across the year. But during the 1990s, advertising schedules had large gaps. Assuming that the campaign was effective (i.e., it had a positive STAS), there were sharp sales increases when it was on the air. But there were sharp decreases when it was not, because consumers would at those times be responding to the advertising for competitive brands. The many gaps in the schedules generally caused a larger number of downs than ups over the course of a year.

If a brand that achieves an average short-term sales increase of 18 percent is on the air for fifty-two weeks, it will end the year approximately 18 percent ahead in sales. In the 1990s, this was most unlikely because total continuity of advertising was virtually unknown. If the brand is advertised for only seventeen weeks—a fairly typical period of advertising a decade ago—the average end-year increase comes down to 6 percent (calculated by simple arithmetic). Continuity Planning is now widely used in the United States, so that there are fewer gaps than before. This means that the drop below the STAS level is now less than it was.

Very little doubt exists that a brand that generates high immediate sales from its advertising can maintain a reasonably high level only if it has a large enough advertising budget to keep on advertising, and if it deploys its media plan with maximum continuity (in the way recommended in Chapter 11). Many brands do not fulfill these conditions and end the year lower at the end than at the beginning, despite healthy short-term effects from their campaigns.

Four elements explain the processes by which advertising works. Three of these have been described in this chapter. The fourth—which, from some points of view, is the most interesting one—will be discussed in detail in Chapter 13.

1. *The Gatekeeper:* Advertising can influence sales, but there must be a short-term effect before a medium-term one is possible. An additional conclusion from the Single-Source research is that high short-term effects are generally associated with high medium-term effects.

2. *Continuity:* Media continuity ensures that the short-term effect is repeated. The more weeks the advertising reappears on the television screen, the better the odds of sustaining the size of the short-term effect.

3. *Medium-Term Effect:* At the end of a year, a brand's sales are often up, but three conditions must be fulfilled for this: (1) an effective campaign, demonstrated by its short-term effect (STAS); (2) an advertising budget big enough to maintain the advertising for a substantial number of weeks on the air; and (3) a media strategy based on the principle of Continuity.

4. *Brand-Building:* A continuation of medium-term effects year after year can lead to a strengthening of a brand in a number of measurable ways. Taking the long view, this is advertising's most important role.

For simplicity, I shall use the acronym *GCMB* to summarize these processes. This is a brutal set of initials. During a recent visit to India, it occurred to me that readers might remember them more easily if they are prompted by the phrase *Good Cooks Make Biryani.* The four processes follow a sequential hierarchy, and each can be measured accurately. These steps were analyzed from a study of good data, and the reasoning is inductive: from the particular to the general.

Many advertising theories move from the general to the particular. They mimic the social sciences and are derived from a combination of imagination, common sense, judgment, and general (but not specific) knowledge. Such theories are often embodied in mathematical models that are used to plan elements of advertising campaigns, in particular frequency patterns, and are often flawed because of the unreliability of the theories themselves. GCMB represents an objective effort to describe the real world. It is based on facts from this rather important source.

Two Very Different Theories

Research into the effectiveness of advertising is carried out in many countries. The many studies that are undertaken differ a great deal in their scientific rigor, but some are good enough to advance our knowledge in small but measurable ways.

Out of the large total number, about three-quarters of the studies come from two countries, the United States and Britain. The United States, not surprisingly, produces most because of the great size of the American advertising market. But most of the American studies are unpublished. In contrast, many more British studies are brought into the public domain. In fact, Britain is responsible for more published research on advertising than any other country in the world. This is because the British organization of advertising agencies, the Institute of Practitioners in Advertising (IPA), has for twenty years actively sponsored the publication of well-researched cases.

Theories of how advertising works—some derived from research but most of them not—have been formulated, described, discussed, and disputed for about 80 years. The field was dominated by American theories until about 1970, when British views about advertising began to be disseminated in most countries where advertising was of any importance. British theories emerged because of the way in which British agencies were changing their working practices to incorporate account planners, whose responsibility was to develop advertising strategy and to talk to consumers about creative ideas before the agency finalized its recommendations.

The British approach to advertising theory was the product of the British educational system, which has always emphasized the liberal arts. Account planners are almost always recruited from the ranks of academic generalists rather than research specialists. Education in the best British universities has always encouraged skepticism of received wisdom, and the competitive nature of British education has always put a premium on originality. I speak as someone who has benefited from such an education although I have lived for more than two decades in the United States. The reason that account planning has not flourished in American advertising agencies is that many, if not most, of the account executives in the leading agencies have MBA degrees. This means that their education has been quantitative and empirical.

In contrast to American practice, the British approach to advertising theory is deductive and intuitive. British theorists have tended to move from the general to the particular, by applying to specific brands the lessons embodied in their beliefs about how advertising works—whether or not these have been validated by a cold scrutiny of market data.

Even the formidable battery of cases demonstrating advertising effectiveness sponsored by the IPA have a strong qualitative flavor, despite the fact that many of the cases also include sales data. In particular, the studies rely substantially on tracking. Although these are quantitative in the size of the samples and the standardization of the questions, the measures themselves—brand awareness, advertising awareness, awareness of brand attributes, attitudes to brands—are totally qualitative.

Surprisingly, no one has studied the total *corpus* of IPA cases inductively. They number almost a thousand and are bound to contain important general lessons. It is regrettable that no one has ever searched for these. There is one small exception. A single researcher combed the cases for how much they relied on econometric evaluation and discovered that, with the passage of time, the cases published were relying *less and less* on econometrics.

Many people see a value in deduction, which may be based largely on qualitative research. Many people also see a value in induction, which relies heavily on quantitative research. My quarrel is that the two separate schools of thought are too often seen as mutually exclusive. Both British and American practitioners are open to criticism. I feel especially aggrieved that so much of the original thinking about advertising that comes from Britain is handicapped by an unwillingness to base generalizations on quantities of observed data.

I will now describe two British theories that are endorsed by many—perhaps the majority—of advertising people in Britain. And as already noted, British ideas about advertising also reach out into many parts of the world.

"Small Steps." In this theory, advertisements start by producing little effect of any sort, but with repetition the influence of the campaign on consumers imperceptibly increases. The eventual result is felt by an enrichment of consumer perceptions; to the extent that these lead to increased sales, the outcome will be the fairly modest sales increase attributable to advertising at the end of a year. Unlike GCMB, the "Small Steps" theory moves from a small effect to a larger one, although there is never any really big effect like the ones that STAS can reveal.

The "Small Steps" theory originated in common sense and was of course connected to the general stability of sales produced by the false reading of retail audit data. However, since "Small Steps" denies the very existence of a powerful short-term effect—something demonstrable with ironclad evidence—the idea is hardly a plausible one.

This would not matter much if the theory were simply an academic exercise. But unfortunately it impinges on how efficiently brands are advertised. Systems exist to test television commercials before they are run on the air, and the results from the best systems have been consistently compared with the sales results achieved by each tested commercial. The research before exposure predicts rather well the sales after exposure. However, the many believers in the "Small Steps" theory are as antagonistic to such research as if it posed a threat to the virtue of their daughters. Almost as seriously, it poses a threat to their view of how advertising works. Because they believe it impossible for advertising to produce a strong short-term effect, they instinctively reject research that demonstrates such an effect.

"Small Steps" is described in the two myths that appear at the beginning of this chapter. Both are quotations from a modest but influential book first published in 1974 and republished in 1998. Because the first clear evidence of a powerful short-term effect from advertising was published in 1995, the author of these myths either did not know about the new research or else chose to continue to propagate his theory despite evidence that might have been expected to pull the rug from under it. Its continued currency is an illustration of the extraordinary conservatism of the British advertising business (a reflection perhaps of British society). One sometimes suspects that the theorists who cling to ancient concepts continue to do so because they have invested so much intellectual capital in them.

"Adstock." This is a more complicated theory. The central concept, "Adstock," is not easy to define, although it echoes "Small Steps" in the idea that advertising's performance can improve over periods of less than a year. "Adstock" is calibrated with a measure of advertising weight, Gross Rating Points or GRPs. But it is a measure not of weight but of the cognitive effect of advertising: consumers' conscious and unconscious memories of an advertising campaign produced by a given number of GRPs (including the impressions made by earlier advertising).

As time moves on, this accumulation of memories erodes quite fast if it is not replenished. Simon Broadbent, who originated the theory, explained it in the following way: "We can think of our consumers' memories holding less and less of our copy point in mind." Typically, the cognitive outcome of 100 GRPs can drop to 50 after four weeks. Using the terminology of nuclear physics, the campaign is then given a "four-week half-life." ("Half-lives" are normally in the four to ten week range.) The original level of "Adstock" can be topped up by additional advertising; indeed, proponents of the theory see this as advertising's most important role.

A paradoxical feature of "Adstock" is that it says two things: (1) that there is a carry-over effect from advertising, and (2) that advertising effects decay. The first of these calls for *less* advertising, and the second calls for *more*. This contradiction causes practical problems when the theory is implemented.

In judging this rather subtle concept, readers should bear five points in mind:

1. As mentioned, "Adstock" was derived from the idea that advertising effects are run down or accumulate over relatively short periods, for example, the "four-week half-life." Facts from the 1995 Single-Source research, which have been amply confirmed by data from many other studies, show that the immediate effect of advertising *on sales* is "in-and-out," with little or no carry-over during periods off-air. Operational plans based on "Adstock" can therefore have dangerous consequences.

The very long term is a different matter, and Chapter 13 discusses the circumstances in which advertising *can* have a cumulative effect on sales. But the process is indirect and operates only over periods beyond a year—far longer than those used for the majority of "Adstock" calculations.

2. If theories about advertising are to have any practical value, they must be concerned with sales. "Adstock" is a measure of a cognitive phenomenon, and not surprisingly it correlates with proven recall of the advertising (i.e., research respondents are checked to ensure that they really recall the campaign they claim to). Recall, in turn, is *not* correlated with sales. To use "Adstock" to predict sales is a much more complicated procedure.

3. "Adstock" is sometimes also used to plan media buying, with occasional unfortunate consequences. Because media buyers assume that advertising effects carry over into subsequent periods, they are encouraged to run advertising at a low level—perhaps too low to have an effect—because they believe that some of the previous advertising is still working. In other cases, air time is bought at "bargain basement" rates and concentrated into wastefully heavy "flights"—blocks of

television airtime—on the assumption that there will be a future benefit from this concentration of advertising money. This is because it might slow the rate of decay, which is a central characteristic of the "Adstock" concept. Both these examples show how advertising funds can be spent inefficiently.

4. The fourth point about "Adstock" will probably surprise readers of this book. During the twenty years since "Adstock" was first used for evaluating campaigns, no one has made any attempt to demonstrate, with the use of observed facts, that it really exists. A new measure would have to be produced to define what "Adstock" really is: the imprint of a brand's advertising on consumers' minds. But with such a measure, it should be possible to demonstrate both the speed of erosion (i.e., the length of the "half-life") and how quickly "Adstock" can be built. A demonstration like this would be a practical help to media planners and might also make the theory a better predictive device than it is at present.

5. The reality of "Adstock" is that it is not a tool for direct measurement. It is a component to be incorporated in mathematical models. In constructing these models, a number of (assumed) causes of sales are compared with actual sales, using the technique of Multivariate Regression, and as a result the contribution of each cause is estimated. The model is then applied to a specific brand and used to forecast its sales over the course of a year.

The method can be valuable, insofar as models that include "Adstock" sometimes produce reasonably good forecasts. This raises the question of whether this practical outcome is a validation of the "Adstock" theory. Not totally, in my opinion. There is still a good deal of muddiness about the concept itself, especially about what it really is, since this is something that cannot itself be measured.

The models include some reliable *observed* inputs (e.g., price, promotions, distribution). The problem with "Adstock" is that it could be acting as a surrogate for repeat purchasing, a behavioral phenomenon that is partly habitual and partly influenced by advertising in its short-term role. It would be interesting to experiment with a model that includes buying frequency in place of "Adstock." Could it also produce reasonable sales forecasts?

Some important statistical processes, such as those involved in deconstructing sales to estimate the relative importance of individual stimuli, can be carried out only by econometric modeling. But other measures can be obtained much more simply by direct observation.

This is true of how we measure the short-term effect of advertising. It is also true of six specific measures of long-term effects. I believe that these give us a much better idea of how advertising works than models derived from "Adstock." If we have a choice between reliable observation and econometric modeling—no matter how sophisticated the model we use—the choice is simple. A model is always a surrogate for the collection of data by direct means, and it is *never* as reliable as direct observation. Colin McDonald, an unusually realistic researcher, once described a model as a "myth with numbers." This is an elegant description and one that is substantially true.

The really important point raised by these theories is what they reveal about the people who believe them. Too much abstract speculation about advertising can lead to a hardening of the intellectual arteries. People become so rigid and backward looking in their thinking that their immediate instinct is to disbelieve evidence that might upset their preconceptions.

Believers in "Small Steps" pay no attention to—and sometimes actively reject—research that undercuts the theory. Believers with an emotional attachment to "Adstock" stretch it beyond its limits, especially into the rather inappropriate field of media buying.

Collecting and conscientiously studying large masses of data in the hope that general patterns will emerge—the process of induction—is regarded as a sterile source for scientific discovery, according to the theory propounded by the celebrated philosopher Karl Popper. He believed that discovery comes from a leap in the dark, and that the only part that data collection plays is in the attempts to disprove an initial hypothesis. If this cannot be done, then the hypothesis holds.

Popper's idea is more popular with the nonscientific intelligentsia than with scientists. Scientists feel insulted by the notion that science is a crap-shoot rather than a process of meticulous and gradual preparation that leads to new knowledge. Scientists also recognize a very large flaw. The theory assumes that proponents of a tentative hypothesis will gracefully bow to contradictory evidence. From my own experience of theorists in all fields (including advertising), they will do everything possible to undermine any evidence that is not harmonious with their own beliefs. They normally adopt 100 percent positions and do not budge from them. The classic statement of Popper's position is that, if we hypothesize that all swans are white, then a single black swan will destroy the hypothesis. From my experience of scientists (and also advertising people), this evidence will not be acceptable because they will make the greatest effort to demonstrate that the black swan is a duck.

It seems right, therefore, to end this chapter with another myth.

"Peace and happiness result from a willingness to admit error, from an accepted fallibility".

13

The Main Source of a Manufacturer's Profit

Myth:

"The lower the price the greater the likelihood that the world will accept standardized modernity."

Lessons From a Visit to a Supermarket

"Commoditization" is an unbeautiful but succinct word that describes rather well the image of the future presented in the myth that appears at the beginning of this chapter. Like most forecasts, it is based on that rather fallible guide, common sense. Common sense will tell us that rational consumers look for the lowest price. Manufacturers therefore compete by offering progressively lower prices, a process that is only possible if they standardize their goods and generate the greatest possible scale economies from long production runs. Consumers are interested only in value for money. This means product parity, low prices, thin margins, and large volumes.

It is an interesting exercise to examine how far we have progressed toward this future world in which the classical ideal of maximum economic welfare will at last be realized.

In October 2002, I visited a large supermarket in Syracuse, New York, to examine the range of ready-to-eat breakfast cereals. I ignored the cereals that had to be cooked, the granola bars, and different pack sizes of individual varieties. Walking down the cereal aisle, I counted *190* different product varieties. I took great care and double-checked my counting. I had carried out a similar investigation in 1984. The number of separate varieties has more than doubled since then.

By different varieties, I mean those with differences in flavor, shape, ingredients, crunchiness, nutrition, amount of sweetener, quantity of "healthy" ingredients (e.g., bran, nuts, raisins), quantity of calcium and specific vitamins, bulk density (the ratio of weight to volume), and whether the cereal contains "fun" ingredients like marshmallows to appeal to children. If there is an obvious similarity between two varieties from different manufacturers, I counted these separately, but I did not find a great deal of *close* copying. When a manufacturer responds to a competitive manufacturer's innovation, it introduces some distinctive features into its own brand. The only examples of one brand imitating another literally is when store brands model themselves on those from the main manufacturers.

The brands came from four major producers (which are responsible for more than 80 percent of the total display), plus some minor players and manufacturers of store brands. Each of the major marketing companies positions its brands in the category with great care, but each responds instantaneously to new product activity by competitors (by offering some differentiation, as explained). The vast number of brands and varieties that has resulted makes it inevitable that each manufacturer will cannibalize its own brands to a substantial degree.

The prices varied widely. Quoting "unit prices," which give a price per pound, these started at $2.27 for Quaker Marshmallow Safari (a brand packed in simple plastic bags) and rose to $5.32 for General Mills Boo Berry. There were in addition a couple of brands that were even more expensive, but these were "variety" packs: collections of individual servings of six or eight different products from one manufacturer. The store brands were, as expected, at the low end. Food Club Crisp Rice had a unit price of $2.34, and its direct competitor, Kellogg's Rice Krispies, was $3.78. Counting the shelf facings (i.e., the number of packs of the brand at the front of the supermarket shelf), there were three of Crisp Rice, compared with seven of Rice Krispies. From what we know about shelf facings (which tend to overstate slightly the market shares of small brands), the manufacturer's brand, Kellogg's Rice Krispies, outsells the store brand, Crisp Rice, by a ratio of perhaps three to one. There is no evidence at all that low prices will persuade the world to accept "standardized modernity."

A visit to most supermarkets in the United States, and also in Canada, Britain, Germany, Australia, and other economically developed countries, will reveal a broadly similar picture. And although the category of breakfast cereals is particularly fragmented, most others show a proliferation of brands and varieties and a wide range of prices.

The myth that appears at the beginning of this chapter—that markets will inevitably move in a "commodity" direction—shows such an egregiously different picture that the reader must wonder about the source of the author's information. Perhaps he was talking about competing stalls selling rice in bulk in an oriental bazaar, but the context of what he was writing makes this unlikely. The author is, incidentally, a famous academic and until his retirement he taught at one of the most prestigious business schools in the United States. The quotation comes from a widely selling book published in 1983.

In the framework of this myth, manufacturers can boost their profit only by increasing their sales volume, in the hope of generating scale economies in production and marketing. But at the same time, competition from more efficient manufacturers—which will reduce prices even further—will relentlessly eat this profit away. This is a most unhappy prospect for companies that market consumer goods.

It is of course an extremely incomplete and flawed view of the real world, however, and the reason is strikingly obvious. The competition in real markets is based on differentiation and not standardization. The economic opportunities provided by such markets stem from this simple fact. (This was all demonstrated decisively as long ago as 1948 by the economist and Nobel Laureate Friedrich von Hayek.)

In the picture of markets portrayed by this chapter's myth, there is no role for advertising because products are not different from one another and the cheapest wins. A system without advertising, or even one that relies decreasingly on advertising, is simply not a description of reality. This is obvious to any member of the public, although the public is generally indifferent about whether there is advertising or not.

Product categories are dominated by manufacturers' brands (or their equivalent in service fields). In food and drug stores, they account for more than half the total numbers, more than 80 percent of total sales volume, and in excess of 90 percent of total sales value. The last two figures are important because they demonstrate that manufacturers' labels, when compared with store brands, "price" brands, and generics, are larger in sales volume and also higher priced.

Generally speaking, higher consumer prices mean higher profits for manufacturers.

Brands have a long history and had become a feature of commercial life well before the end of the nineteenth century. When goods began to be produced in large quantities in factories, brands were introduced to identify a manufacturer's products. This was important when the United States was in an early stage of development and communications were difficult. Factories were geographically distant from retailers and consumers, so the latter did not know the manufacturers at first hand. Brands identified. They also guaranteed homogeneity and quality. In addition (and, in fact, the main reason they were first employed), they provided legal protection. No competitive manufacturer could copy the formula of Ivory soap—and still less use its brand name—without finding itself in the gun sights of Procter & Gamble's lawyers.

Added Values—What Advertising Contributes

Chapter 3 was devoted to brands, and in particular to how added values are what make the difference between brands and unbranded commodities. It is now time to develop some of the ideas contained there. But first, a brief recapitulation.

- A brand is a composite of two things: its functionality, which comes from the contents of the box (or the function carried out by a service), and its added values. Functionality is easily observed and measured. This is less true of added values, which represent impressions in the minds of consumers: an accumulation of reasons why the brand is bought, and attitudes to it according to a number of different aspects and criteria.

- An unbranded product is functionally acceptable, although generally not liked quite as much as a well-established brand. A brand possesses both functionality and added values. A small but increasing number of store brands have added values connected with the name and reputation of the store.

- Added values are not a fanciful concept. Their reality can be demonstrated by product testing to compare consumers' responses to brands in two separate guises: when they are unidentified, and when they are in their normal containers.

A brand's strength is ultimately derived from how much it is bought repeatedly by its users. This is obviously true of brands sold in food and drug stores, and also of commonly used services like transportation and communications systems. It is even true of high-ticket items like cars if these are sold in mature product categories (as is the situation in the United States and many other countries).

If a brand continues to satisfy its users, it will be bought repeatedly. This will continue until a competitive manufacturer introduces a brand that is functionally superior, which will almost certainly cause the original brand to be bought less often, unless it is also improved. Functionality is fundamentally important, and this importance continues through the life of the brand. Repeat purchase of a brand leads to the growth of added values in consumers' minds. This process takes place in almost imperceptibly small increments. A measurable effect can be felt only in the long term, over periods of years and not months. These accumulated added values encourage the next purchase, and the process continues by which purchasing and added values resonate against one another. This resonance goes on until it is blocked by a change in consumers' buying patterns. Until this happens, the process is smooth and harmonious, satisfying both the consumers (because they like the goods) and the manufacturers (because they like the profits).

Advertising helps this process to a very major degree. It does two things to increase the resonance described in the previous paragraph. Its *short-term* effect boosts sales directly. And it also grows the store of added values by its ability to reinforce consumers' perceptions of a brand's nonfunctional qualities; this is a *long-term* effect.

The way that advertising deepens consumers' perceptions of a brand's nonfunctional qualities is how we describe advertising's long-term effects. It is the "Brand Building" that forms the last stage of the GCMB process described in Chapter 12. Advertising does this job in six measurable ways. Because some of these ways are related to each other, they are simpler to understand if they are grouped in pairs.

Penetration and Purchase Frequency. Advertising can increase a brand's penetration (i.e., the proportion of households that buy it in a defined period). It does this by demonstrating the advantages of the brand so as to prompt some non-users to buy the brand at least on a trial basis. Advertising can also boost a brand's purchase frequency (i.e., how often buyers purchase it during a given period). It does this by addressing existing buyers and giving them ideas and encouragement to use the brand more often. This is a prime objective for large brands in many categories—for example, food brands by using recipe advertising, gasoline brands by featuring tourist destinations in the advertising, and upscale charge cards by featuring luxury shopping.

A direct relationship exists between a brand's penetration growth and the increase in its market share. But penetration growth eventually reaches a plateau. There comes a point at which a brand, if it is large enough, runs out of potential users because virtually everybody knows about it, and those who do not like it will not use it.

When this happens, purchase frequency provides at least some compensation. Rate of usage is relatively uniform for the bottom four-fifths of brands in any category, so that larger brands are distinguished from smaller ones solely on the basis of their penetration. But when a brand grows large enough to be in the top quintile (i.e., the one-fifth of brands comprising the largest ones), its purchase frequency kicks up. In this top quintile, despite the fact that penetration growth has probably flattened, purchase frequency does not stop growing. This means that manufacturers are getting extra business from existing users, which is something that can be achieved fairly cheaply in advertising terms. (Attracting new users is a more difficult task no matter how large or small the brand.)

When Dove was launched (initially as a bar), its average annual volume growth during its first three years of national distribution was *almost twice* as high as during the subsequent three years. During the first period, the brand was growing as a result of penetration; during the next period, as a result of purchase frequency. This is a typical pattern for that rather rare *genus*, the successful new brand. Dove is now the leading brand by value in its category in the United States and a very important name internationally.

High purchase frequency, because it generates sales volume, is one reason why large brands are more profitable per unit than small ones are, *and this extra profitability is to a large degree driven by consumer advertising.*

Price Elasticity and Consumer Prices. In Chapter 3, we discussed how added values reinforce a brand's distinctiveness. As these values are growing in consumers' minds, the marketing company can afford to lift the price of its brand because consumers will be increasingly reluctant to stop buying it and buy a substitute. In the language of economics, the brand's price elasticity is reduced. There is good evidence that advertising can actually accomplish this.

Because manufacturers are protected in this way from losing too much business when they increase their prices, it is not surprising that large successful brands—which represent about 15 percent of the total in all categories—have prices at least 10 percent above their category average. The mechanism by which this is accomplished is that these brands need trade and consumer promotions much less than smaller and weaker brands do. Because promotions reduce retail prices and eat into manufacturers' profit, manufacturers try to resist pressure from retailers to promote all the time. Strong brands are manufacturers' best counter in negotiations with the retail trade. When negotiation becomes tough, retailers will eventually realize that they simply cannot live without strong manufacturers' brands because of their large sales volumes, and manufacturers will of course remind them of this.

Large, successful brands sometimes have direct costs slightly above their category average because of their superior product quality. But against this, such brands will benefit from above-average economies of scale in manufacture and marketing.

Large, successful brands, because of their high prices, will therefore almost always be more profitable per unit than small, less successful brands are. *And advertising, again, has contributed to this extra profitability.*

Advertising Elasticity and Advertising Intensiveness. Advertising elasticity is extremely difficult to calculate, but it has been computed for large numbers of brands. It is a measure of how much sales will go up if the advertising budget is increased by a given amount. The hard part of the calculation is to confine the effect to the advertising alone, excluding all other factors that could influence sales.

On average, advertising elasticity is low, showing a five-to-one relationship between advertising and sales. (This estimate is based on a broad sample of more than 130 brands.) A 5 percent boost in advertising typically produces a 1 percent increase in sales. This is a medium-term effect, felt over the course of a year. Any degree of advertising elasticity assumes an effective campaign; the advertising elasticity of an ineffective campaign is of course zero. With normal brands, increased advertising is not profitable in the medium term, because the profit on the extra sales is generally less than the cost of the extra advertising.

However, the situation can sometimes look better if we add long-term effects to the medium-term ones. This generally low level of advertising elasticity can be increased slightly by the growth in a brand's added values, which is, as explained, a long-term effect of advertising.

In other words, sales become gradually more responsive to a boost in advertising pressure. When this happens—when the advertising elasticity has been raised above the average level—the additional sales mean that the extra advertising *can* become profitable. And again, the addition of other long-term effects may make the situation even better.

Advertising intensiveness measures the proportion of a brand's net sales value (NSV) that is devoted to media advertising. If the proportion is small, this frees up a greater margin for profit; if it is large, a smaller margin. As explained when advertising budgets were discussed in Chapter 8, large brands spend a lower proportion of NSV on advertising than small brands do. Large brands therefore generate more profit margins because of the relatively small size of their advertising investment. This is a genuine economy of scale.

The ways in which successful advertising builds added values strengthen brands in the long term, and this can increase advertising elasticity and reduce advertising intensiveness. *Both of these effects have a direct payout in terms of increased profitability for the brand.*

All the discussion so far has been about the long-term effects of advertising on brands, and how it is that the *brands* provide buoyancy and profitability to a manufacturer's business. I have not looked at any direct long-term effect of advertising on its own on sales and profit.

This approach has often been taken by other analysts, and they have generally examined the problem by implicitly following the "Small Steps" theory, discussed in Chapter 12. The myth of "Small Steps" visualizes advertising as having an almost imperceptible effect at first, but one that grows in minute progressions until it becomes measurable at the end of a year. The theory clearly fails to explain the real facts of how advertising influences sales over a year, in particular the drop from the short-term effect to the end-year effect. But "Small Steps" may come nearer the truth when it is used to explain long-term year-by-year sales growth, which is incremental.

It is, however, difficult to test it empirically. This is sometimes attempted with the use of econometric models, but these are invariably complex, with so many explanatory variables that there is often contamination between them. This suggests strongly that the various factors influencing sales are operating synergistically and are having the general effect of strengthening the brand itself.

Models can provide subtle insights; observation generally provides simpler ones. Models are complex to set up and interpret; observation less so. If I have to choose between models and observation, I generally choose the latter, so long as the observed data do not distort reality. The information on which we base recommendations for action must be unambiguous even if it is limited (although it must, of course, not be misleading). For this reason I think it is both simpler and more productive to cut the Gordian Knot and rely on a single unifying concept to address the long-term effect of advertising. This concept is obviously the brand, whose increasing strength can be measured in six simple ways (although we should not exclude the possibility that econometric modeling may also be able to show us something, as I shall shortly demonstrate).

To summarize these six ways: Advertising can influence long-term sales growth by boosting a brand's penetration, until a ceiling is reached. *Penetration is measurable.* Advertising can increase purchase frequency, and with it profitability. *Purchase frequency is measurable.* Advertising can reduce price elasticity and enable the manufacturer to maintain high consumer prices by cutting back on sales promotions: all with an obvious effect on profitability. *Price elasticity and prices are both measurable.* Successful advertising can increase advertising elasticity and make it possible to reap the scale economies of low advertising intensiveness. *Advertising elasticity and advertising intensiveness are both measurable.*

If, as I am suggesting, increased advertising elasticity and reduced advertising intensiveness mean *more sales for every advertising dollar,* then we might be able to find a way of demonstrating that this productivity is greater for large strong brands than for small weak ones. In Chapter 10, I discussed the concept of advertising payback, a technique developed by the well-known organization Marketing Management Analytics (MMA). Payback represents the net return from the dollar investment in advertising. It is calculated by estimating the sales increase attributed to that advertising and deducting the direct and indirect costs of producing the extra sales volume. An authoritative but unpublished series of MMA estimates shows that the advertising payback for large strong brands is on average *twice as high* as that from small weak ones.

Note my repeated emphasis on measurability. One of the greatest problems with how brands are planned is the cloudy and imprecise way in which they are described. The typical language includes such phrases as "brand equity," "core brand values," "high share of mind," "brand stretching," "psychographic targeting," and other rich and evocative phrases. It is not very easy to plan these in a businesslike fashion.

My analysis of brands is intended to be straightforward. It depends on observation and not modeling. I do not intend that it should do more than demonstrate to organizations that manage brands how advertising can contribute to their long-term profitability. It is indeed difficult to dispute that the main source of a manufacturer's profit is its brands. These provide the multifaceted differentiation that is needed to compete successfully in mature categories.

Brands are planned according to the overall strategic blueprint of the marketing company. Within these limits, the success of brands is due to two groups of people: those responsible for product design and physical production, and those responsible for advertising and day-to-day marketing operations. During a brand's introduction and growth, the first group of people is the more important because of the absolute necessity to offer something functionally superior to the competition, in at least some respects. When the brand is up and running, the advertising and marketing people reach a position of equal—perhaps even greater—importance, because it is their job to transform a skeletal brand into a real one. Brands can generate growth, staying power, and profitability for a company. Advertising is able to contribute to these things in a substantial way.

This chapter must end with a coda. The picture I have painted of advertising has been extremely positive. It must, however, never be forgotten that successful advertising campaigns represent a minority of the total. The number of ineffective or questionably effective campaigns is disgracefully high, and the proportion that work demonstrably well does not seem to be increasing. Everybody concerned with the advertising business should be alarmed and not merely troubled by this situation. It is therefore appropriate that Chapter 14 should address one practical method of improving matters. It is not the sole method we should use, but it is an important one.

Part V

Researching Advertising—Before and After It Is Run

Three Myths:

"There is no kind of reliable advertising quality control procedure [for] filtering out the duds and passing only the winners."

"The difference between the number of customers who can remember your current advertising and those who cannot, shows how many have been pulled over to the usage of your product by your advertising."

"While . . . advertising, sales promotions, and personal selling are effective in creating brand image, conveying information, and/or creating awareness, going direct with these same tools can generate an immediate behavioral response."

These are all total fallacies.

14

Looking Before You Leap

Myth:

*"There is no kind of reliable advertising quality control proce-
dure [for] filtering out the duds and passing only the winners."*

Research and the Creative Process

In the advertising business, the creative always takes first place
in importance. But although Stanley Resor, the man who made the
J. Walter Thompson Company the first modern advertising agency,
went so far as to say that "everything else is plumbing," he did not imply
that plumbing is a totally unimportant activity. If our advertising
plumbing describes (among other things) the research used to measure
campaign effects, this can be very helpful indeed.

This chapter discusses pre-testing, which enables us to eliminate
ineffective creative ideas before we spend money on screening them.
Chapter 15 describes the research used to track campaigns while they
run and that can help us diagnose how advertising is—or is not—working. Chapter 16 looks backward at the ancient lessons of direct response
and how these might still be useful to us as we struggle to make all other
types of advertising as effective as possible.

An executive with a senior job in one of the international divisions
of a gigantic marketing company once said at a meeting I attended:
"There's no need to research this advertisement. We only research ads
we have doubts about." The agency was gratified. It should not have
been. The remark was rooted in the assumption that experienced

advertising people can safely rely on their instinctive and educated judgment to predict whether or not a campaign will be effective.

This is a very questionable belief.

A leading figure in the media research world, Leo Bogart, and two colleagues once examined the predictive powers of eighty-three advertising decision makers (brand managers; advertising managers; agency account executives; and creative, media, and research people) in New York, Boston, Cincinnati, Detroit, and Los Angeles. The researchers discovered that although the experts could judge perfectly well whether or not an advertisement would be noticed, they were hopeless at forecasting its selling ability. (The predictions had of course been checked against the facts.)

Other investigations have found the same thing. But the strongest evidence of the unreliability of expert opinion is that 95 percent of new brands fail and 60 percent of ongoing campaigns have little or no effect in the marketplace. All these brands and campaigns had been evaluated by decision makers who were as experienced and talented as those consulted in Bogart's study, and had received their blessing. Subjective judgment alone is never enough. The strongbox described in Chapter 6—the box that contains the secrets of *how* an advertisement can actually produce sales—still remains securely padlocked.

What is obviously needed is some reliable way to research advertising before it is run. However, such research suffers from two problems. The first is the complexity of the task. For one thing, advertising does not operate in isolation to produce sales. Research into advertising alone can often, therefore, mislead us. And what people in the advertising business sometimes call "cut-through"—advertising's supposed ability to seize attention in a cluttered environment—is hardly an important consideration when we realize that brand purchasing and television viewing are both characterized by what has been aptly called "low involvement." As was pointed out in Chapter 2, when consumers buy most brands, the process does not mean that there is a conscious weighing of the pros and cons. Most television viewing can also be best described as a fairly superficial engagement with the audience.

But the second problem is even greater and is a real impediment to progress. Advertising people, especially those who work in advertising agencies and most especially creative people, do not like one important type of advertising research. They are not so much "underwhelmed" as aggressively antagonistic toward it. The word "test," especially as it applies to the pre-testing of finished commercials to produce scores, immediately increases their blood pressure.

Although this attitude makes for great difficulties, it is to some extent understandable. The tests that advertising agency people hate so much employ what they see as a weak methodology to make judgments about advertising: judgments that can lead to the rejection of proposals that were the product of hours of dedicated labor and that had been endorsed by the agency experts. (If they had not been, the proposals would not have been presented to the clients in the first place.) Besides the emotional investment in the advertising idea, there is also the financial investment in the finished productions. There is an emotional element here as well.

Yet despite the technical difficulties—not to speak of the delicate feelings of the people who write the advertisements—the fact is that 60 percent of advertising has little or no effect. (This figure has been discussed in Chapters 1, 6, and 12). When the mechanical problems and personal prejudices are weighed in the balance against the need to do better—to improve the return on clients' massive investment in advertising—the call for improvement is a very much weightier consideration. The clients that spend (or waste) such large amounts of money should drive bulldozers through the methodological and personal obstructions in order to find a solution to the problem of locating which campaigns will work and which will not.

Research into advertising is carried out in three stages, as follows: The first one is aimed at helping creative people produce ideas and to discriminate at a very early stage between the more promising and less promising ones. This type of research is relatively uncontroversial. It will be discussed in the next section of this chapter.

The second stage is research into finished advertisements, with the aim of forecasting effectiveness. This stage is predictive, and it is the only part of the advertising research process that is. It is looking before you leap, and it is the research that causes the problem with agencies. It has the dreaded word "test" attached to it. It will also be examined later in this chapter.

The third stage takes place after the campaign has begun to run on the air. Consumers' knowledge and attitudes are tracked regularly to provide feedback from the campaign. This provides an important input to the next round of creative planning (usually planning for the next year). Like the first research stage, the third does not raise too many objections from agencies, although some measures are far better than others and clients and agencies do not necessarily favor the best ones. This research has many points of interest, and Chapter 15 is devoted to it.

The Emergence of the Focus Group

In the United States during the early 1960s, advertising agencies began to use qualitative research to help with the first stage of their work on developing campaigns, after the strategy had been agreed. This process is still a part of agencies' normal operating procedures. Typically, two or three creative ideas—different responses to the same strategy—are worked out for television advertising in the form of scripts or story-boards or animatics (storyboards put onto videotape); and in the form of layouts for print campaigns.

These schematic advertisements are exposed to qualitative research: either individual interviews (known as "one-on-ones") or, more commonly, focus groups. The samples typically comprise twenty individuals for one-on-ones, and six groups of eight people each for focus groups. All respondents are, of course, members of the target group for the brand that is being advertised.

The questioning is not rigid. The field workers (known as "moderators" or "facilitators") use an interview guide to lay out the ground that should be covered, and they encourage respondents to use their own words, which are usually recorded on audiotape. The groups themselves are also often recorded on videotape so that the observers can watch the participants' body language. Each piece of research is sensitively reported. The reporting is more an interpretation of the findings by the moderator/facilitator than a straightforward tabulation of the data (as is done with larger scale quantitative surveys).

This sort of research uses small samples. Large ones are impracticable because of the high cost per interview and also because the results are always needed quickly. However, because of the small sample sizes the findings cannot be projected to represent the population as a whole. This limitation is accepted because the purpose of the research is to provide insights and enlightenment and not proof of anything at all. The research is efficient at detecting problems: miscommunication of existing messages or communication of unintended ones. Individual advertising ideas are generally amended and sometimes even thrown away by creative people because they caused problems to a relatively small number of respondents.

The research is used to evaluate how interested consumers might be in different advertising ideas, and how easily these communicate. Communication is a specialty of one-on-ones because, if we attempt to use groups to test communication, one member of the group who understands the point will immediately give the game away. A very important feature of this research, especially focus groups, is that it is "green-thumbed." The creative proposals become catalysts for discussion. Because of the interaction among group members, the advertising ideas they are looking at can trigger additional ideas, and creative people often find these very valuable. The actual language that is used in focus groups sometimes re-emerges in advertising copy. Creative people (and sometimes also account executives and even clients) spend many interesting hours in their rather stressful lives observing groups of consumers discussing the agency's campaign ideas from the other side of a one-way mirror. All major agencies have these installed in their offices.

This participation by creative people provides the real clue to why qualitative research is so popular. It is carried out essentially to make their lives easier, and they are persuaded to accept it on the grounds that it is more helpful than threatening. Significantly, the word "test" is never used to describe this sort of qualitative research. It is generally paid for by the agency and not the client, and the moderators/facilitators are often on the agency payroll.

When account planning was introduced in British advertising agencies during the late 1960s, account planners latched onto qualitative research and used it to develop a close working relationship with their creative colleagues. Account planners often carry out the qualitative research themselves, and this is also true in the small number of American agencies that have followed the British lead and established account planning themselves.

The more account planners became associated with small-scale qualitative research, the more this reinforced their antagonism to the types of research described as "tests." Qualitative and quantitative research are only too often regarded as mutually exclusive, as either/or. This is a curious misconception of their separate roles. The two types are complementary, not competitive.

Qualitative research is valuable in developing and refining campaign ideas. But it suffers from a very serious imperfection. In the marketplace, advertising is *used* by consumers. It is looked at or not looked at; acted on or not acted on, totally at consumers' discretion. No one instructs them to look at an advertisement except when research is being carried out. Whether or not they will do so in their normal lives depends on the brand and the advertisement itself. An advertisement is a fleeting stimulus that is missed in many if not most circumstances, and it is virtually impossible to describe psychologically why it is or is not "caught" by consumers—and by which consumers.

Advertising research that is not rooted in this reality cannot provide an explanation of the real world. Qualitative advertising research, despite what it is able to do, is based on "forced exposure." Consumers are told to look at an advertisement. (In the same way, some types of advertising research using quantitative methods are based on asking people to focus their memory and attention on advertisements they might have seen.) Both qualitative research and these quantitative systems are handicapped by the very important thing that they cannot reveal: whether or not people will look at the advertising at all.

All that we can expect from "forced exposure" research is that, *after the most important thing that happened* (i.e., after consumers' attention has been caught by an advertisement), the research will tell us something about whether and how it is working. Because this type of research is not concerned with measuring consumers' attention, its field of operation is narrowly limited. And if consumers' attention is not caught in the first place, all the findings of "forced exposure" research are valueless.

A Last-Minute Health Check

We now consider the type of advertising research that produces such violent sparks when it is discussed in advertising agency circles.

Assume that a creative proposal has been developed with help from the best qualitative research, and assume that this proposal has been taken to its final form in a series of television commercials enriched with expensively acquired production values. Because qualitative research is nonpredictive, and because the senior marketing manager of the client company is realistic enough to know that the judgment of advertising experts is fallible, he or she is now faced with a tough decision. The production cost of the commercials may have been high, but the screening cost is very much higher: perhaps ten times as much. The decision to be made is "go" or "no go." It is not surprising that the executive in question will look for some type of last-minute health check of the advertising: an objective reassurance that the decision to "go" is correct (or, if the worst comes to the worst, a solid reason for saying "no go" despite what has been spent on film production).

This reassurance (or otherwise) will be provided by a certain type of quantitative test. Some quantitative research is flawed (as explained) because it is based on telling consumers that they are being asked about advertising. In fact, over a period of about thirty years, ending in the late 1980s, the most widely used type of quantitative advertising research suffered from this handicap. This was "Day-After-Recall-Testing" (DART), which was eventually proven not to predict sales. For this reason, major advertisers stopped using it.

Testing, if it is to be reliable in predicting sales, must totally exclude all elements of prompting, just as it must avoid "forced exposure." There is more than one method of testing the selling power of an advertisement using indirect means. The system I shall describe is remarkable because it has been validated through a comparison of predictions against marketplace performance.

The method is proprietary and is offered by an organization in Evansville, Indiana, called **rsc THE QUALITY MEASUREMENT COMPANY**. It is called ARS (an acronym for Advertising Research Systems) and has been used for almost half a century. This is, incidentally, the type of research referred in the section on "The Locked Strongbox" at the end of Chapter 6. This method was developed shortly after World War II by a highly original behavioral psychologist called Horace Schwerin. Although the system has always been controversial (to say the least) among advertising agencies, it has been employed to good effect by many major clients because they believe that it works. In many cases, the clients have proven its effectiveness.

The test is carried out either in a cinema where the audience views the big screen, or in a meeting room where the audience looks at television monitors. The audience consists of at least 500 adults who have been invited to see an entertainment show lasting an hour. Interspersed in the program are some commercials, including a single commercial for one brand. This is the subject of the test, although the audience is not told this. Before the program begins, there is a lottery for a stated number of dollars. Everybody in the audience has a chance of winning, but the money has to be received in goods. Everyone marks a card on which he or she chooses individual brands, the value of which will add up to the total prize money. One of these brands is the subject of the test. At the end of the show, there is another lottery of exactly the same type, and a simple questionnaire is completed by the audience.

The result of the test is calculated by comparing the preference for the advertised brand in the second lottery with the preference for it in the first. Any increase can be attributed to the influence of the single screening of the advertisement: which was (as explained) one of a number of advertisements for different brands that were shown. There is never any mention of the purpose of the test, and the audience leaves the test location unenlightened. Of course, the lucky prize-winners will have received their prizes in the form of goods.

The idea of the test is extremely simple, although the logistics make it fairly expensive to carry out. The test produces a single finding, but this answers the really important question as far as the advertiser is concerned: whether or not the advertisement is likely to produce sales. More than 30,000 tests have been carried out in six different countries, and the more than 30,000 separate scores have been analyzed in many ways. Norms, calculated from a number of factors, provide "expected outcomes" for each brand, and these help with the decision as to whether or not to use a commercial as part of a major campaign. This decision will be substantially governed by how its score compares with the expected outcome.

The method is often called "persuasion testing." This is an inappropriate name, because it conveys the idea that advertising works by persuading (i.e., by overcoming apathetic or even resistant attitudes). Advertising actually works in a much less intrusive way, by evoking previous favorable experiences of the brand. I prefer to call the system "pre/post preference testing," an accurate and objective although clumsy title.

The many opponents of the system argue inexhaustibly that the method must be invalid and a dangerous waste of the client's money. Believers in the "Small Steps" theory consider multiple exposures are needed to make an advertisement effective (untrue); they believe that the method discriminates in favor of rational advertisements and against emotional advertisements (also untrue); and they believe that it undermines the agency's position as primary decision maker about what advertising should be run (true but justified).

It is not fruitful to spend much time on these and other objections, for a very simple reason. *We have evidence.* If a rational person is asked to balance the relative weight of theoretical arguments on the one hand, and firm evidence on the other, the balance will tilt in only one way. The fact that many advertising professionals come down in favor of the theoretical arguments is an interesting commentary on their working methods.

The ARS organization has always realized the importance of factual validation. But reliable sales measurement calls for properly conducted scanner research carried out soon after a commercial has been exposed on the air. This has been possible on a large scale only since the late 1980s. Bimonthly measurement via the old-fashioned retail audit was useless because it could not capture advertising's immediate effect. When scanner measurement began to be commonly used, the ARS researchers began assembling cases. They put together *all* the cases for which data could be provided, whether the results were strongly positive, weakly positive, or negative. There was no "cherry picking."

Over the years, more than 2,000 cases have been collected, although the ARS clients have put an embargo on releasing the majority of these, even in a disguised or even aggregated form. There remain more than 300 cases for which data can be published. In each of these, the size of the "pre/post" shift has been compared to the size of the brand's market share increase or decrease soon after the tested advertisement was run. Any possible contaminations (e.g., from sales promotions) are accounted for, so that the result is a serviceable measure of the predictive power of the ARS scores.

Looking at all the cases together, there is a good statistical relationship between the size of the "pre/post" shift and the subsequent change in market share. The simplest way of describing this correlation is that it achieves a score of 7 on a 10-point scale. A positive "pre/post" shift will forecast a positive test result; and the size of the shift is a good prediction of the actual change in market share. The aggregated data have been supplemented by a number of detailed individual cases that track the "pre/post" scores and market shares over time, and these cases all identify the brands in question. They make interesting (and persuasive) reading.

The overall success rate of the system is far greater than any unguided judgments could provide, no matter how experienced the judges. The myth that appears at the beginning of this chapter, that no system will eliminate the duds and select the winners, is patently untrue. Worse, it is counterproductive. People who believe it are deliberately removing an important instrument from their research toolboxes. In making decisions about advertising campaigns, decision makers need all the help they can get.

The research produces consistent results. When commercials are retested (as has been done with more than 1,000 of them), differences in scores between test and retest are not significant. Most important, the system does not discriminate in favor of—or against—any particular type of brand or style of advertising. It works equally well for established and new brands; large and small brands; food, household, proprietary drugs, and personal care products; and thirty-second and fifteen-second commercials. It does not favor predominantly rational or predominantly emotional advertising.

As readers can infer from the way the lotteries are carried out, the system is primarily suitable for everyday products that fill the normal homemaker's shopping basket. But such repeat-purchase packaged goods are an important and advertising-intensive group of product categories. No one has been able to make the system work with any advertising medium other than television. But because television is the dominant medium for packaged goods, the system's inability to measure print advertising is not disastrous, although it would obviously be desirable to find a method of doing so.

The research scores are easy to understand and act on. But diagnostic information has been produced rather sparingly, although the research company makes constant efforts to use the system to provide richer details. In any event, diagnostic information is the province of qualitative research, and (as mentioned earlier) qualitative research and quantitative pre-testing are complementary and not competitive techniques.

This sort of testing is used far more widely in the United States than in Europe, especially in Britain. This is partly a result of the larger American advertising and research budgets. In Britain, however, something else is at work. Account planners, who are so important in British agencies, never conceal their negative feelings toward quantitative pre-testing.

This has an interesting outcome. Pure Single-Source research has been used in a number of different countries to measure the immediate effect of advertising on sales. In most countries there is a strong effect in the cases of 30 to 40 percent of brands. But among this group of strongest campaigns, the Short-Term Advertising Strength, or STAS, measures of market share improvement are a good deal higher in the United States than they are in Britain and Germany. In other words, the best campaigns in America produce relatively more immediate sales than the best campaigns in these two large European countries. I believe that the superior performance of the American campaigns is partly the result of effective pre-testing: a procedure that enables the clients to screen out the duds and concentrate on effective advertising as this has been predicted by quantitative pre-testing. American advertisers are obviously more energetic in driving their bulldozers through the obstructions than their European counterparts are.

This chapter has repeatedly emphasized how important it is to research advertising in a disguised way, so that consumers' attention to advertising will be natural and not forced. It would be an advantage if this approach could be followed in all advertising research, qualitative as well as quantitative.

During the 1990s, the Los Angeles agency Chiat/Day, which was a lengthened shadow of Jay Chiat, one of the few commanding figures in the advertising business at the end of the twentieth century, carried out a most unusual piece of qualitative research for its client, the fast-food chain Jack-in-the-Box. The researchers piled focus group members into a bus and told them that they were being taken to eat in McDonald's. The respondents were surprised when they arrived at Jack-in-the-Box. The researchers were, of course, interested in consumers' immediate and frank reactions: They noted some disappointment, some relief, some indifference. These reactions told the researchers more about consumers' unvarnished responses than they would have learned from hours spent with the consumers in the comfortable surroundings where most focus groups take place. In research as well as in advertising, it is the immediate response—which is often highly unexpected—that has the greatest value of all.

After going through the process described in this chapter, the advertising is run in the marketplace. The next type of research is devoted to tracking its influence on the perceptions of those consumers who have (one hopes) seen the campaign.

15

Consumer Perceptions—
and the Cash Register

Myth:

"The difference between the number of customers who can remember your current advertising and those who cannot, shows how many have been pulled over to the usage of your product by your advertising."

Why Do Advertisers Track Consumer Perceptions?

Ready-prepared foods are very popular with American consumers. They comprise a large and variegated group of product categories, both fresh and frozen. I shall talk about the leading brand in one of the largest of these categories. Its name cannot be revealed, but I shall call it brand KK. The category is growing modestly, and KK's sales are keeping pace. In the most recent year, KK's volume grew by 2.5 percent over the year before, and its sales when tracked weekly over the past three years show a modest upward trend despite the usual weekly ups and downs. Its lead over its three main competitors remained equally strong over the whole three years. KK has a substantial advertising budget, and the campaign has a demonstrable influence on sales.

The manufacturer of KK, like all major players in this and other categories, is closely interested in following the sales of all its brands (and also those of its competitors). What matters most is sales to final consumers and not just sales to the retail trade. In particular, manufacturers measure sales before the beginning of any advertising campaign, sales during the campaign, and—most important—sales afterward. Even if a manufacturer cannot afford the expense of Pure Single-Source research, sales estimates based on consumer panel or retail audit research will give a crude indication of the success or otherwise of its campaign. Experienced marketing and advertising practitioners, however, will not be too confident that all the immediate sales effect is due to advertising, nor that the entire effect of advertising is captured in an immediate sales gain.

Nevertheless, consumer sales, if they are properly monitored, will reveal a great deal. To show real sales movements, they must be measured at short intervals—ideally weekly—to disclose their full volatility. And as the week-by-week sales (or market share) figures are averaged to eliminate erratic movements, we can begin to see longer-term trends.

The simplest way to smooth the fluctuations is by calculating a moving average. This is an elementary statistical technique, and it is always useful. If we are measuring averages over thirteen-week periods, the starting point is *the end* of the first thirteen weeks. We calculate it by totaling the thirteen weeks' sales and dividing by thirteen, to give an average weekly sales figure for the period. The next stage is to take the total and deduct the figure for week one and add the figure for week fourteen, then divide again by thirteen. (The thirteen weeks have now moved along by a week.) After this, we take away week two and add week fifteen, as the period moves along by yet another week. And so the process continues until it enables us to see a trend progressing forward. These immediate sales measures and averages are still the ones most commonly used to estimate the effects of advertising.

The more directly the advertising works, the easier it is to detect the relationship between advertising and results. In Scotland, the Health Education Board ran a television advertising campaign to encourage people to make a telephone call to seek help to quit smoking. The number of inquiries followed the pattern of television advertising so closely that the relationship between the two was quite unmistakable. This is in fact the sort of pattern we have always seen with direct response advertising.

With campaigns that work less directly, which are of course the norm for most consumer goods, the relationship between advertising and effects is less obvious but can often still be seen. A series of commercials for Nestlé instant coffee, featuring a man and a woman who became romantically involved after one of them had borrowed a jar of the coffee from the other, became an advertising icon in the United States and Britain and also in a number of other countries. Its effect on sales in Britain was strongest when tracked among heavy television viewers: the people who had been exposed to an above-average number of different commercials in the campaign and as a consequence would have seen more of the love story. This differential effect is persuasive evidence that the campaign was working.

Nevertheless, no matter how close to the day of buying the measurement takes place, nor how carefully the figures are tracked over time, they will show only *what* has happened. This is important, but we need to know much more if we are going to plan future advertising efficiently with the help of research. In addition to the what, we need to know *why* and, in particular, *how* any changes have taken place.

In the case of KK, the improvement in sales was accompanied by a fall during the last year in the amount of television advertising: from a total of 1,720 Gross Rating Points (GRPs) to 1,440, a reduction of 16 percent. The brand's sales were deconstructed by econometric techniques, and television advertising's contribution to sales per GRP was estimated to have increased substantially. The campaign was obviously working and was yielding a greater sales return for each dollar spent on the television advertising.

This is something that the marketing people in the manufacturing company could really sink their teeth into. With KK, most of the reasons for the success were related to media factors, in particular the continuity with which the campaign was planned and executed. From this it could be inferred that the brand was succeeding because consumers' purchase frequency was increasing. But far more commonly, when a campaign seems clearly to be working (or not working), advertisers feel the need to dig more deeply into sales and explore the responses of consumers directly. These are, after all, the people at the receiving end of the advertising. This brings us to the processes of measuring changes in consumers' knowledge of and attitudes toward advertising campaigns; and their knowledge of and attitudes toward the brands themselves, and also their usage of them. (Usage and attitude surveys are generally abbreviated with the initials U&A)

This research is carried out through repeated surveys among consumers. We do not interview the *same* consumers every time because the cost of calling back is too high. Each survey is based on a sample of the same size and demographic structure as all the other surveys. Most important, the same questions are asked, so that the findings from one investigation can be compared reasonably precisely with the findings from the others.

The frequency of fieldwork ranges from once a week to once a year. Only the weekly and monthly surveys can be described as continuous tracking (i.e., there are no gaps in the periods covered). When the research is carried out weekly, it is often reported as a four-week moving average because of the larger size of the sample accumulated over four weeks. Less frequent surveys, such as those carried out every three months or every year, are sometimes called "dipsticks": investigations carried out at regular but infrequent intervals. It obviously makes sense to spend the large amount of money needed for continuous tracking only if the figures produced by the research are likely to change rapidly. This is true of some but not all measures of knowledge and attitudes.

Consumer Perceptions of Advertising

Tracking originated in Britain with the system called the Advertising Planning Index, which was first used as long ago as the early 1960s. During the 1970s, the Millward Brown system of tracking advertising awareness became rapidly popular and virtually established Britain as the home of tracking techniques.

Tracking has, however, been carried out in the United States only since the early 1980s, and as late as 1998 American managers were found to favor behavioral data from scanner research and media modeling rather than using tracking. Tracking was seen to be concerned with means to an end and not with what matters, which is consumer behavior. It can, however, be used as some sort of surrogate for behavioral measures in categories where it is difficult to collect behavioral data, such as certain products and services outside the field of repeat-purchase packaged goods.

The most common type of continuous tracking still relates to consumers' awareness of advertising: a measure in essence of the impact of the creative content of a campaign on the consumer. Such research can measure spontaneous (i.e., unprompted) awareness; in other cases, a list of brands is used as a prompt for a question such as: "Which of these brands have you seen advertised on television recently?" (This is the Millward Brown approach.)

The purpose of the research is to measure what advertising the respondents had seen or heard during the previous week or so. The figures are often adjusted, to factor in latent recall (e.g., a "base" or long-term recall level that sometimes exists). Even more important, the figures are often also weighted to account for differences in media expenditure, because a heavy campaign is likely to produce a higher awareness level than a light one, irrespective of the creative quality of the two. Small brands are also bedeviled by small sample sizes, which make the figures unreliable.

The most important characteristic of continuous tracking of advertising awareness is that the figures can indeed change quickly, and for this reason the substantial expense of continuous data collection can sometimes be justified. And this actual expense can often be reduced if a number of different product categories are covered in a single set of interviews.

When a new shampoo called Decoré was introduced in Australia with a sixty-second commercial, spontaneous awareness of the advertising rose quickly, and in less than a month it reached 45 percent. The campaign then moved to a thirty-second commercial and the level of spontaneous awareness responded very weakly and took another two months to reach 50 percent. A month after the campaign began, the brand's market share had shown no response. It then climbed steadily and rapidly to 12 percent at the end of two further months. These figures indicated clear success, at least in the launch phase of the brand.

Did the information on advertising awareness provide a useful insight into what was happening? The answer is "yes," within narrow limits. These limits are that advertising was being studied as an end in itself. It certainly made an impression on people and probably triggered their buying. But how it did this is unclear. By far the most important role of advertising is to influence consumers' buying behavior—single and repeated purchasing—which is in turn connected with their perceptions of the brands themselves. *There is no simple connection between advertising awareness and these more important effects.* The steep rise in awareness of the sixty-second commercial for Decoré predated the sales increase, making it reasonably certain that it was advertising in all its aspects—creative, budget, and media—that was driving the sales. This was a good argument to continue with the campaign. The role of the thirty-second commercial is more difficult to establish. This shorter commercial was doing very little for advertising awareness, but sales were continuing their upward progression while it was running.

This example amplifies what I have already said about the problem with advertising awareness: the weakness and complexity of the relationship between advertising awareness and consumer behavior. Awareness of advertising does not ring the cash register directly enough for it to be used as a key component of a marketing strategy. With new brands, it is quite valuable to know that steeply growing advertising awareness is likely to lead consumers to purchase the brand, at least on a trial basis. But with ongoing brands and familiar advertising campaigns, awareness of advertising will be influenced to a substantial degree by whether or not a consumer uses the brand already. This is the result of selective perception.

This points to the profound fallacy in the myth that appears at the beginning of this chapter. It is clear that the author of those words had ongoing brands in mind because he refers to a brand's customers. Such people will almost certainly be conscious of the advertising for the brand. If awareness of the advertising ever drives usage, it is equally— or even more—likely that usage of the brand drives awareness of the advertising. The most appropriate policy recommendation in these circumstances is to try to build usage directly and not be too concerned with whether or not people remember the campaign. Concentrating on awareness could, in fact, get in the way of a more profitable style of communication.

Besides the value of tracking advertising awareness for new brands, there is another circumstance in which studying advertising awareness over time can make a much more positive contribution. Some very long-lasting campaigns, by their very success, encourage the client and agency to be complacent. In reality, the effect of long-lasting campaigns can sometimes almost imperceptibly fade. They begin to resemble wallpaper: it is still on the wall but no one notices the pattern anymore.

Oxo is an old and successful British brand of bouillon and soup cubes made by a company that researches its advertising campaigns punctiliously. Oxo used one notable campaign for a period of seventeen years: a campaign that was continuously successful and indeed became a classic. Toward the end of this period, advertising awareness was found to be weakening, despite the fact that sales were still strong. Before long, U&A research detected an erosion in favorable attitudes toward the brand; it was also found that, although the overall consumer penetration remained more or less unchanged, the number of regular users was beginning to fall slowly and the number of infrequent users to be rising. The eventual result would inevitably have been a reduction in the brand's volume sales. But the client and agency had seen the warning signs and had begun working on a new campaign. This was exposed nationally before the productivity of the old campaign had been totally exhausted, and the brand was given a new lease on life.

With Decoré, the advertising awareness data helped the advertiser discover the reason for its initial success, and it justified the continuation of the campaign. With Oxo, the diagnosis provided by tracking advertising awareness was of even greater value. By providing advance warning, the weakening awareness figures enabled the client and agency to take remedial action before the brand found itself in real trouble. And because the Oxo research was being used to study long-term changes in consumer perceptions of the advertising, it was carried out at "dipstick" intervals, thereby saving the large amounts of money that would have been needed for continuous tracking.

Consumer Perceptions of Brands

We now take a broader look at advertising's role in the marketplace. We will no longer study advertising as a means to an end, that is, sales, but more the degree to which it influences consumers' knowledge of and perceptions of *brands*. This brings us much closer to understanding the purchasing process.

We measure consumers' spontaneous *awareness* of brands by collecting their responses to a simple question: "What brands in this product category can you think of?" (The research is normally carried out among category users.) The data are analyzed in two ways: counting any brand named (which provides "share of mind" awareness), and counting only the first brand mentioned (which provides "top of mind" awareness). Prompted awareness is generally not worth investigating, because the figures are usually all very high because users of a product category know at least the names of most of the brands on the supermarket shelf.

Consumers' *perceptions* of different brands cover both their functional features and, more important, what the brands mean to them in nonfunctional terms. We collect this information by showing consumers of the category a list of functional and nonfunctional attributes and asking them to rate each brand according to every attribute on the list. Sometimes respondents are asked to nominate the brands they rate best, second best, and worst by each of the criteria, and we average the results.

One criticism that is made of this research is that it fails to cope with advertising that works with low-involvement goods and services, which account for a large share of total advertising. The brands themselves are likely to have a more subtle relationship with their users than bald statements of specific perceptions are able to capture. There is, in addition, the problem of interview fatigue. Some of the statements describing perceptions are rather complicated, and there is a limit to the amount of detail that can be discussed in a twenty-minute interview.

The research sometimes goes further and asks questions that attempt to measure consumers' *commitment* to a brand. It is not certain that the findings are much better than those that can be produced by simple direct questions about the quantities of different brands the respondents actually buy.

The same criticism also applies to attempts to measure *intention to purchase,* in answer to the question "Which brand will you buy next time?" The answers that come out are known to reflect actual purchasing in the recent past more than any true intention to buy in the future. It therefore makes more sense to measure recent purchasing directly.

Awareness and attitude research related to brands has two important characteristics. First, awareness figures (and also, to some extent, attitudinal measures) tend to go down when new brands enter the category. The reason for this is cognitive. With low-involvement products, consumers seem unable or unwilling to expand their total knowledge of the category when new brands are introduced. If a newcomer makes an impression, existing brands pay the price. A successful new brand will therefore reduce the "share of mind" of all the others.

The second point is that all the figures move slowly, which means that annual "dipstick" figures are quite good enough to measure any changes. This slow pace of change is proof that advertising's long-term influence on how consumers view brands is extremely gradual (although it is inexorable if the campaign is working properly).

Here is an example of these types of research and how they can be used. Listerine is the longtime leader in the mouthwash category in the United States and Canada. Shortly after Procter & Gamble launched Scope, which posed a very serious threat to Listerine's pre-eminence, the "top of mind" brand awareness of Listerine among Canadians dipped from 45 to 35 percent. Not surprisingly, the arrival of Scope caused much fluttering in the dovecotes of both client and agency. After an extensive but worrisome and very rapid exploration of creative ideas for a fresh Listerine campaign, a powerful new series of commercials was launched that did two things: they underscored Listerine's strength in curing bad breath, and they encouraged purchase frequency, by telling people to use Listerine twice a day.

The data shown here are Canadian, but the American figures are very similar. Within a year of the start of the new campaign, Listerine's "top of mind" brand awareness had increased to 38 percent, and within two years it had recovered its original level of 45 percent. More important, perceptions of the brand were consistently strengthened across a whole range of attributes. And more important still, research into consumer behavior showed that the proportion of Listerine users who used it with heavy frequency (eleven times a week or more) went up from 25 to 33 percent.

Another example is the De Beers advertising campaign for diamond jewelry described in Chapter 6. The familiar campaign based on the slogan "A Diamond Is Forever" has been used with great effect for more than sixty years. During the 1990s, the advertising was directed specifically at selling higher-price jewelry. This strategy was successful worldwide. During the period 1990 through 1995, the average price per piece of diamond jewelry increased from $800 to $900. And the aggregate value of sales went up, although there was a slight decline in the total number of individual pieces sold.

During this period, in the United States (where good data are available), the image associations of diamonds strengthened to a measurable degree. The price-related association "worth the expense" remained stable at 65 percent (thus providing justification for the gradually increasing prices of the individual pieces of jewelry). The proportion of people associating diamonds with "an expression of love" rose progressively from 69 to 81 percent. Association with the belief that "diamonds are more beautiful than any other stone" went up from 53 to 58 percent. And the proportion of people endorsing the belief that diamonds are the "best way of marking an important occasion in one's life" went up from 52 to 61 percent.

What do these examples tell us? Four points emerge fairly clearly:

1. Awareness of an advertising campaign can be useful in only two rather extreme circumstances: with new brands and campaigns (which need continuous tracking) and with very long-lasting campaigns (for which "dipstick" research is sufficient). Continuous measurement costs a great deal of money, which must be absorbed as part of the high start-up costs of a new brand. Such an expense is hardly justified with most ongoing campaigns.

2. Brand awareness is generally more valuable than advertising awareness, because it focuses on something closer to the end result of

advertising: its influence on consumers' perceptions of brands. Measurement of brand attributes is an even more valuable tool, and for the same reason. For both these measures, "dipstick" research is sufficient.

3. The most important insights come from evaluating together three separate measures: brand awareness and knowledge of brand attributes (both cognitive measures) and purchasing (a behavioral measure). With Listerine and De Beers (and a number of other specific examples I have come across during my career), it was these three separate but mutually supporting types of information that provided ironclad evidence that the advertising was working, and that it was working as planned. These measures take a step beyond a brand's sales—which describe the *what*—and they illuminate the *how*.

4. The key point about these measures is their interaction. Purchasing a brand influences consumers' knowledge directly, and heightens their interest in it. Because of selective perception, users will tend to notice a brand's advertising, and their knowledge of it will therefore increase more. Purchasing also influences people's attitudes. They will develop warmer feelings as they strive to reduce cognitive dissonance. All three measures need to be looked at. If they are all moving in the same direction, then we may not need to worry too much about the relationship between them. But if they do not, this may point to problems. Increased purchasing accompanied by static or declining image perceptions may mean that consumers are buying the brand increasingly on promotion. Improving perceptions and stable purchasing may mean price or distributional problems. Strengthened brand awareness and no other improvement may point to an inadequate advertising campaign.

Brand-related measures, which can be collected by "dipsticks," are more valuable than advertising-related measures, which involve expensive continuous data collection. It is therefore difficult to understand why advertisers concentrate so much of their research budgets on the continuous tracking of advertising awareness. The probable reason is that advertisers like to receive a regular report card: one that is extremely easy to understand. The heavy expense of continuous tracking makes it certain that advertisers pay attention to the figures. They should, however, consider the value of what is reported on the card: in particular the very fragile connection between advertising awareness and sales.

British advertising theory is still rooted in the idea of "Small Steps," which I discussed with much skepticism in Chapter 12. If advertisers and their agencies believe in "Small Steps"—the idea that advertising's effect grows all the time in gradual and barely perceptual increments— they may be persuaded that they need a continuous (and measured) advertising presence so as to avoid interrupting the supposed progression of the advertising effect. If—as I believe—the "Small Steps" theory is a fallacy, one of the main props supporting the continuous tracking of advertising awareness is removed.

In view of the complexity of measuring advertising effects, the best guiding principle for clients should be to concentrate on the end results of advertising activity. American advertisers, with their greater interest in behavioral research, have assembled a better tool kit of useful methods for planning advertising to build brands, sales, and profits.

A Footnote on Sales Promotions

This chapter has concentrated exclusively on measuring the effects of advertising. There is a further important aspect of this. As discussed in Chapter 9, sales promotions account for three-quarters of the total amount of money spent by major manufacturers on A&P (advertising above the line plus promotions below the line). In turn, a huge proportion—perhaps 90 percent—of promotional expenditure is devoted to direct price cutting.

If we track price cuts and a brand's weekly sales over the course of a year, we normally see a very direct relationship between the two. A dip in price usually means an immediate surge in volume sales: albeit a strictly temporary effect. Periods of consumer advertising can also be related to weekly sales, but the response of sales is usually far less pronounced.

The most interesting outcome of this analysis is the light it sheds on the interaction between the two stimuli, lower prices and consumer advertising. In most circumstances, the two activities are run in different periods during the year. It seems to be a policy of most manufacturers to cover the calendar as completely as possible with one activity or the other. When promotions are used, advertising is absent, and vice versa. In this normal situation, there is no synergy between the two activities and the trend in volume sales is usually static or even declining, despite the sharp short-term effect of the price reductions.

The situation is very different when advertising and promotions are employed at the same time, with the aim of encouraging mutual support between them. (The two activities need only coincide in time, and the advertising should not be used to publicize the promotion *per se.*) The advertising nudges the buyer into purchasing the brand in store, and the lower price in that same store will provide an additional push. During my professional career I have encountered very few cases of manufacturers using media advertising and promotions in mutual support. But when this happens, the trend in volume sales is often steered modestly upward. Very few manufacturing companies and advertising agencies follow this policy, because the facts are so little known. They are not known because, in the normal process of measuring advertising effects, researchers tend to concentrate totally on single isolated variables, and not necessarily the most important variables at that. This is a fundamental problem with concentrating on consumer perceptions and paying too little attention to behavioral outcomes. The next chapter focuses almost entirely on the effect of communication on consumer behavior.

16

Wheels and Their Reinvention

Myth:

"While . . . advertising, sales promotions, and personal selling are effective in creating brand image, conveying information, and/or creating awareness, going direct with these same tools can generate an immediate behavioral response."

An Abandoned Heritage

Every year, at least seven companies spend more than $1 billion each on media advertising in the United States. In 2001, Procter & Gamble (P&G) spent $1.7 billion, and its expenditure on sales promotions was even greater. This organization, which many people consider to be the most knowledgeable marketer of consumer goods in the United States and indeed the world, would be extremely interested to learn that these vast dollar expenditures are actually being devoted to "creating brand image, conveying information, and/or creating awareness." In other words, P&G is spending the money on softening up consumers rather than selling to them.

The quotation at the beginning of this chapter is rather a strange piece of prose, but it is possible to extract a clear meaning from it. It is saying that the only type of advertising/sales promotion/personal selling that actually does manage to sell is the absolutely direct variety. However, such directness is virtually never practiced by large consumer goods companies, for a very good reason. We have plentiful evidence that a single appearance of a conventional television or magazine advertisement can produce a large increase in sales.

This is the simple and obvious reason why P&G uses so much media advertising for selling Crest, Folgers, Pampers, Tide, and all its other brands. The normal type of advertising used for such brands can move merchandise. To P&G and most other major American advertisers, advertising is a relentlessly commercial activity that must be justified by its contribution to sales and profit. Many companies also believe that psychological perceptions of a brand—awareness of its properties and the image associations surrounding it—are created and nurtured more by consumers' actual experience of using the brand than by the advertising.

The quotation, which comes from an advertising textbook used in American universities, baptizes students with an idea that will be quickly and abruptly corrected once they get a job in the advertising business. The statement is a myth and that should be the end of the matter. But the idea that media advertising is merely a background influence on sales—concerned with such things as image building—is still believed by many people who should know better. Within the advertising business, there has for a long time been an undercurrent of feeling—one rarely mentioned explicitly—that media advertising is a soft and indirect stimulus whose contribution cannot be measured. This belief is especially associated with television advertising, which since the 1960s has grown progressively more important as an advertising medium for major brands of consumer goods. In studies of the results of television advertising, there is an insistent tendency to look for "longer and broader" effects (a particularly British fixation). This concentration on indirect and long-term benefits is something that has developed over more than three decades. But it was not always so.

Until about 1960, advertising campaigns for large national brands were run mainly in print media, especially in magazines: magazines that had far higher circulations than such journals today and that served a general nonspecialist audience. Newspapers were also used for national advertising, although to a lesser degree. Print campaigns were strongly supported by advertising on radio, which also had a general audience, and listeners paid much more attention to the messages on air than radio listeners do today.

With print and radio advertising, advertising messages are communicated through the written or spoken word. And although words are very often used for an emotional purpose and used to great effect in this way, the underlying characteristic of the written and spoken word is that it carries a degree of rationality.

The source of the skills deployed in the print advertising used so effectively during the decades before 1960 came from the old tradition of direct response: that advertising is a source of information and a tool to sell. Brand advertising was stylistically very similar to direct response advertising; a number of noted practitioners, James Webb Young and David Ogilvy in particular, paid tribute to direct response because of the lessons it had taught them. And although most print advertising in that period was not for goods sold by direct response, the *style* of most print advertising came from a common heritage. The results of direct response advertising were always measurable. And even with general advertising in magazines, there were various serious attempts to study effects and relate the advertising to sales. For instance, the Starch organization started measuring readership of print advertisements during the 1920s. During the 1950s, it attempted to relate readership figures to sales; although it was many years before a way could be found to analyze the data, a positive connection was eventually found between the two series of figures.

One thing more than anything else caused the change in emphasis away from the printed word and from the influence of direct response. This was of course the emergence of television. By the end of the 1960s, this had become the most influential medium for widely sold consumer goods. Although during the 1960s the best work of leading advertising practitioners like William Bernbach and David Ogilvy continued to be in print media, magazines were beginning to be marginalized, eventually becoming merely a supplementary medium. Newspapers and radio remained important only for local advertisers.

Much of the television advertising during the 1960s had a verbal and rational orientation. A positive reason for this was the discovery that television could demonstrate a brand's functional features. But there were also more questionable uses of the medium: commercials using the "slice of life" and Unique Selling Proposition (USP) techniques, both of which were perpetuated through the use of flawed research. But starting in the 1970s, television became a medium much more heavily dependent on visual imagery, with a very limited use of words. At the same time magazine advertisements also moved away from using words and toward a greater reliance on pictures. They increasingly began to resemble page-sized billboards. Meanwhile agencies were beginning to favor qualitative evaluation of advertising at the expense of quantitative; qualitative research is a diagnostic device rather than a means of measurement. The result of all this was that attempts to relate advertising to sales began to fade.

After the 1960s the shift of emphasis in a visual direction was perfectly obvious, but the reasons for it were not totally straightforward. A highly experienced American creative man who spent his career in Europe said this about television: "technique now replaced emotion (and conceptual thinking) and selling slipped further down on the list of priorities. You couldn't win a prize at Cannes with sales results!" About print advertising he said: "television didn't kill the copy department; bad writers did." This touches on a problem of which, as an educator, I am constantly aware: a pervasive and increasing weakness in public literacy.

Bernbach's most celebrated campaign was for the introduction during the 1960s of the Volkswagen "Beetle," or "Bug." The advertisements that gained the greatest plaudits were in magazines and used at least 150 words: no trite attempts at image building, just sinewy but inviting prose. The launch campaign for the new "Bug" almost forty years later was run by another agency. The form of the magazine layout was similar to Bernbach's but there were virtually no words at all. The agency was clearly oblivious to how Bernbach's advertisements actually worked: by using arresting layouts to lure readers into involvement with the copy, where they were told in a user-friendly way why they should buy the car.

These evolutions affected the culture of advertising agencies, and this culture in turn bred a continuation of a soft, visual style of advertising: It emphatically rejected direct advertising in all its ramifications. A factor that re-emphasized the importance of long-term as opposed to short-term effects was a point I have already made: the industry's inability to trace easily a connection between television advertising and sales. Because agencies were now relying on qualitative evaluation of advertising, the only available way of measuring sales was through bimonthly retail audits that smoothed out all short-term fluctuations. This made the immediate effect of advertising essentially invisible. The advertising business had to wait until the arrival of scanners in the 1980s before week-by-week changes in sales could be measured; and until the development of Pure Single-Source research in the early 1990s before we could detect the connection between these short-term sales changes and media advertising.

During the 1970s and onward, advertising agencies began to resemble show business organizations: less involved in writing advertisements than in producing spectacular thirty-second commercials. At the same time, agencies began to lose their craft skills in writing advertising for media other than television: a loss that David Ogilvy publicly deplored in a widely read book published in 1983; the title of the relevant chapter in his book is "Wanted: A Renaissance in Print Advertising."

Advertising for national brands began therefore to be focused on television, on visual imagery, and on long-term effects measured (if measured at all) by tracking studies. In all this evolution, salesmanship was not much to the fore, although Ogilvy—who was a highly informed observer—thought that salesmanship was the distinguishing characteristic of the best American advertising. But as it was seen by the rest of the advertising industry, salesmanship was the concern of the quaint archaism of direct response. If direct-response advertising bequeathed a heritage, practitioners of general advertising soon dumped it into the trash can of history. In the cases in which major agencies had direct-response clients, this advertising was often relegated to specialist organizations that were forced to trade under their own names and to dissociate themselves from the names of the agencies of which they were a part.

The myth that appears at the beginning of this chapter eventually became supported, at least in part, by advertisers of mainstream goods and services and their agencies. They certainly accepted the part about the role of advertising in creating an image, but there was less agreement about direct advertising. This was seen to be effective for limited categories of goods, but its relevance to general advertising was continuously questioned.

In essence, advertising was thought to start and finish with "creating brand image, conveying information and/or creating awareness." The proponents of Integrated Marketing Communications (IMC) have always emphasized the large and growing importance of direct response, especially using direct mailings to lists of prospects (a technique known as "database marketing"). This looks inward into the brand with the aim of increasing the rate of purchase, rather than outward into the market in order to boost penetration. IMC practitioners would have a difficult row to hoe, as we shall discover later in this chapter.

Is Direct Response an Exclusively Specialist Technique?

This question of whether direct response is an exclusively specialist technique provides the main focus of this chapter. There are serious misconceptions about direct-response advertising, and we must start by sketching its most important characteristics.

Practitioners of mainline advertising do not have much regard for direct response for two reasons, both of which are concerned more with perception than with reality. First, direct response is considered to be different in all ways from general advertising: in particular in its objectives and in its method of operation. The second reason stems from the direct-response advertisements themselves. They appear to many advertising people to be dull, old-fashioned, and (for want of a better word) "tacky."

Most direct advertising is for goods and services sold by mail order, a business that has in the past been associated occasionally with dubious products and questionable business practices. The classic description of mail order as "salesmanship in print" (or television) still applies, but most people concerned with mainline advertising think the word "salesmanship" too pedestrian to describe the work they do for print and, more especially, for television.

Direct-response advertising did originate in mail order during the nineteenth century. At the time when the American frontier was moving westward, the geographical movement of the pioneers outstripped the geographical expansion of retail organizations to provide them with everything except everyday necessities (which were sold by small dry-goods stores in the frontier towns). Mail order was firmly established by 1900 and was carried out both through print advertising and through catalogs that offered a vast range of farm equipment, household durables, clothing, and other goods as varied as firearms, self-improvement systems, and even complete houses shipped in separate sections for building on the newly occupied homesteads.

As mentioned already, the style of direct-response advertising influenced the style of general advertising in print media, and this influence was still being felt until the 1960s, about the time when television advertising was becoming dominant. During the whole of the twentieth century and beyond, direct-response advertising itself did not lose its importance. Indeed, it grew at much the same pace as general advertising, and its growth was also more continuous. In the years when mainstream advertising flattened, direct response still continued to increase.

The largest single advertising medium for direct response is direct mail, which is not counted in the estimates of advertising expenditure in the main media such as those quoted in Chapter 9. In 2001, direct-mail advertising was estimated to be worth almost $45 billion. We should add to this total the direct-response advertising on television and in newspapers and magazines, plus most of the advertising on the Internet. (Direct-response advertising rarely employs radio.) These calculations suggest an aggregate expenditure for direct-response advertising of a figure approaching $60 billion. This is a very serious sum of money: larger than total advertising on television (which overlaps with direct response, as explained; the actual overlap is approximately $1.3 billion).

Direct response is defined as advertising that makes a sale directly, via the mail, the telephone, or the Internet, and also by prompting people to visit a retail store. It also includes inquiries about high-price goods and services that will (or will not) lead to a sale. The conversion rate of inquiry to sale is carefully monitored, and great emphasis is always placed on high-quality inquiries that produce sales rather than low-quality inquiries that do not. In addition, vast numbers of general advertisements contain a Web site address to encourage the public to find out more about what is being advertised, but these have not been included in this present review.

How does all this affect general advertisers and their agencies and how they carry out their business? To judge this, we must look at the most important characteristics of direct response. There are three: (1) *measurability*; (2) the fact that extra advertising rapidly produces *diminishing returns*; and (3) a *style* of advertising that is unique to direct response today although it was less so forty years ago.

Measurability. Direct-response advertising is a pure stimulus because the sale (or inquiry) is not influenced by other factors. The advertising effect is uncontaminated. In this respect, it is different from general advertising for goods sold in retail stores. With the latter, in-store activities like displays and store-related stimuli like coupons and rebates make the influence of advertising hard to assess. The difficulties of measurement are made even worse by competitive activity. With direct response, besides the fact that there is no retail link between advertiser and end-consumer, most goods and services sold are not engaged in competitive warfare on quite such an intense scale as we see with repeat-purchase packaged goods.

With direct response, the cost per sale can be measured by simple arithmetic: by dividing the number of goods sold from a specific advertisement into the cost of that advertisement. As a general rule, direct-response advertising pays its way, because only advertisements of proven selling ability are used widely. Is it so strange to believe that this criterion should apply to *all* advertising?

Because it is so easy to measure the results of direct response advertising, the guiding precept of the business is experimentation. Advertisers test alternative copy; different sizes in print and different lengths on television; alternative media vehicles; different direct-mail lists. The unit of measurement is always cost-per-response. Direct advertisers are not inhibited by the high absolute price of certain media vehicles. The cost-per-response from a publication or television daypart with a large audience and high exposure cost can often be lower than that from a publication or daypart with a small audience and low cost. Testing creative alternatives with television is much more expensive than with print advertising because of the cost of the television production, but it is often done nevertheless.

Testing is the lifeblood of the direct-response advertiser. "Never stop testing, and your advertising will never stop improving" is, appropriately enough, an adage that David Ogilvy always followed.

Diminishing Returns. The effectiveness of a direct-response advertisement is driven by the creative idea. The proof of this is that if a direct-response advertisement is going to work, it will work with a single exposure; repetition will not help matters. And it is an absolute rule of direct response that the same advertisement should not be used in the same media vehicle within days or even weeks of its first appearance. If it does run too soon afterward, the response will fall off catastrophically. Because direct-response advertisers know enough about the field to avoid repetition, it is difficult to find examples to demonstrate this point.

However, I have private knowledge of a remarkable example. During the 1970s, a leading general agency in London was appointed to handle the direct-response advertising for a collectible item costing about $10. The agency, unaware of how sharply the responses would fall off, ran a single advertisement with a greater frequency than a direct-response agency would permit. Four national newspapers were used, with seven insertions in each over a six-month period. The responses fell away sharply and progressively from the first exposure, and at the end of the six months the advertisement was producing only 5 percent of the original response!

The best prospects—the fish swimming at the top of the pool—are always caught more easily than those lurking in the depths. All the fish are well dispersed and do not swim in shoals. We must therefore lower our fishing lines into all parts of the pool. Translating this metaphor into advertising language, direct-response advertising schedules aim for the maximum possible coverage with no repetition, until enough time has passed for a substantial number of new prospects to enter the market.

Style. It is easy to describe the style of direct-response advertising. Its first characteristic is length: long headlines and long copy in print advertising and above-average spot lengths on television (60, and sometimes even 90 or 120 seconds). The orientation of the advertising is more verbal than visual and more rational than emotional. The offer made to the consumer and how he or she can buy it are always presented with total clarity.

There is also a high standard of craftsmanship in the print advertising, with close attention to attracting and keeping readers. A number of stylistic tricks are used, such as short paragraphs, brief sentences, cross headings, and bullet points. The television films can best be described as "serviceable": simple communication without frills. They are rarely enriched with expensively acquired production values that are so important when the communication is substantially visual. All good direct-response advertising concentrates on the essentials of what should be communicated to achieve a sale. This is probably the best description of salesmanship.

These principles are all familiar. The only thing that needs emphasizing is that they did not emerge by chance. They were the end result of decades of experimentation by myriad advertisers. In contrast, advertising for mainline goods and services is put together with the use of very different guiding principles.

The first fifteen chapters of this book have concentrated on mainstream advertising. However, a number of the points made in these chapters have a clear bearing on direct response. In particular, readers of Chapter 11 should now be able to detect certain unmistakable harmonies between what we now know about mainline advertising and what we have always known about direct advertising.

Both types of advertising are measurable. Both can achieve an immediate effect. With both types, one exposure does the job, which means that the short-term effect is driven by the creative content of the advertising and not by media weight. Finally, because the superior productivity of Continuity Planning has been demonstrated and widely accepted for mainstream goods and services, their media strategy has followed the direct-response principle of maximum reach and minimum repetition, and achieved significant successes through doing so.

These important signals about how advertising works—which are practical enough to be called lessons about how to do it—were all well-known by direct-response practitioners decades ago. But the lessons had to be expensively relearned by mainstream advertisers—the wheels had to be reinvented—through the use of research techniques developed during the 1990s.

This is not the end of the points of affinity between the two types of advertising. Two other harmonies are very much fainter, although this faintness does not mean that there is nothing there; it is more likely that the similarities have not yet been fully revealed. Among other things, they could help us understand why the policy of IMC has not yet fulfilled its promise. Equally important, they could help us make some real improvements in how we discriminate between advertising ideas to select the best. These harmonies between the two types of advertising are relevant to the creative work of mainstream agencies. The first concerns the style of this creative work itself; the second involves the testing of creative alternatives by exposing them experimentally in the marketplace.

It is naïve to propose that advertising for mainstream goods and services should make a major shift toward rational arguments and away from emotional ones, and toward verbal signals and away from visual ones. Advertising for low-involvement products will not attract any attention from consumers if it is strongly and explicitly biased in a rational/verbal direction. But there are concealed ways in which the rational and verbal components of mainstream advertising can be strengthened without automatically turning off consumers' attention. This requires practiced skill. But to illustrate the importance of rationality, here are three independent arguments that all bear on it.

First, when consumers buy, some rationality is involved although consumers may not often articulate it. In particular, repurchase of a brand bought on an earlier occasion must be substantially rational because it is based on satisfaction with the brand's performance in use.

A second and more subtle point has emerged from recent research from the field of neuroscience. This confirms that rationality plays a part in brand choice, but that consumers must be led *indirectly* into absorbing rational arguments from an advertisement. The mechanism is through the very emotional and visual elements that get attention in the first place: these disarm the consumer and permit a tiny element of rationality to be slipped into the communication. The relationship can be expressed by saying that rational arguments are best enclosed in emotional envelopes.

The third point is that if we examine objectively the campaigns that are shown by Pure Single-Source research to be effective, and if we compare these with those that are not, the effective campaigns are often distinguished by an element of rationality that is absent from the ineffective advertising.

What practical steps can we take to nudge mainstream advertisers and their agencies a little further in the direction of rationality? It is not at all easy. The mind set of practitioners of general advertising is directed at developing a *single* advertising idea. This is the work of those creative people in the agency who are thought most appropriate for the advertised brand and who are guided by qualitative research that reveals something about consumers' responses to alternative ideas. The exploration of alternatives is carried out at the earliest stage of idea development, and what is sold to the client is the end result of a process of elimination based on judgment. This method is full of uncertainties stemming from the fallibility of the qualitative research (not to speak of the fallibility of the judgment).

Did practitioners of general advertising always do things this way? The answer is "no." It was once quite common to experiment with alternative ideas in the marketplace, and the results were often strikingly effective.

During my last decade at J. Walter Thompson, I had personal experience of creative and/or media experiments for at least seven substantial brands. Here is one example, which dates from 1980. As I write these words, I have in front of me thirteen color advertisements that were run in national magazines in Britain for a range of Kraft foods: seven types of cheese and five different salad dressings. The campaign was experimental and originated as a media test, but it was soon seen to be equally concerned with the creative content of the campaign.

Each of the thirteen advertisements featured one or (more commonly) a selection of the Kraft brands. During the 1970s, Kraft was a large advertiser in terms of its total expenditure, but it marketed so many brands that the budget for each was in danger of being below the threshold of effectiveness when the brand was advertised on its own. The agency's thinking moved toward running a single campaign featuring a selection of the foods, showing how they could be used together to make simple dishes. The advertisements in fact featured a range of unusual snack ideas. (Completely separate research had indicated that British housewives were devoting more of their cooking to making snacks than to preparing substantial family dishes.)

There was much discussion about the campaign within the agency and with the client. It was eventually decided to measure the impact of the campaign with the use of a simple device. Each advertisement had a coupon in the corner (with a key number to identify the actual advertisement), and readers could send this coupon to Kraft to receive a free recipe booklet.

The detailed findings of the experiment are no longer available. However, I personally supervised the analysis and I have a clear recollection of what was discovered. There were two major findings. First, the overall response rate was extremely high, although there was naturally some variation among the different subjects in the campaign. The second point was even more striking. There was no evidence at all that the effectiveness of the advertising was declining over the course of a year.

This, then, is a practical example—and a very simple one—of an important media/creative experiment carried out for a major advertiser. The campaign itself could not be considered a true direct advertising campaign, and it was measured by its effectiveness in generating sales for the different Kraft brands, which were monitored in the usual ways. The measure of coupon returns was a useful supplement. The important point was the harmony between the sales figures and the response figures from the coupon offer.

Higher sales reflected at least partly increased penetration. Coupon returns were connected with increasing business from each customer. It was a classic process of experimentation, with a multiple measurement of effects that provided evidence to support the continuation of the campaign. And the experiment was, of course, carried out by a mainstream advertiser.

IMC—Does It Have a Promising Future Behind It?

The doctrine of Integrated Marketing Communications (IMC) was first developed during the early 1980s, and it has been propagated continuously since that time in books, journal articles, conferences, and university teaching programs.

The idea behind IMC is totally logical. It is assumed that major marketers of goods and services engage in many marketing activities: a range that includes product design, packaging, consumer advertising, database marketing, personal selling, trade advertising, trade promotions, consumer promotions (the strongest influence on consumer price), sampling, product placement, demonstrations, events, and public relations generally. The doctrine of IMC lays down that all these things should be executed as expressions of a common strategy. They should all march to the same drum beat, and this will result in mutual cooperation and eventual synergy.

A second part of the doctrine foresees a gradual shift of emphasis from advertising in broad, nonspecialist media toward the much more narrowly focused medium of the database. Databases are usually made up of regular and occasional buyers of a brand, and such concentration obviously eliminates or at least reduces wasted coverage. This is a seductive idea, but we must remember that database marketing concentrates on *existing users* in order to increase business from them. However, for all but the largest brands, penetration (i.e., the number of users) can also be increased and this can make a major contribution to growth. Because this source of business is excluded from database marketing, it is unwise to rely on databases unsupported by media advertising. Media can address non-users to interest them in the brand.

In view of the obvious common sense that guides IMC, it is remarkable that it has not been implemented at all widely. Very few marketing organizations pay even lip service to it, and even fewer carry it out wholeheartedly. There are three reasons and these are not difficult to discover.

First, database marketing is obviously more suitable for some types of goods and services than for others. The real problem is with low-priced everyday goods that are traditionally advertising intensive. It is one thing to sell a book costing $30 or more using database marketing, where the cost per contact could be a dollar. It is quite another thing to sell a pack of shampoo costing $4.79. With database marketing, the cost per contact is still a dollar; when it is advertised in the mass media, however, the cost per contact is a fraction of a penny.

Part of the fallacy in the quotation at the beginning of this chapter is that the types of product for which image-creating media advertising is traditionally important can be effectively sold by direct means. The major manufacturers of low-priced products, such as Procter & Gamble, Unilever, Nestlé, and Philip Morris/Kraft General Foods, have made continuous efforts to make economic use of databases, but their energy has borne little fruit. They persist in their efforts with undiminished vigor, but their successes are relatively few.

Unilever recently put out a series of elegantly produced mailings, some with product samples, for one of its most important brands. This is Dove, brand leader by value in the toilet soap category (although Dove is strictly speaking not a soap but is produced by a different formula). Dove is a highly esteemed brand whose users are well defined demographically. But like so many similar efforts for packaged goods brands, the Dove program eventually languished. Philip Morris has had better luck with Marlboro, probably because of the restrictions in the use of advertising for cigarettes in the main media. The most interesting example of all is Gevalia coffee, a brand from Kraft General Foods. This gives every sign of being a viable operation. It employs database marketing, and the secret is automatic monthly supplies sent by mail to people who have signed up as a result of direct-response advertising on television and in magazines. The brand is, of course, marketed totally separately from Maxwell House (also from Kraft General Foods), which is distributed through retailers.

For higher-priced merchandise—clothing, certain types of food, books, CDs, and DVDs—database marketing can make economic sense, especially if consumers buy from catalogs. The Internet, which can be an important medium for producing business from existing addresses, is capable of generating high volume sales. However, doing this on a profitable basis is generally more difficult.

Where IMC should come into its own is with relatively expensive goods and services, especially those bought repeatedly: airline travel, hotels, credit cards, banking, and insurance services; a few infrequently purchased durables like computers; and in the important field of business-to-business marketing. With all of these, the high value of the transaction makes the process economic.

There is also an excellent opportunity, which many car companies successfully exploit, of using IMC to nurture potential buyers' interest in specific car models. But the selling still takes place, as it always has, in the dealer's showroom.

But even if we narrow the field of IMC to these select goods and services, there are still things standing in the way of its full use. This brings us to the second impediment. If all the various marketing activities should be marching to one drum beat, who is going to beat the drum? It *should* be the client. But the problem with most client organizations is that day-to-day marketing operations are carried out at a low level in the company hierarchy. The brand managers, even the most senior and seasoned ones, lack the authority and "clout" to dictate an integration of the whole range of marketing activities, especially because they would be expected to exercise this authority over both outside organizations and internal departments, all of which have discrete responsibility for individual programs. (These organizational problems are discussed in more detail in Chapter 18.)

What makes the job of the brand manager even more difficult is that advertising agencies are no longer in a position to offer a range of services, because the era of the full service agency has come to an end; agencies have now become disconnected even from matters of such operational importance as media planning and buying. The variegated activities connected with IMC are more than agencies can afford to offer even on a fee basis, especially because they often cannot compete effectively with outside specialists on either quality or price. The holding companies that emerged during the 1980s and 1990s to control agencies in groups now all own subsidiary companies doing business in promotions, package design, and public relations. But clients have shown no great eagerness to fulfill their IMC needs by such "one-stop shopping."

This leads to the third and most serious impediment to the development of IMC. The cultural difference between general and direct advertising is just as strong today as it has ever been during the past thirty years. Advertising agencies are still in the world of show business, and they have been backward in addressing the question of what business they are really in. People who have never worked in agencies are quite unable to appreciate their deeply rooted conservatism (a conservatism that has been compared by one cynic to that of the Roman Catholic church). Agencies are full of talented, sensitive, and interesting people. But philosophically, these men and women have been stuck in a groove for more than thirty years: a groove that has become deeper as the range of functions carried out by advertising agencies has become narrower.

This problem is especially evident when attempts are made to exploit the Internet as a medium for direct selling. There are great practical problems in using it for this purpose, but this does not mean that they can never be solved. Nobody denies the extraordinary potential of the medium. Yet the people who have so much to gain from making it work—the mainstream agencies—have virtually given up the effort.

They use Internet banners for image building. This is a totally unsuitable medium for the job, and there have been no successes. But this use of the Internet is close to the traditional focus of agency work, which has always concentrated so much on image building. Agencies have always used television for this purpose and they can think of nothing better than attempting to do the same in a totally different medium.

I am at a loss to know how agencies will respond to an environment that is now quite different from what it was in 1970. The only thing I would be willing to bet on is that change will come about only as a result of unwelcome economic necessity. This is a point that will be picked up in Chapter 19.

Part VI

How Advertising Is Managed

Four Myths:

"The new Republic of Technology homogenizes world tastes, wants, and possibilities into global-market proportions, which allows for world-standardized products, giving the global producer powerful scale advantages."

"As the trend toward globalized marketing and advertising strategies continues, more companies are likely to move more toward centralization of the advertising function to maintain a unified world brand image rather than presenting a different image in each market."

"Advertising is our single most important activity."

"The relationship between a manufacturer and his advertising agency is almost as intimate as the relationship between a patient and his doctor."

These are all unusually egregious fallacies.

17

The Global Village

Myths:

"The new Republic of Technology homogenizes world tastes, wants, and possibilities into global-market proportions, which allows for world-standardized products, giving the global producer powerful scale advantages."

"As the trend toward globalized marketing and advertising strategies continues, more companies are likely to move more toward centralization of the advertising function to maintain a unified world brand image rather than presenting a different image in each market."

How Manufacturers View International Business

During the past two decades, the fortunes of the advertising business have waned, then waxed, then waned again. These cyclical movements, which have been more pronounced than during earlier periods, have brought changes in how the business is directed and organized. The ways in which advertising has been controlled and coordinated internationally have moved away from the excessive regimentation of earlier years toward a greater realism (as discussed in this chapter). To manufacturers, advertising has gradually declined in importance, at least in the esteem of the CEOs of major client companies (as shown in Chapter 18). This has not helped improve advertising efficiency. Nor has the present plight of agencies (examined in Chapter 19). To these organizations, the state of the industry has brought problems that still remain unresolved.

Heineken, the second-largest-selling beer in the world, has one of the most internationally familiar brand names. The beer comes from an old-established Dutch organization that brews in twenty different countries and sells its product in sixty. During the 1990s, the company asked three people, including myself, to study the brand's position in various countries and write a detailed recommendation on whether its advertising should run on an international basis, that is, with the same campaign used (suitably translated) in a number of different countries. The three people all worked separately, with no mutual consultation. Only the client was able to judge the degree of consensus. Because Heineken has not subsequently run any international campaigns, it is possible to infer that there was some harmony among the views of the outside specialists, and also between those views and what the company itself believed.

Heineken was an advertiser experienced enough to realize the folly of thinking exclusively about the economic advantages that international advertising might eventually provide for its own business. These are spelt out enthusiastically in the two quotations at the beginning of this chapter. The Dutch organization was, of course, conscious that its brand varied greatly in market share, penetration, consumer price, and image from country to country. Heineken was also well aware that too many large manufacturers have pursued economies of scale so single-mindedly and so blindly that the only result has been the dissipation of vast sums of money in unsuccessful international ventures.

A manufacturer's success in reaping the enticing advantages of international marketing—a huge scale of output, low costs (and low consumer prices) per unit, large and increasing profits, and eventually a uniform presence and image worldwide—does not depend on its own ambition and effort. It depends totally on the people in different countries who will buy its goods and services. And success depends particularly on how well it is able to detect and satisfy what these consumers want, remembering that many have incomes, tastes, and habits very different from the incomes, tastes, and habits of people in other countries.

It is helpful to begin to study this complex subject by defining some terms.

International Advertising. This is the best portmanteau phrase to describe advertising campaigns that are used in a number of countries (although not necessarily everywhere). A number of other descriptions are sometimes used for different types of international campaigns, but it is not necessary to complicate the discussion by using them.

Originating and Receiving Countries. Most international campaigns are written in the largest and most sophisticated advertising markets, the United States and Britain. One reason for this is that both countries use English, which is the international language of business. The receiving countries are those that translate and run the campaigns. The decision to run international campaigns is normally mandated by the international advertiser and the head offices (but not the local branches) of its advertising agencies.

International campaigns are rarely asked for by a manufacturer's local operating company or its local advertising agency in any market. One of the problems afflicting the use of these campaigns is the *amour propre* of local agencies. They resist outside ideas, for emotional rather than objective reasons: an attitude commonly summarized with the acronym N.I.H. (which stands for "not invented here"). Here are the words of a senior agency executive who spent most of his long career in the field of international advertising:

> Creative people exist to create. They want to be able to claim authorship of famous campaigns, they want to feature in the trade press, to win awards and to earn the respect of their peers, and to assemble a portfolio of successful campaigns. . . . Adaptions of international campaigns, however successful, do not have the same resonance. This can be a serious consideration. If an agency has the reputation that it exists mainly to adapt international campaigns it becomes difficult to attract outstanding creative talent, and even more difficult to retain them. This can also have an effect on international collegiality.

An international campaign is only rarely planned as an international campaign. It normally begins as an existing local campaign that was successful in its originating market, and the advertiser decided on pragmatic grounds to use it more widely.

International Brands. Brands in all countries can be put into four groups. The first two on this list are those that are most directly important to the discussion of international advertising (although the other two are also indirectly relevant):

- First, international brands marketed by international companies that employ international advertising campaigns.
- Second, international brands marketed by international companies that do *not* employ international advertising campaigns. There is normally much discussion about whether these should join the first group.
- Third, local brands marketed by international companies, and that for obvious reasons do not use international campaigns. The number of these is not declining; indeed, manufacturers are always on the lookout for brands that could eventually become international properties.
- Fourth, local brands marketed by local manufacturers, and that (again obviously) also do not use international campaigns. There are rare exceptions: when campaigns are "borrowed" from brands marketed by different manufacturers in other countries. This procedure is sometimes recognized for what it is: plagiarism.

In every country, all four types of brands are sold. But the relative importance of these groups varies country by country. In virtually all countries, the *smallest* group of brands is the first one on the above list: international brands that use international advertising campaigns. This easily observed fact should bring a touch of reality to any debate about international advertising. Not all these brands that run international campaigns are important. But some are old-established; some have a wide consumer franchise; some are category leaders; some are highly profitable; some are growing and demonstrate great potential. However, the numbers are always relatively small.

International brands like Kodak, Ford, Nestlé, Shell, Singer, and some others came into use before World War I. More arrived during the interwar period: a variety of consumer brands from Unilever, Gillette, Kellogg's, Quaker, Carnation, Heinz, Mars, and Pond's. Heineken reached all over the world and was sold in a specially built Dutch windmill at the New York World's Fair in 1939. There were a few durables, such as those from Philips, Hoover, and Electrolux; some brands of gasoline and tires (but not car models); and a number of international airlines, all still tiny. One of the most powerful international brands of all (although an unorthodox one) was the British Broadcasting Corporation (BBC).

International advertising campaigns began in a small way during the 1920s. Unilever began its celebrated campaign for Lux bar soap which featured movie stars as early as 1927. (The campaign is still used in many countries outside the United States, and Lux keeps its position as the largest-selling soap in the world.) J. Walter Thompson began its international operations during the late 1920s on the back of General Motors (GM) business. The agency promised GM that it would open an office wherever the client set up an assembly plant. However, the Great Depression, World War II, and the years of recovery did not encourage the spread of either international brands or international advertising campaigns.

Both took off extremely rapidly during the 1960s, being given a boost by the success of the European Economic Community (now called the European Union). The advantages to manufacturers, such as those described in the two quotations at the beginning of this chapter, began to be widely propagated. To make this point less kindly but more accurately, the brainwashing began. Globalization—an extreme form of internationalism—became an article of faith both for manufacturers and for the head offices of advertising agencies. Two major agencies in fact almost became insolvent because their ambitions outran the success of their policies.

Not all international brands succeeded, and this was even more true of international advertising campaigns. The high tide of international advertising was reached during the 1970s. But having burned their fingers so often, advertisers began, at that time, to treat such campaigns more circumspectly. When manufacturers used international campaigns, they began to amend them substantially to fit local conditions. Research carried out during the mid-1980s into the advertising policies of international manufacturers showed that the proportion of "fully standardized" campaigns had fallen from the earlier peak of 70 percent all the way down to 10 percent, while the proportion of international campaigns that had been adjusted to local conditions had grown from 10 to 55 percent. And the proportion of totally local campaigns had risen from 20 to 35 percent. International advertising seemed to be in retreat. But this is a misleading impression. What was happening was that ineffective international campaigns were being abandoned; as clients and agencies learned how to handle them properly, however, effective international campaigns began to grow more and not less important.

Two factors bear directly on the success or otherwise of international campaigns: considerations of culture and economics. The second is by far the more important. Cultural factors, although they are widely discussed, do not carry much weight from a practical point of view. They will be discussed first.

Different Tribes

Consider France and Britain, two countries that are close neighbors and now connected with a tunnel under the English Channel. Yet they are different in many ways—in race, language, education, religion, law, habits, the structure of the society—all the product of centuries of different histories. It is as if the two countries are inhabited by different tribes. Consider the United Kingdom and how this country now contains four distinct tribal homelands of its own—England, Scotland, Wales, and Northern Ireland—which have become more separate during the past decade. And now compare Britain with a totally different country like China. The differences multiply. These factors are generally thought to have a bearing on the viability of international advertising campaigns. But are the differences insuperable? Or can they be overcome by making changes in individual advertisements?

It may surprise many readers that, except in one special case, international campaigns *can* be used to address tribes as different as the ones just described. In many cases adjustments are necessary. Kenichi Ohmae, an experienced and sensitive commentator, makes the point that a brand must be transplanted in a foreign soil so that it will develop organically in its new environment.

As an example, this is how this process is carried out in the advertising for Lux soap:

- Films are made, wherever possible, featuring local movie stars, and these are used alongside films featuring international stars.
- Alternative scenes can be inserted in the films used in specific countries; for example, in Far Eastern markets, the traditional trappings of Hollywood are emphasized.
- Washing sequences are sometimes differently handled in different countries; for example, in Arab countries, it is unacceptable to show too much of a woman's skin.
- Verbal claims also vary; for example, in Japan commercials cannot claim that a movie star uses Lux, merely that she recommends it, and the Japanese language does not easily handle shades of meaning between two extremes: it is possible to say "good" and "bad," but not "good enough." Japanese advertising is

more emotional than that in other countries. It totally eschews hard selling. This is one of the reasons why advertising from foreign countries, especially the United States, is so rarely used in Japan.

- In many countries, trade union restrictions demand that local film technicians must be employed in making films that will be used internationally.

In all countries there are problems of translation from the English language, and we should remember that the vocabulary of English is much larger and richer than that of most other tongues. Local branches of international agencies cope with these difficulties by employing local copywriters who are less concerned with generating big ideas than with understanding the subtlest nuances of two languages: English and their own. Ideas can generally be communicated effectively in local languages, but this is not always done by a literal translation of the words. The *intention* can usually be completely realized using more idiomatic phrasing in the local language. (The copy used in a foreign country is normally then translated back, that is, put literally into English, and this version can be scrutinized in the advertiser's head office in its home country.)

A positive advantage of internationality is that the foreign origin of certain brands can have its own appeal. American Express, McDonald's, Burger King, Levi's, Nike, Coca-Cola, Pepsi-Cola, and Marlboro all carry an unmistakable American flavor: a national symbolism that appeals equally positively to most Western countries (or equally negatively to countries less enthusiastic about the United States). National origin is also exploited with a few brands from Australia (Foster's), Germany (BMW), France (Chanel), and Britain (Burberry and a number of brands of Scotch whisky).

A rather unusual piece of evidence exists about how people of different cultures respond to advertising, and such response is *uniform*. We know from the field of direct advertising that response rates to specific advertisements are remarkably similar in different places. If advertisement X does better than advertisement Y, and if Y does better than Z in one country, the same will be true in most others, irrespective of the extent of the cultural differences.

The examples I have given have all come from my personal experience. With the exception of the special case that will shortly be described, it is most unusual for cultural differences to put a roadblock in the way of international campaigns. The Lux campaign has been used for decades with great success in more than thirty countries. The same is true of the De Beers campaign for diamond gemstones. McDonald's has been introduced in many countries; it has gone into India using chicken and various types of vegetables in place of beef. And Timotei shampoo, a Swedish brand for daily hair washing, and advertised with the use of blond Nordic models, was successful in nearly twenty countries and was market leader in Japan, where all the target consumers have dark hair.

Timotei was developed by the local Unilever operating company in Sweden. It is not the only example of a Unilever brand that originated in a small country. Unilever has now, in fact, dismantled its Co-ordinations, which once controlled the marketing of its brands internationally. This organizational change was made to encourage local market initiatives. In the future, not all important brands will come out of the United States and Britain.

The special case in which international harmonization remains very difficult—something I have already referred to—is the large and complex category (or categories) of branded foods. Eating habits in different countries remain stubbornly idiosyncratic, and they are very slow to change.

People drink instant coffee in Britain and Spain; ground coffee in Germany and Scandinavia. Cold breakfast cereals have met considerable resistance outside the United States, Canada, Britain, and Australia, although Kellogg's has made great efforts to make them popular in many other countries. The leading brand of beer is different in every country. Wine drinking varies to an enormous degree among countries. In Australasia and Britain, people eat more butter than margarine; in the United States, they eat more margarine than butter. Americans eat cheese as an hors d'oeuvre; the French and British eat it at the end of a meal; Germans, Scandinavians, and the Dutch eat it for breakfast. Mild Cheddar cheese sold under the name Kraft P'tit Québec has a market only in French-speaking Canada; it has been a failure in other parts of that country. Only Australians eat Vegemite yeast extract for breakfast. Oxo cubes—a brand used in two-thirds of British homes—are sold nowhere else. The British eat lamb; the Germans do not. In the United States, the leading brand of canned soup is condensed (Campbell's); in Britain and the Netherlands, it is full strength (Heinz and Unox respectively). Examples could be multiplied.

The underlying principle for marketing companies to follow is to be very cautious about extending their food brands internationally, and even more cautious about using international campaigns to advertise them. Large manufacturers are, of course, fully conscious of this limitation, and this accounts for the large number of local brands, especially of food, that they market in different countries (the third group of brands in the list at the beginning of this chapter).

The points made here are not widely known—or at least not widely accepted. The more common view—at least as this is reflected in the literature of international advertising—is that cultural differences matter a lot, but they are disappearing, as "the new Republic of Technology homogenizes world tastes, wants, and possibilities." Illuminated as it often is with a sparkling metaphor, the population of every country is thought to be growing so similar to that of every other country that all the people in the world are beginning to inhabit a Global Village. But what indeed is the reality?

In a host of countries, the past decade has seen a splintering of once-homogeneous populations into factions that are as often as not in conflict with one another. Think of the Soviet Union, Yugoslavia, Israel, Indonesia, and Spain. Think even of Canada and the United Kingdom. The United States continues to provide a home for millions of legal and illegal immigrants every year. Spanish is already established as the second American language, and by the middle of the twenty-first century Caucasians in the United States will be the minority (giving a neat twist to the way in which the euphemism "minority" is used today). In every country, it seems that fission is the order of the day. Socially and culturally, population subgroups want to have less and less to do with one another. Only if they see some sort of economic benefit, as with the European Union, are they willing to come together to harmonize policy. The Global Village—that rather flashy description of someone's vision of the future—is so out of touch with reality that it could only have originated in academia. Which it did.

As far as international marketing is concerned, the real differences among countries are economic and not cultural. These differences provide a clue to how some international brands and some international campaigns are effective, and some are not.

A Brand's Position on Its Competitive Map

The following are two briefly summarized cases. I am describing these merely to illustrate a general principle that emerged repeatedly during the years in which I was personally involved in international advertising.

The first is Pan American Airways (Pan Am), once an extremely important name in the airline industry. Pan Am, led by the legendary Juan Trippe, was one of the merchant venturers of the twentieth century, pioneering air travel across the oceans during the 1930s, 1940s, and 1950s. But Pan Am and its closest rival, TWA, had no real access to internal routes within the United States, which severely limited their business. Domestic airlines such as American and United were able to tap into a much larger and more rapidly growing market.

During the early 1970s, Pan Am launched a stylish advertising campaign to persuade Americans to travel out of the country, thus filling empty seats in the new Boeing 747 airplanes. The argument used was motivating and not discriminating (i.e., concentrating on the pleasure of traveling overseas rather than on Pan Am's competitive advantages). Because Pan Am had such a large share of the overseas travel market, the strategy was viable. Pan Am would have much to gain from an expansion of the total market.

J. Walter Thompson handled the Pan Am business worldwide, and one of the conditions laid down by Pan Am was that all the creative work used anywhere had to originate in the agency's New York office and be translated as literally as possible. In due course, the local offices of the agency were directed to run the American campaign urging people to travel overseas. The trouble was that Pan Am's situation in the market was quite different overseas from what it was in the United States. Because Pan Am carried passengers only to and from the United States, the airline had only a tiny share of overseas travel within each foreign country. In every case, the market was dominated by local airlines that, in Europe, were taking holidaymakers in large numbers to the Mediterranean. The Pan Am advertising was in fact doing their job for them, and Pan Am itself was gaining virtually nothing. What made the matter worse was that the Pan Am campaign was written for television, a medium not available for advertising in some European countries. The campaign was therefore run in movie theaters, which had a youthful audience that was not even in the travel market.

This is an example of international advertising carried out to a crazy extreme, driven by a fixation on centralized control and a belief that differences in local conditions do not matter. The failure of the international campaign—due totally to the strategy on which it was based—contributed to J. Walter Thompson's loss of the Pan American business shortly afterward.

The second example is a brand of bar soap that I am not allowed to identify. This was a deodorant protection soap, planned for the American market, where deodorant soaps represent the largest single market segment. The brand did not offer benefits superior to other brands, although the advertising attempted to make a competitive argument through a very distinctive tone of voice. Not surprisingly, the brand did not succeed in test market.

It was then launched in two European countries, in both of which deodorant soaps were relatively unimportant. New advertising was developed that attempted to educate the consumer about the benefits of deodorant soap. The brand was promoted with massive price reductions, and the temporarily high level of sales obscured the fact that the advertising was not working. The brand therefore failed again. The European advertising was then brought to the United States, where market conditions were of course quite different from the conditions in the countries where the brand had failed. The campaign was now changed again to make the argument more discriminating, but the creative idea was weak and the brand was again unsuccessful.

The brand stumbled from experiment to experiment over a period of thirteen years! The cost of all this—in money, in the time of talented (and highly priced) people, and in overall frustration—can only be imagined. The repeated failures were due mainly to unsound strategy and in particular to the multiple attempts to transfer a campaign built for one type of market to a totally different one; the strategic mistakes led the agency to produce creative ideas on a "hand-to-mouth" basis.

Success with international advertising demands that the brand in question should be positioned in approximately the same way in all the markets where the advertising will run. Here are five guideposts to define positioning a little more clearly.

Incomes. Average per capita incomes matter a great deal. Countries with low personal incomes have undeveloped consumer goods markets. If the economy has life in it, all successful brands can share in overall market growth and the advertising can encourage this by concentrating on motivating, product-related benefits. On the other hand, in countries with high personal incomes, there is little overall market growth and brands have to fight for market share, which means a style of advertising concentrated more on discriminating, brand-related benefits. But there are interesting exceptions. India has low average personal incomes, yet there is a substantial advertising industry engaged in selling goods and services to the 10 percent of the population—100 million people—who have discretionary income and can therefore afford to buy advertised brands. Advertising for these goods can concentrate to some degree on discriminators.

Brands' Average Shares of Market. It is a little known fact that a large brand in a small country will have a *higher* share of market than a large brand in a big country, where categories are crowded. This is an additional factor causing advertising in bigger countries to discriminate. On the other hand, advertising in the smaller countries can be more concerned with general product benefits. This is an indirect reason why so much European advertising is softer and less hard-hitting than the majority of American advertising.

Novelty. Innovation often makes international campaigns practicable, especially if it relates to functionally innovative products that in effect create a category (e.g., Coca-Cola, McDonald's) or a market segment (e.g., Timotei, Diet Coke). With both types of brands, consumers in every country are in the same position of being confronted with something new and something without any direct competitors.

The Young. Unusual affinities also exist between different countries in the presence there of certain demographic groups. The most important of these is the young, who have similar tastes and lifestyles in different countries, and at least some discretionary income because they have no family responsibilities. It is said that a young person in the United States is more similar to a young person in Japan than a young person in America is to an old person in America (and the same holds for Japan). This all helps us understand the success of international campaigns for jeans, athletic shoes, fast food, and soft drinks.

The Affluent (or *the Internationalists*). The other important demographic group comprises well-established, affluent men and women, especially businesspeople who travel. Again, these have much in common with their counterparts in other countries; this helps us understand the success of international campaigns for diamonds, watches, charge cards, credit cards, vodka, and airlines.

The Role of the Advertising Agency

According to the best available evidence, the success of an international advertising campaign depends mainly on the uniformity of a brand's position in the market, country by country. But remember the importance of per capita income in determining that position, the special cases of innovative brands that create categories and segments, and finally the particular importance of brands that appeal to the young and to the affluent.

Adding together the types of brands for which international advertising is appropriate, my own guess is that the number represents only about 10 percent of the total, although the percentage of the *international* brands marketed by *international* companies is much higher—maybe 25 percent—if we include those that are positioned in a similar way internationally even if the actual names vary in different countries for legal reasons. Many of these brands are important and are likely to produce healthy profit over a long period.

But even if the marketing conditions are right, not all international campaigns are as successful as those for De Beers, Dove, and a selected few others. The degree of success is really driven by the intrinsic effectiveness of the campaign. If a campaign has a clear and proven track record, this is a compelling reason to try to exploit it more widely: which is why the best procedure is to roll out successes rather than attempt to write international campaigns unconnected with consumers in specific countries. But the downside of starting in one market and moving the campaign out from there is that a good deal of time can be lost. (The Timotei campaign took six years before it had got to eight countries.) This entails the danger that the concept might be stolen by wide-awake competitors, as mentioned when I earlier discussed the four separate types of brands.

The production cost of international campaigns is invariably high because it is always thought important to enrich the films with production values of high aesthetic quality. There are thought to be scale economies in production (as suggested in the first quotation at the beginning of this chapter), because the total production costs of a film can be shared between a number of countries. But the situation is not quite as simple as it appears.

A top-quality film production costing $2 million, which is syndicated among 20 countries, averages a $100,000 share per country (although contributions are normally calculated more equitably according to the value of the brand's sales in each market). To the $100,000 must be added the local costs of developing the script, the film editing, the sound recording, the optical work, shooting the pack shots, and printing the show copies. These additional costs could very well double the film production budget to a total of $200,000.

In small countries, where film production companies are forced by the low screen time budgets to simplify filmmaking so as to scale down production costs, it is perfectly possible to produce a new film for $200,000. The local film would not stand out as being particularly weak compared with other films on air, but it would not have production values approaching those of the international film made for a group of markets. The advantage of international film production to the local markets is not a matter of cost saving. The advantage is more subtle and more powerful. It is that, for the same money, the local market can obtain much better advertising material than it could otherwise get. This eventually boosts the value of the screen time investment and means a greater bang for the advertising buck.

Despite all that is written about scale economies, international campaigns make little economic sense to international advertising agencies. The reason is that, as the agency's responsibility for a brand extends into smaller and smaller markets, the agency's profit in each of them progressively shrinks. This of course reduces the overall rate of profit that the agency earns from that brand. Agencies are required by their clients to staff their local branches with expatriate executives who earn high salaries, because these people are needed to provide a standard of service to which the client is accustomed in large markets. The cost of these people always outweighs the saving in the time of locally employed creative people through the importation of campaigns; much work has to be carried out on these, as explained earlier. In some cases, the agency agrees with the client to handle a brand in all countries, although in some offices the budget may be so small that there is no way that the agency can run the business at a profit. Uniformity is a costly business for agencies.

Why, then, do agencies accept international business? The reason is simple. An international agreement with a single client to handle one or more of its brands on an international basis cements the agency's relationship with that client. It is difficult for an agency to be fired by any client if the two parties are connected in perhaps twenty markets. If the relationship is frayed in some countries, it will be strong in others.

This introduces the concept of the "club agency." Large advertisers normally employ a number of different agencies, each of which handles a brand or group of brands in all countries. (Unilever has four such agencies.) The agency is persuaded to invest time and resources in increasing its knowledge of the brand or brands, and this means that each agency's expertise with those brands becomes deeper and stronger. This is in the client's interest. In the long term, it is also in the agency's. In any event, manufacturing companies have such policies in place, and everybody must learn to live with them. This goes for the marketing specialists within manufacturing companies and—even more impor-tant—for advertising agencies. Clients and agencies are the subjects of the next two chapters.

18

The Cinderella of Business

Myth:

"Advertising is our single most important activity."

Advertising and the CEO—A Faded Relationship

GlaxoSmithKline, a firm at the leading edge of the drug industry and the third-ranking public company in Britain, is the product of a number of mergers between separate and strong American and British businesses. One of its component parts was the Beecham organization, which had originated as an old-fashioned British manufacturer of patent medicines, but which eventually became a prominent player in toiletries, health drinks, and pharmaceuticals of all types. Its most rapid growth took place during the 1950s and 1960s, when the head of the company was Henry Lazell, a CEO of legendary resource and drive.

The quotation that begins this chapter has been reliably attributed to Lazell. Because the thought behind it was disseminated throughout his organization, it is clear that Lazell himself believed it. Yet in the supposedly more complex and sophisticated world of the twenty-first century, the aphorism appears a naïve myth. It represents a belief that died out with Lazell's generation of business leaders. Lazell was larger than life, and even if he was not totally typical he had a number of contemporaries who thought about advertising in a similar way. In 1958, Lord Heyworth, chairman of Unilever, devoted his annual statement to stockholders to describing Unilever's use of advertising. Heyworth, like Lazell, had no professional background in advertising. Yet his brief essay remains even today one of the most strongly argued defenses of advertising's contribution not only to a large business but, more important, to competitive capitalism in general: in particular to reducing consumer prices in the long term.

American business leaders were, if anything, even more enthusiastic about advertising. During the hundred years from 1860 to 1960, many were closely involved in their companies' advertising activities and supported their use of advertising with great vigor. The names Harley Procter, John Wanamaker, Gerard Lambert, George Washington Hill, and Charles Revson come to mind, and there were many more. Even Franklin D. Roosevelt claimed that he would have relished an advertising career.

The situation is different today. The only people who now demonstrate and publicize the value of advertising—and they often do the job thoughtfully and well—are agencies and agency trade associations. But because they are directly interested parties, their endorsement carries much less weight than endorsement by client organizations whose brands have been built and sustained by advertising. During the last thirty years or so, however, it has been difficult to identify CEOs of manufacturing and service companies who have been willing to nail their colors to the advertising mast. This is bad enough in itself, but it is also a symptom of something more serious: that advertising has a very low priority on their working agenda.

Top business executives give the nod to the recommendations of their subordinates. And they approve the advertising budgets, although in doing this they are not much concerned with the explicit purpose of consumer advertising, that is, to influence consumers. As I argued in Chapter 1, CEOs are more interested in two quite different objectives: attacking their competitors by matching and exceeding their competitors' advertising expenditures, and leveraging their own advertising investments to influence the retail trade. Top business executives supervise advertising in a remote fashion (as will shortly be described), but they do not participate in any way in the untidy and often exciting process of advertising development.

The unfortunate side effect of this separation of functions is that most CEOs of large companies are not actively conscious of advertising's enormous potential: the role it can play in maintaining the sales of large brands, boosting the sales of small ones, and strengthening consumer franchises and thereby increasing manufacturers' long-term profitability. These contributions were totally familiar to Lazell, and they were the reasons he was so emphatic about the importance of advertising to his business. And since his day, they have been amply confirmed by objective research that has also shown that effectiveness depends on the advertisements used. Some work and others do not (and both types can be identified).

As I write these words, I have in front of me the latest issues of nine leading periodicals and newspapers directed at senior decision makers in the business world (including those people who have ambitions to be decision makers). The publications I am looking at are *Barron's*, *Business Week*, the *Economist*, *Forbes*, *Fortune*, the *Harvard Business Review*, *Money*, *Strategy and Business*, and the *Wall Street Journal*. I have concentrated on those directed at general managers because these executives allow advertising to be handled by people lower in the hierarchy. I did not therefore include the two leading advertising trade publications, which are read by people in advertising agencies, by brand managers, and by media sellers, planners, and buyers.

The issues of my nine publications contain a total of 796 editorial pages (excluding paid-for advertisements). The features and articles cover well over 100 different topics: many general ones (e.g., the state of the economy, international trends, entrepreneurship, the management of human resources) and also a number of subjects of specific interest (e.g., high-tech businesses, airlines, prescription drugs, energy). Any discussion of advertising—either as an industry in its own right or as a contributor to other businesses—is almost totally absent. Advertising-related topics cover *two pages* of editorial, which represent less than one-third of one percent of the editorial matter in the nine journals. This is not absolute proof that high-level decision makers separate themselves from the hurly-burly of advertising, but it is clear confirmation of my own observation that this is the case.

Slowly and almost imperceptibly over a period of more than three decades, advertising has become the Cinderella of business. The interesting question is *why?* There are a number of identifiable causes, but the most important one stems from the different cultures of manufacturing companies and their advertising agencies.

Two Cultures

The advertising agency "thrives on a very different culture. The product company, whether in goods or services, is always more structured and hierarchical than the advertising agency should be. The producer will also be steeped in its product, whereas the agency is more sensitive to wider trends in the market."

These words were written in the late 1980s by Sir David Orr, also a chairman of Unilever and one of Lord Heyworth's successors. Orr's view is extremely well informed, but in my opinion he does not go far enough. The most telling difference between advertisers and their agencies is that they think differently. Manufacturers and service companies invariably think along rational lines, and their most effective tool for making decisions is quantification. On the other hand, advertising agencies do their best work by using intuition and imagination, which are of course nonrational faculties. Their thinking may be directed by a brand's advertising strategy—which is a formal document—but the advertising ideas that stem from it generally go far beyond the strategy and shoot off at sometimes quite unexpected tangents.

Advertising agencies have a patchy record of success in producing effective campaigns, but good agencies get it right more often than they get it wrong. Their successes are due to their culture, and I am totally convinced that if agencies were staffed with people who think in the same way as their clients do, they would never produce work that made any impression in the marketplace. The reason why in-house agencies faded away was because their thinking was too close to that of their clients, who were also their owners.

Agencies' ability to mobilize—and to focus—their nonrational mental apparatus is their most important stock-in-trade. Yet when client CEOs make decisions, they are accustomed to dealing with quantitative projections beforehand, and quantitative results after the decisions have been made and the policies put into effect. Precise numbers are simply not available for advertising, at least at the present state of the art. The greatest single problem with client-agency relationships is how to squeeze the agency's ideas into the straitjacket of the client's evaluative procedures. And agencies' instinctive antagonism to quantification makes it even more difficult for them to accept the constraints of this straitjacket.

The dialogue between client CEOs and their advertising agencies was once much stronger than it is today. The situation changed after the 1960s, for two simple and related reasons. The first is that before the 1970s or thereabouts, CEOs were impressed by the talents and personalities of the most senior people in agencies and they often accepted and trusted their advice. In the years following World War II, Marion Harper, Rosser Reeves, Leo Burnett, David Ogilvy, William Bernbach,

Jack Tinker, Mary Wells, and a few others with the same magic touch (or perhaps the same show business flair) were firmly established in the advertising pantheon. And although their approach to advertising was classically intuitive and imaginative, they were listened to. This was for the very reason that they *were* temperamentally so different from the client CEOs. The two parties had complementary qualities, but at the same time they both had personalities of a similar weight and stature. The concept of "partners in business" had a real meaning for both clients and agencies.

One of the most striking changes that has taken place in the advertising business during the past two decades is the business's loss of cachet. The giants of the past have all disappeared. The financiers who now manage agency groups are more similar to than different from the CEOs of the client organizations. They think along the same lines, but they are seen as running smaller, less capital-intensive operations than those of their clients. And their businesses are not always considered particularly solid.

The second reason for agencies' loss of cachet is that, at the time when the stars in the advertising firmament were fading from the scene, the clients themselves were developing their marketing skills. They were also receiving much basic, timely, and easily implemented counsel from management consultants. The strategic advice they were receiving from their agencies was therefore becoming almost superfluous.

The Straitjacket

The brand management system was originated by Procter & Gamble during the 1920s. We do not need to go into the historical details, but because the system is today so prevalent in large businesses worldwide it is difficult to appreciate just how original and ingenious it appeared when it was first introduced.

The great merit of the system is that, by focusing on the brand, advertising plans can be coordinated (with varying degrees of intimacy) with all aspects of the process by which brands are brought to market: product features, packaging, production, selling, shipping, pricing, promotions. The strings controlling all these activities are in the hands of the brand manager.

But although all the strings are in the brand manager's hands and he or she must work out in the greatest detail how to pull them, it is actually somebody else who does the pulling. Brand management is a staff and not a line function. Specific actions are *recommended* by the brand manager, but it is the more senior people in the company who actually authorize every detail of how the brand manager will carry them out. The brand management system put the tools in place for Integrated Marketing Communications. But the gap—which still exists—between theory and practice is the result of brand managers' lack of executive authority to implement the doctrine in practical terms.

Brand managers are invariably young, and because their experience is limited they are not very knowledgeable. They learned to be aggressive and competitive at the business schools from which they graduated. But they did not learn much about advertising there: MBA programs in most American universities devote only about 5 percent of the course work to advertising, usually under the guise of "marketing communications." Brand managers are nevertheless the main point of contact between the client and the advertising agency, and there is invariably a close day-to-day working relationship between the two.

This single point of contact should in theory make life easy for the agency, but there are frustrating difficulties. The fullest involvement with the agency's recommendations takes place at the level of the brand manager, who is at the bottom of the client's management hierarchy. The brand manager is allowed to reject the agency's plans, and he or she can steer the agency in a particular direction, for example, based on guesses about what superiors' responses to advertising ideas are likely to be. But the brand manager is never empowered to say "yes" without reference to the superior ranks. All the brand manager can do is to move the agency's recommendations through the various layers of the client's chain of command (there are sometimes as many as six of these), until they are approved or amended or rejected by the CEO, who is in ultimate control of all major expenditures.

The brand manager must develop considerable skill to be successful in moving agency recommendations upward through the client organization. Most important, the different cultures of client and agency have to be melded. The brand manager does this by fitting ideas that started as intuitive and imaginative into a format that is rational and often quantitative: the format with which CEOs are accustomed to working. In other words, it is the brand manager's job to put the agency's ideas into the client's straitjacket. The brand manager's working tool is the written recommendation. This is succinct—often only one page in length—but supplemented by references to supporting research, and such a recommendation has to be persuasive if it is to be approved. When there is no research that bears directly on any aspect of a recommendation, the phrase "judgment suggests" implies that non-rational ideas have been subjected to rational evaluation (whether they have or not).

One of the most important jobs of a brand manager is to make sales projections, because these determine all the budgetary plans for a brand for the years ahead. In making such projections, brand managers must hazard guesses about the sales effect of their advertising. Agencies are not involved in this, mainly because they would be horrified at the dangers of such prognoses, and they probably do not even know that such sales estimates are being made.

Many client organizations have clearly defined and sometimes quite rigid policies about the form and content of their advertising. Some also have their own favored research techniques for pre-testing, which exclude the possibility of using alternative methods. It is the brand manager's task to make sure that the advertising proposals and the way they are researched conform to the requirements laid down by the company. This is not popular with the agency, and the acronyms by which the systems are identified often have a rather depressing effect on the people in the creative departments.

As far as most CEOs are concerned, the system appears to work smoothly. They are persuaded that it makes logical sense of an untidy process characterized by flair, inspiration, and emotion. Because brand management is firmly in place, and in many companies seems to have worked for decades, CEOs are content to let well alone. They pay attention to the logic of the recommendations they are given; they glance at the summarized research; they weigh the judgment of the managers in the layers between brand manager and CEO: the people who will already have given their general endorsement.

In this process, however, CEOs do not necessarily bring their critical faculties to bear directly and in full detail on the actual content of the advertising. As I have suggested earlier in this chapter, CEOs spend very little time on advertising, and one suspects that this time is devoted to routine evaluation of other people's recommendations rather than studying the advertisements themselves coolly, contemplatively, and at leisure. CEOs may not be particularly interested in advertising, but they usually have much more experience of it than their subordinates do. It is therefore wasteful to discard this experience needlessly.

The system is like a lightly oiled piece of machinery. But paradoxically, the smoothness of its working is considered more important than what comes out the other end. The system permits huge sums of money to be wasted on ineffective advertising. As demonstrated in Chapter 12, only 40 percent of advertisements generate a measurable short-term effect; and this is a precondition for any medium-term and long-term benefit. The first thing that advertising has to achieve is, therefore, an immediate effect on sales: either visible growth or a demonstrable protection of existing volume. To look at advertising's success rate in a slightly different way, *60 percent of advertisements do not fulfill this condition.* This is the best possible reason why CEOs should start thinking about advertising far more seriously than most of them do at present. But what may hold them back is an unstated belief that advertising does not, after all, matter very much in the larger scheme of things.

Does Advertising Matter?

Business decisions are made on the basis of data. As a general (although not universal) rule, the sounder the data the sounder the decisions. When actual figures are not available (e.g., if we are looking into the future), then estimates or at least targets must be used, although these are of course fallible.

The simplest figure to describe advertising's importance to a company or a brand is the advertising to sales (A:S) ratio, or advertising's share of net sales value (NSV) for a particular year. The figure is actual if the year has passed; estimated if the year is to come. A common ratio for repeat-purchase packaged goods is 5 percent (or a percentage point or two on either side). For some packaged-goods categories (e.g., proprietary drugs and cosmetics), the figure is a good deal higher. For some completely different types of businesses (e.g., cars and retail stores), the ratio is much lower.

A firm with an A:S ratio of 5 percent will spend 95 percent of its receipts on other expenses. It is not surprising that CEOs fix their attention on these larger sums. Despite the huge quantities of money invested in advertising—seven American advertisers each spend upwards of $1 billion on advertising above the line—CEOs are inclined to delegate responsibility for it and concentrate on the activities that make up the 95 percent.

A company's NSV is used to cover three separate expenditures. The first is direct costs (i.e., the basic costs of production, mainly for raw materials, labor piecework, packaging, and transportation). The second element is the indirect costs, or the firm's general overhead (payments for buildings, equipment, head office salaries, and a number of other things). These must be paid whether any goods are produced or not. The third element is the amount of money (if any) left over. It is a residual that is used to cover three items: advertising above the line, sales promotions below the line, and profit.

Direct and indirect costs remain fairly stable although they rise slightly as a result of inflation; and direct costs (and eventually indirect costs also) will also go up gradually as output increases. The size of the residual and the relative size of its components are much more volatile. Most volatile of all is the mutual trade-off among these three components. If advertising spending is cut back without affecting sales, profit goes up by the same amount. And if more money is spent on advertising, there is less available for promotions and profit unless advertising boosts sales significantly. It is obviously wasteful to spend more money on advertising if there are going to be no extra sales, or even if the extra profit on any additional sales is going to be much less than the cost of the extra advertising.

Measuring the effects of advertising therefore becomes a major priority, despite the methodological difficulty of estimating its short-term sales productivity, not to speak of the even greater problem of estimating the dollar value of its long-term effects. And there is another important consideration. The amount of money that many manufacturers spend on advertising is broadly similar to their earnings, so that there is a fairly direct percentage trade-off between the two. Assuming in a particular case that the two are equal, a 20 percent boost in advertising that produces no extra sales will cause profit to come down by 20 percent. This simple calculation should bring some alarming reality to discussions of advertising budgets. *Everything* depends on whether or not the advertising works. And these effects must be measured in dollar sales and dollar profit, and not with the use of a soft tracking of consumers' awareness and perceptions.

The trade-off between advertising and profit demonstrates that advertising is far more important than is usually imagined by leading business figures today, although Henry Lazell and his contemporaries were much more conscious of the leading role that advertising played in their businesses.

We have now reached what I believe to be an important pair of conclusions. First, the odds are 60:40 against a company running effective advertising. Second, there is a double penalty for exposing advertising that does not work:

1. The opportunity-cost of the higher sales that might have come from using something better.

2. The opportunity-cost of the very significant profit that might have come in by not spending the money on the advertising that did not work. Of course, zero advertising carries a long-term penalty, but this is no worse than the penalty from ineffective advertising—and the latter costs money.

It would be presumptuous to tell CEOs how to handle this double problem. However, I believe that four topics need to be put on their agenda.

Judgment of Advertising. A more sensitive and continuous evaluation of the agency's advertising proposals calls for the client to locate experienced people who can do the job. It also means finding ways of fitting them into the company's decision-making hierarchy without spoiling its mechanical efficiency. As I have already suggested, CEOs themselves would be well advised to take a closer interest in the quality of the advertising ideas on which they are going to be spending their budgets.

The Client's Advertising and Pre-testing Policies. On the assumption that advertising proposals will receive a much more serious, sensitive, and experienced evaluation from the client than they receive at present, advertisers will feel less need for rigid "how to" instructions about styles of advertising and methods of pre-testing. Agencies will certainly welcome a loosening of the straps of the straitjacket.

Measurement of Advertising Effects. The leading companies marketing consumer goods in the United States have made great advances in measuring advertising effects, through the use of scanners to measure sales and econometric analysis to isolate advertising's specific contribution. The systems are far short of perfect, however, and increasing their precision calls for talent, resources, and a dedicated belief that their promise will one day be amply fulfilled.

Agencies' Prejudices Against Quantification. The work of clients is rooted in quantification. The culture of agencies encourages an almost total reliance on a qualitative approach. The first and second items on this agenda are concerned with moving clients further toward the agencies' position. But quantification is still important. The aspect of agency work that has relied most on quantification has been media planning and buying. These functions are being quite rapidly transferred from agencies to independent companies, and these organizations are more committed to econometric analysis than most agencies are. In addition, agencies today carry out virtually no quantitative research. This was something that played an important part in their operations before the 1960s.

If agencies can now be persuaded to turn the clock back and make an intellectual contribution to measuring how well their campaigns are working, both clients and agencies will benefit. Econometric analysis is, at the moment, carried out by specialist organizations hired by the clients. There is no reason at all why agencies should not cooperate with these specialist companies. And with agencies being paid on a fee basis—which is now an extremely common practice—they should not be out of pocket.

The issues discussed in this chapter should now be handed over to the people who will grapple with them. Every firm will handle these agenda items in a different way, and indeed a number of organizations are already tackling certain of them; in recent years, clients have been more proactive than agencies in improving advertising practice. The only point I must, however, re-emphasize is that improving advertising efficiency is an urgent and very important problem. And it sits squarely in the hands of CEOs of companies that spend a lot of money on media advertising above the line, which means all corporations engaged in the mass marketing of consumer goods and services.

19

Volcanoes and Their Extinction

Myth:

"The relationship between a manufacturer and his advertising agency is almost as intimate as the relationship between a patient and his doctor."

A Fascinating and Rather Sinister Business

Business books have been very popular for decades, and this popularity has attracted many talented writers. I do not mean technical works describing business organizations or their operating methods. What I am thinking about are stories about the human dramas of business successes and (more especially) business failures. The books' titles give the clue to their contents. From the many feet—or yards—of such works on library shelves, here are half a dozen examples, with their dates of publication: *Never Complain Never Explain* (1981), about Ford; *The Big Store* (1987), about Sears Roebuck; *Merchants of Death* (1988), about tobacco; *The Greatest Ever Bank Robbery* (1990), about the savings and loan industry; *The Aspirin Wars* (1991), about over-the-counter drugs; *Soap Opera* (1993), about Procter & Gamble.

A remarkable feature of popular business books is that many of the earliest—and most widely selling—works described a much smaller type of enterprise than any of the major industries and firms listed above, and one totally different in character. These were books about advertising, and advertising agencies in particular. Here are four examples: Vance Packard's *The Hidden Persuaders* (1957); Martin Mayer's *Madison Avenue, USA* (1958); Rosser Reeves's *Reality in Advertising*

(1960); and David Ogilvy's *Confessions of an Advertising Man* (1963). There have been many others, some with picturesque titles.

The advertising books are all engagingly written, although not more so than those that deal with larger and more important businesses. Why then were advertising books so popular in the 1950s and 1960s? What was there about advertising that tickled the public's palate?

I can think of two connected reasons. The first is that advertising is much more in the public's face than the activities of even the largest industries that market goods and services. All members of the public are confronted with hundreds of advertising messages every day (although few of us dwell on how many—or how few—of these have any effect). Advertising has therefore a high public profile, although its omnipresence carries what many see as a real danger. This is the second reason why advertising interests the public. Advertising is commonly thought to make us buy both things we want and things we did not even know we wanted; many people believe that it does this by controlling us in unseen ways. (I am talking about perception and not reality.) What I once heard described as "psychological engineering" (!) is fascinating and also rather sinister, and it seems to home in on the American public's deep-seated interest in the workings of the human mind.

The four books about the advertising business that I mentioned show that their authors were convinced of advertising's effectiveness, although none of them provided anything approaching robust evidence of this. Packard's delightfully named book *The Hidden Persuaders,* which was about motivational research and how this can supposedly be used to manipulate the public, amply lived up to people's expectations of mysterious forces at work.

The clients of the bigger agencies in the 1950s and 1960s—as Mayer, Reeves, and Ogilvy knew them—were stable organizations, many of them very large. Most although not all operated in the various fields of repeat-purchase packaged goods. (Other types of goods and services have become increasingly important on the advertising scene since that time.) Most of them advertised for a simple purpose: to sell soap (or whatever they were in business to manufacture). Clients employed their agencies for the long haul, although agencies were occasionally fired. This usually caused a considerable stir because it was so rare.

Agencies themselves were also stable, with billing volumes that grew steadily but not dramatically every year. Many agencies were well established, a number dating from well before 1900. They were all privately owned and most were very prosperous (although quite how prosperous was not widely appreciated). Their financial strength was a direct result of the way they were paid: by commission on the value of the press space and the television and radio time they bought on behalf of their clients. This system was universally employed and was assumed to be a permanent fixture of the business. In retrospect, this payment by media commission—which was a historical anachronism—must appear to an objective observer an astonishing phenomenon.

Advertising agencies opened their doors during the mid-nineteenth century as organizations that worked for magazine publishers. An advertising agency meant an agency that sold magazine space, and in doing this they often showed simple advertising ideas to help persuade clients to give them business. Agencies were paid by the magazines that employed them, and this was done by granting them a commission on the value of the space they sold. By the beginning of the twentieth century, agencies had begun to resemble their present form, in that their main function was to plan and write the campaigns for advertisers that sold their goods and services to the public at large. Agencies were no longer in the business of selling media space. Nevertheless they continued to be paid as if they still were. But the commissions they were earning were by now paid on the space (and later the time) they were buying on behalf of their own clients, the advertisers.

The centrally important point about the commission system was that it was a fixed rate. This was 15 percent of the gross cost of space and time for advertising billings *of all sizes*. If a client spent $1 million, the agency received 15 percent, or $150,000; if it spent ten times as much—$10 million—the agency also received 15 percent, or $1,500,000.

A $10 million advertising account requires more work from the agency than a $1 million account, but not usually ten times as much. This means that, the larger an account grows, a uniform 15 percent commission will make it increasingly profitable to the agency in both absolute and relative terms. This is why large agencies were always so anxious to preserve the system. But the clients were much less enthusiastic, and there is good evidence that even as long ago as the 1920s many clients believed that agencies were earning too much money at their expense.

The system was the result of a comfortable arrangement between media owners and advertising agencies. Both parties were exercising their market power to preserve a quiet life, which was brought about by ensuring that agencies operated as a cartel, eliminating price competition. If clients bought advertising space without an agency, they would still have to pay the full gross cost of that space. It is surprising that the Federal Trade Commission did not label this as undesirable if not illegal behavior. It certainly ensured that the scale economies of advertising agency operations would benefit the agencies exclusively, and this is what the clients resented. With all of the many other outside purchases that clients made, they received lower prices as they bought larger quantities. This was the case with raw materials, office supplies, and capital goods of all types, and there were even volume discounts on the press space and television time the agencies purchased on their behalf. Advertising agency services were the shining exception to the rule that the more you buy, the lower the rate you pay.

As agencies emerged from space selling and adopted their modern role of writing campaigns, their working principle became increasingly "full service." This meant a total involvement in all advertising functions: planning market research, writing strategy, generating creative ideas, supervising press (and later film) production, media planning, and media buying. During the 1930s, 1940s, and 1950s, agencies were fully involved in producing radio and television shows sponsored by their clients, but this is no longer part of their job. However, agencies also became involved in so-called collateral work, such as package design, print production, and public relations, and they earned separate fees for this work. The "outside" costs of market research fieldwork and creative production were also charged to the client (generally with a mark-up), although the planning and supervision of these activities were part of the agency's full service.

The combination of increasing commission income and full service meant that agencies tended to become overstaffed, as they strove to justify their obviously large and growing revenues. This meant increasing the layers of account management, hiring people to carry out a variety of rather strange administrative functions, and setting up a number of support departments such as home economics, information services, legal counsel, staff training, international coordination, and others. Agencies would even hire people with a prominent reputation or specialist skills even if they had no jobs for them. It was hoped that such people would create their own business, which would generate income for the agency. I never once saw this policy pay off, mainly because the newcomers got little cooperation from existing members of the staff, who always jealously protected their own turf.

Another prominent feature of the business was that client entertaining became a practiced art and far exceeded the occasional two-martini lunch. I revisited J. Walter Thompson, London, during the late 1990s, with some important clients of the agency. What surprised me most was that we were offered a picnic lunch off paper plates!

Such was the business that I encountered at the beginning of my own career. I found it genuinely interesting and more than a little glamorous. But if one were to take a more jaundiced view, the old-style agencies might have been described as fat, rich, complacent, uncompetitive, and producing work that was long on craftsmanship but short on originality. David Ogilvy, who was running a vigorously competitive agency in the 1950s and 1960s, called them extinct volcanoes. This was unkind but not totally untrue (hence the title of this chapter).

Agencies on the Big Board

Before the 1960s, agencies were privately owned. Their stock was in the hands of their proprietors, except for small amounts distributed to senior, long-serving employees. When an individual retired, he or she had to sell all the stock owned back to the company and it was in due course sold to someone who was still employed. Stock purchases and sales were made at "book" value, that is, based on accountants' conservative estimates of the company's equity: its net worth after liabilities had been deducted from assets.

Over time, the "book" value increased if the agency was successful, and the proprietors were able to retire with modest fortunes when they eventually stopped working. However, some of them stayed in harness until they were long past their best: perhaps in the hope that the value of the stock would climb much higher.

A major change took place during the 1960s. Agency proprietors, David Ogilvy being the most prominent, began to see the advantages of offering stock in their companies to the public. The first agency to go public—in 1962—was a small, high-profile operation, Papert, Koenig, Lois. It no longer exists, and this should not surprise us too much in view of the problems that publicly owned agencies soon began to encounter. Agencies were floated publicly because their proprietors guessed—with good reason—that the open market valuation of their stock would be much greater than its "book" value. Agencies' comfortable earnings would impress investors, and there were two other factors at work. First, to institutional investors the advertising business appeared buoyant, the leading agencies had well-known names, and they were led by prominent figures in the business world: A number of agency heads were better known than the CEOs of some major corporations. Second, individual investors were interested in the advertising business (as has been discussed earlier) and might therefore put some money into it.

Public flotation therefore provided agency proprietors with a ticket to an opulent retirement in the sun, collecting antiques and playing golf, or—like David Ogilvy—holding court in a French chateau. One after another, the stock of the majority of the large agencies was offered to the public. Most were listed on the Big Board of the New York Stock Exchange; others were traded over-the-counter.

Serious fortunes were made, although these were small in comparison with the sums accumulated by a host of operators rolling the dice on Wall Street, and also by numbers of senior people in large (and sometimes even in modest) industrial corporations. The advertising agency business had traditionally been small, specialist, and professional, with some cultural resemblances to firms of lawyers, accountants, and management consultants. Agencies now quite rapidly joined a bigger league, although only as rookie players. Agency CEOs were not at home in the world of finance, and this in due course caused problems.

As the high-profile individuals in the advertising agency business left the scene, the business's cachet began to fade: a point discussed in Chapter 18. The quotation at the beginning of this chapter about the client-agency relationship resembling that between patient and doctor began to lose any connection with the real world. The words are David Ogilvy's and date from 1963, but he had no way of knowing how much the business would decline in importance in the estimation of clients within a couple of decades.

The detailed publication of agencies' earnings, which was required now that they were public companies, powerfully reinforced clients' feelings that agencies were making too much money. Many clients had begun to question the 15 percent commission system when massive television budgets began to provide the most luxurious pickings for their agencies. And after agencies became publicly owned, when their profits were fully disclosed, 15 percent was irreversibly doomed. Agency CEOs were also forced to accept the harsh discipline of publishing their companies' earnings on a quarterly basis, and the market's sensitivity to profit reductions and shortfalls below expectations had damaging effects on the value of the stock, which naturally diverted the attention of agency CEOs from the professional concerns of their clients. This outcome was most unfortunate, because it eroded the credibility of a business that had been created by quintessential professionals: dedicated and occasionally charismatic crusaders for the cause of advertising as a business-building force for their clients.

Total advertising expenditure was stagnant for much of the 1970s, and large agencies now found themselves with falling incomes because commission rates were being ratcheted down. Despite the efforts of agency managements to focus on their company finances and at the same time on their clients, agency stock prices were pummeled. This made the organizations vulnerable to predators in the market. Financiers eventually took command of the largest advertising businesses, and the industry is now dominated by international groups, in some cases controlled by financial holding companies. These embrace not only advertising agencies but also market research companies, public relations consultancies, design offices, and a raft of specialist communications firms. Most important, they include media organizations that were set up to handle all the media buying for the advertising agencies in the group.

The separation of media buying from advertising agencies was one of the most important trends in the American advertising business during the 1990s. It was begun for the seemingly sensible reason that it maximizes buying power so as to squeeze lower advertising rates out of the media. For decades, some large clients had used the Agency-of-Record system. With this, the media *buying* for every brand a client advertised was carried out by a single member of the client's agency roster, but the media planning was always done by the agencies handling the separate brands. However, completely independent companies set up to plan and buy media emerged in Britain during the 1970s and early 1980s. They were started by agency media executives who realized—with justification—that their talents were not being fully used by their agencies. Besides the cost advantages they could garner through buying media space and time in very large volumes, they foresaw a valuable opportunity in using their specialist skills in an increasingly complex media environment. Media organizations were originally independent of agencies. But as they became successful and profitable, the agency groups moved in. Most, but not all, media organizations are now part of agency conglomerates.

Because the media buying organizations work so closely with the clients, they are directly concerned with the basic advertising strategy for brands, to the exclusion of the agencies handling those brands. Agencies have most to gain from working with a carefully developed strategy, particularly if it is based on good facts and is "green-thumbed." Agencies' separation from the strategy of the brands they handle has been a real impediment to their effectiveness.

The growth of agency groups has proceeded to such an extent that, of the twenty-seven leading American agencies (according to a list published by the trade journal *Advertising Age*), twenty-three are members of such conglomerates. The overall result of this concentration has been an improvement in the operating efficiency of advertising agencies. As a result of pressure applied to the managers of individual operating divisions, the groups have been healthily in the black for a number of years, especially during the prosperous years from 1995 through 2000. Great problems have emerged, however.

The most insidious (but perhaps most predictable) effect of the outside ownership has been on agency morale. As has been easily observable for more than a decade, there has been an almost universal and quite perceptible loss of family feeling and internal cohesion: a weakening of corporate culture within the agencies. This loss has been permanent, and there have been very few exceptions. The only agency I know fairly well that has managed to maintain and indeed strengthen its culture is FHV/BBDO, Amsterdam, a part of the Omnicom network. This reinforcement is the result of a strong spirit of independence allied to very careful planning to foster proactive thinking by everybody in the agency. The result is evident in the work that is produced, and the agency itself radiates a spirit of confidence and optimism.

But most agencies have suffered in morale and have been subjected to a weakening of their intellectual resources. Advertising during 2001, 2002, and 2003 has been (and may well continue for a further period) in its worst slump since the Great Depression. This is partially because of general business stagnation, a short- and medium-term phenomenon. But overlaying it are longer-term problems. Chickens—or perhaps blackbirds—have come home to roost.

Three Items for an Advertising Agency's Agenda

The concluding section of this chapter is addressed specifically to advertising agencies or, more specifically, to a single large agency. I am more comfortable addressing an individual agency albeit a hypothetical one that can be taken as typical of the genre. Such an agency may be part of a group controlled ultimately by a holding company, but it is managed as an independent entity. CEOs of advertising holding companies know quite well that the success of their businesses depends on the success of the individual parts of it, not on the CEOs' own contributions in imposing financial controls, spreading wisdom throughout the network, and arranging business referrals among individual business units, that is, cross-selling.

To an individual agency, its expertise is not common property; it is proprietary. Good agencies have *amour propre* and are jealous of their identity, their methods, and their culture. The coming of the financial holding companies has not changed these basic facts in any way.

The long-term problems of the advertising industry can be addressed only by individual agencies, each in its own way. This is why I am discussing these problems as agenda items and not as discrete difficulties for which neat and general solutions can be found. Because of the pressures on all agencies since they got to grips with the difficulties raised by public ownership, they have not had the time or even the inclination to think through their difficulties in a considered way. They have not planned strategically but simply reacted to adverse conditions— normally by reducing costs, which has often meant cutting into the muscle as well as into the fat. In the 1960s, American agencies usually employed twenty staff members per $10 million of billing; the figure today is five staff members and often many fewer people. Agencies' solutions to their problems have almost always been inadequate and badly timed.

Despite the temptation to do so, it is unwise for an individual agency to continue to believe that the industry's problems should be tackled by somebody else: by other organizations within the group of which it is part, or by some competitive agency or by well-meaning professional associations. The time has really come to work differently. An individual agency must work alone and operate exclusively for its own benefit (which, if one believes in Adam Smith's Invisible Hand, will eventually benefit everybody). In tackling the problems, the most fundamental challenge that my agency faces is to change its mind set and plan proactively. There are three specific issues for the agenda, which I shall describe with an acronym, SIA:

Strategy

Income

Accountability

I shall discuss each in turn.

Strategy. Clients have been perennially dissatisfied with agencies' inability to develop a proper strategy for the brands they handle. Agencies seem unable to grasp what strategy means to a client: a set of objectives calibrated in terms of sales and profit. Agencies think almost exclusively in advertising-related terms, such as brand awareness, advertising awareness, attitudes to brands, impact, "cut-through." As I attempted to demonstrate in Chapter 4, the first question that an advertising strategy for a brand should address is: "Where is the business going to come from? What is the source of our business?" Business is about boosting or protecting sales, increasing or maintaining a consumer franchise, generating rising profit from sales volumes that may be static. All other parts of a strategy stem from the answer to this first question. The focus should be on behavioral data and objectives rather than on psychological ones. Quantification is more important than qualitative insights. The agencies' fondness for the latter makes it difficult for them to understand fully their clients' way of thinking.

During the 1990s (as explained), the jobs of planning and buying media became increasingly separated from advertising agencies and were put in the hands of specialist media organizations, some (but not all) owned by advertising holding companies. This process continues. What this process has meant is that matters of strategy are increasingly determined by the clients and discussed most seriously with the media organizations, which are of course accustomed to working with hard numbers. In the most extreme cases, the advertising plans are decided between clients and media specialists, and the advertising agency is then given instructions to prepare advertising to appear in specified media vehicles on particular dates. The way in which the media organizations are increasingly involved with clients at a strategy level harks back to the nineteenth century, when agencies were engaged exclusively in media operations. The wheel has turned full circle.

The idea has even been raised by knowledgeable people that this system will soon lead the clients and media organizations to shop around for creative ideas among different agencies on a job-by-job basis. Readers of this book may be reminded of Coca-Cola, a company that has been operating in this way for a number of years. When clients and media groups develop strategy together, this provides an important element of continuity in circumstances when the relationship between clients and creative agencies can be volatile.

This is not a happy prospect for advertising agencies. Perhaps more seriously, it is not a happy prospect for our chances of producing good advertising. It goes against the principle of planning campaigns for the long term. It encourages the selection of campaign ideas on the basis of superficial and uninformed criteria. It is not good for the operating efficiency of agencies, not to speak of their morale! Morale influences an agency's effectiveness to a surprising degree.

The "S" of the SIA acronym is the first item that should be put on the agency's agenda. It seems to me that my hypothetical agency should mobilize its best talents to consider the issue in a detached and unhurried fashion and try to find a realistic method of bridging the interests of clients, media organizations, and the agency itself; strategy is, or should be, of major interest to all three of these parties.

Full involvement in strategy means that my agency must become more interested in—and more adept at handling—statistical quantification than most agencies are at present. An important aspect of this is that my agency must overcome its prejudice against the quantitative pre-testing of commercials. Agencies' infantile opposition to this type of research has cost their clients dearly, because of the large amount of ineffective advertising that the clients have been persuaded to run in the marketplace: advertising whose ineffectiveness should have been identified at a very early stage. As I aimed to demonstrate in Chapter 14, quantitative pre-testing would have made this possible in many cases.

Income. Sixty percent of advertising is ineffective. Advertising agencies are mainly responsible for this high failure rate, and the reason is that they are underfunded. The success rate was probably no better during the time when agencies were making large profits from 15 percent media commission, but the advertising world has changed since then. We know far more about evaluating advertising effects, and this should go a long way to improving our overall effectiveness by helping us to locate unproductive advertising, dump it, and then find something better.

According to reasonably up-to-date information, a dwindling 9 percent of the billings of major advertisers are still placed by agencies compensated by the traditional 15 percent commission, and 26 percent are placed by agencies paid by commission at reduced rates: commonly about 9 percent. The remaining two-thirds of all advertising is run by agencies that are paid in other ways, mainly by labor-based fees. These are set in the following way: The agency charges the number of hours spent on a particular client's business and multiplies this by the hourly salary of the people involved. The agency then loads these labor costs with three add-ons: the direct overhead (the account group's expenses, e.g., for office space, telephone, and travel); the general overhead (the cost of running the agency: a comparable calculation to that for a manufacturer's indirect cost); and profit.

Of these systems, labor-based fees are by far the most equitable and efficient, although they are rather complicated to use and difficult to negotiate with clients. The system means that the agency's income is related to its effort (or at least the time it spends) on the client's business. The agency is never likely to be out of pocket. And the client in turn will benefit from the scale economies of large budgets by paying the agency fairly for its services but mopping up excess profit. For instance, agencies no longer reap the revenue from holding their clients' money: the bank interest they used to earn for the two-week period between receiving their clients' payments and paying the media bills.

The advertising industry is moving quite fast toward fee-based payment, and improvement in agency incomes must come through higher fees. I must reiterate the need for agencies to receive more money to address realistically advertising's inadequate record of success. Far too little is spent at present on campaign development and on examining alternatives, both through laboratory testing and marketplace exposure. More money is needed for three specific purposes.

First, my hypothetical agency needs to be beefed up with a small extra number of talented and experienced (and expensive) people: some to increase the agency's creative output, and others to contribute substantially to strategy and evaluation. The second need is for funds for experiments of all types: in filmmaking and for testing creative ideas. The third call on funds is something that will bring benefits only in the long term. During the 1950s and 1960s, agencies attracted young university graduates as talented as—or more talented than—those hired by their clients. This has not been the case during recent years, and agencies badly need a stream of young people who have high potential. (The British agencies' association, the Institute of Practitioners in Advertising, is looking into this problem on an industrywide basis.)

Higher agency fees represent only a small amount of extra money to a client, and this is far less than the benefit that would be received from eliminating ineffective advertising and by making advertising that is currently effective more effective still. But no client will accept this point unless there is something a good deal stronger behind it.

No client would be willing to put on the table for consideration any proposal to boost an agency's fee income unless serious progress is made toward solving the problem of accountability, the "A" in the SIA acronym. This is a difficult proposition. However, if accountability *can* be provided, persuading clients to accept an increase in agency fees may not be as tough as it might at first sight appear. Paying agencies by results interests clients. Beginning in the early 1990s, major clients have been putting incentive systems into action, and these are being improved with each year's experience. Performance-related-fees (PRFs) are commonly received by media organizations, but of course measuring the efficiency of their buying is a simpler matter than measuring the effectiveness of an agency's campaigns. Solving the problem of "A" would be the best way of making it quite practical to reward agencies according to their productivity.

Accountability. This word has become such a cliché of the advertising business that I am embarrassed to use it, although I cannot think of anything better. As it is used—only too commonly—by advertising practitioners, it is surrounded by a cloud of imprecision, abstraction, and optimism. In very many cases, the progress of an advertising campaign is measured through continuous and open-ended tracking of awareness and attitudes. If brand awareness is going up or if brand associations are becoming more favorable, the advertising is assumed to be accountable. This is not what I mean by accountability, and I believe that many clients share my view.

The word "accountability" originated in the world of finance. Financial accountability means two things: first, a finite period during which accountability is calculated; and second, a comparison of financial input and financial output. We have not yet found a completely reliable way of doing this for advertising, but we have made progress.

The immediate short-term effect of advertising can and should be measured with a reliable technique, ideally Pure Single-Source research. Assuming that only the effective campaigns are allowed to pass through the gate, we now face the difficulty of measuring the joint effect of the creative/budget/media combination over a finite period, usually twelve months.

Econometric analysis (as described briefly in Chapter 10) is the best way of doing this. The calculation that is most useful for practical purposes is the advertising payback: a comparison of the advertising input (in dollars) with the net output directly caused by this advertising, the dollar value of which must be estimated by taking the value of sales attributable to advertising and deducting direct and indirect costs. The procedure is complicated and not free of pitfalls.

This description of the method gives rather an optimistic picture of the present state of the art. The starting point is a hypothesis of a statistical model, using sales as the variable that needs to be explained. The relative importance of the causes of these sales is derived from regression analysis, and the different causes can now have different weights attributed to them. Predictions are then made and tested against reality. The model is refined and the process of prediction and refinement continues. Most models we use today are in the earlier rather than the later stages of this process. The problem with econometrics is that it is a work in progress and it will be a long time before it can be considered as bulletproof.

A separate problem is that the findings of econometric models are usually described in a technical way and are hedged around with intricate qualifications. They are therefore used most by marketing specialists—usually staff advisers—in client organizations. It is very unlikely that their findings are fully absorbed by the CEOs who have to make the ultimate decisions about advertising.

One general conclusion emerges from econometric investigations. With rare exceptions, advertising does not pay its way in the medium term. The dollar value of the payback produced by the advertising is almost always smaller than the cost of the advertising itself. If we are prepared to make extreme assumptions about the long-term effects of advertising, we can sometimes inflate the figures by including the extra effect of advertising from previous years. When we do this, advertising in about a quarter of all cases can be shown to yield a positive return (i.e., more dollars from advertising-related payback than dollars invested). But the method of calculating this is controversial and I think it is best to concentrate on the conventional medium-term (i.e., one-year) measurement.

When the advertising is effective, the medium-term payback for most brands of repeat-purchase packaged goods is usually in the range of 50 to 70 cents per dollar of advertising investment. Turning these figures around, the cost of the advertising net of the value of the payback recovered is between 30 and 50 cents per dollar.

An immediate—but highly dangerous—response to this conclusion is that manufacturers should stop their advertising and add the advertising budget to profit. But this ignores the opportunity-cost. It does not take into account advertising's defensive role: its ability to maintain a large enough volume of sales to keep production costs low so that the goods can be marketed at competitive prices. A manufacturer should tackle the difficult job of estimating the likely consequences to overall revenue of abandoning advertising. In most cases, it will be found that such a course is unwise, if not disastrous.

It must be remembered, however, that we are talking here about effective campaigns. In the all-too-common circumstance that the advertising is ineffective, the total sum spent on it is a net charge against profit, and the sooner the campaign is changed the better.

Two other points are also worth noting. First, in fields other than packaged goods (e.g., apparel and telecommunications), payback levels can be significantly higher. Second, the payback from trade and consumer promotions is always smaller than that from media advertising. This comparison should make it easier to distribute funds between advertising and promotions more rationally than is normally done today.

Turning now to specific estimates of the medium-term payback for advertising, what is the best way in which this information can be used to provide accountability? Because a net loss should be seen to be normal, the best way is to look at the figures *comparatively*. Some campaigns produce better returns than others. If in a particular year the payback is 60 cents on the dollar, and in the next year a fresh campaign yields 70 cents, then the second campaign is more effective and the agency should receive some reward for this. It is going too far to calculate the increase in effectiveness as precisely as 17 percent (the proportion by which 70 is greater than 60 cents), but there is really no doubt that the new advertising is working more strongly than the old.

I have gone through the principles of accountability extremely briefly, but it will be useful at this stage to summarize my proposed agenda items for my hypothetical agency. Four tasks are to be accomplished:

1. To measure accurately the immediate short-term effect of advertising. This gives a health check on the creative content of the advertising and enables us to eliminate ineffective campaigns at the starting gate.

2. To use econometrics judgmentally, with the client, agency, and outside research company working cooperatively to improve and refine the techniques.

3. To estimate the opportunity-cost of abandoning advertising; in most cases, this calculation will provide a sharp statistical reminder of advertising's importance.

4. To make the most productive use of payback estimates of campaign effectiveness; this is best done by using the data comparatively. Improvement should mean extra compensation for the agency.

Accountability means that we will always have to work with difficult concepts. This makes it even more crucial that they should be described lucidly but without oversimplifying important points: an art that not many econometricians have acquired. (Advertising agencies can perhaps do better.) The huge merit of econometrics is that it gives us our best shot at quantifying what advertising means to a brand. If at every stage of planning and exposing a campaign the client and agency make the right decisions, advertising is the factor that can turn a promising brand into a great one. Econometrics can give us our report card on the progress we are making to achieving this goal.

If, during the next twenty years, econometric techniques develop as fast as they have during the past twenty, we shall by the early 2020s have a reliable—or certainly reliable enough—method of measuring advertising's effects over the short and medium term, and this will make it possible to calculate its financial productivity. A payback will remain difficult to calculate, but the concept is easily grasped and this makes it an admirably practical tool to help CEOs of client companies make decisions about their advertising.

Accountability should also make it possible, at last, for advertising agencies to be more comfortably rewarded. I believe that there are extremely good odds that this will lead to more efficient advertising practice and a reduction in the disgracefully high waste at present associated with the business.

Part VII

Sources of Information

Myth:

"Americans want more information. . . . In a knowledge-based economy the most important domestic political issue is no longer the distribution (or redistribution) of wealth, but of the information and media that produce wealth."

One of the most popular of all misconceptions.

20

The Expanding Universe of Information

Myth:

"Americans want more information. . . . In a knowledge-based economy the most important domestic political issue is no longer the distribution (or redistribution) of wealth, but of the information and media that produce wealth."

No one can deny that the amount of information available to people has exploded during the past two decades, largely as a result of how we collect facts on computers and disseminate them via the Internet. The quotation given here refers to matters of public policy, although the point could equally well be made for all other human activities. But the statement contains an enormous trap for the unwary. The technical improvements in the delivery of information have led many simple souls—who include most of the commentators who have published their thoughts on the subject—to conclude that members of the public have an unrequited thirst for information and (even more implausibly) that they are as a result better informed than before.

My own professional observation, through my work as an educator, has raised rather large questions in my mind about such a charming and optimistic idea. The fact that we are drowning in *information* does not mean that most of us have actually become better *informed*. Our greatest need is to digest what we have already. This is far more urgent and important than the need to acquire ever-larger quantities of data.

Advertising represents a small microcosm of the wider world of knowledge. There is a large total accumulation but only a small amount that is original, sound, well presented, and processed in such a way that it can guide operational policy.

A Small Corpus of Valuable Literature

The number of books, monographs, and journal articles about advertising is very large and rapidly growing. Quality varies greatly. From the point of view of increasing our total knowledge of the subject, a remarkable number of works are counterproductive because they propagate myths: something that will not surprise readers of this book. In addition, many contributions are ephemeral and inconsequential; and a good deal is accurate but tells us nothing new. But some of the published literature genuinely advances the sum total of our knowledge, and although the flow of such work is little more than a trickle, a modest but respectable body of work has been built up over the years.

The purpose of this chapter is to tell readers about the factual underpinnings for everything I have said in this book. The Bibliography lists 107 different sources, organized alphabetically by authors' names. The works in this Bibliography are mainly in the last group listed in the previous paragraph: those that have revealed something new. But there are a few exceptions, because I feel that the sources of the myths that are quoted in every chapter should also be disclosed.

The Bibliography contains a number of my own published works. I hope that readers will forgive my vanity, but I have two reasons for doing this. First, I have been fortunate enough to have made a small number of discoveries myself. Second, much of my work is devoted to collecting and summarizing the findings of other people's research: research that, in most cases, is more important than mine. I provide full details in these works of where all this research is published, so that readers can go to the originals if they want to find out more. The sources are often to be found in many different places, some difficult to locate. My syntheses, therefore, provide a convenient way into this wide-ranging research.

I shall now march through the chapters and give references to the works in the Bibliography that support my facts and arguments. Each chapter in this book is divided into sections. In this chapter, each section of the other chapters is covered by a separate paragraph of sources. When I refer to "this book," I mean *Fables, Fashions, and Facts About Advertising* and not any other specific source listed.

Chapters and Sources

Preface: An inventory of the state of advertising knowledge can be found in Jones, *How Much Is Enough?*, Chapter 10, which also contains a very extensive bibliography. The various fables listed in the Preface are discussed in later chapters of this book. Direct response is the main topic of Chapter 16. The details of Hopkins's monograph are given in the Bibliography.

Chapter 1: The introductory myth comes from the Kotler, *Marketing Management*, p. 22 (a quotation from an advertisement for American Bell). The anecdote about the company that markets six brands in the single category is based on private information. Jones, *How Advertising Works*, Chapter 26, shows that the advertising for 20 percent of brands boosts sales significantly over the course of a year; and that for a further 20 percent protects and slightly increases sales. (The average shares of market of the brands in the two groups are 3.6 and 8.6 percent, respectively.) The high failure rate of new brands is detailed by Jan Slater, in Jones, *How to Use Advertising to Build Strong Brands*, Chapter 13. The stagnation of category growth is discussed in Jones, *How Much Is Enough?*, Chapter 2. The reference to *The Economist* refers to the issue of March 9, 2002, p. 20.

Oligopolistic competition is described in Jones and Slater, *What's in a Name?*, Chapter 2. The most important contribution to our understanding of competitive innovation was made by von Hayek, "The Meaning of Competition." The increasing strength of the retail sector was first signaled by Schultz and Dewar, "Retailers in Control." The importance of Wal-Mart to Procter & Gamble is detailed in Stephanie Thompson and Jack Neff, "Wal-Mart Weighs Wholesale Food Division," *Advertising Age*, January 6, 2003, pp. 1 and 19. An instructive view of how shoppers do their shopping can be found in Underhill, *Why We Buy*. The increase in the proportion of Advertising and Promotional (A&P) budgets that has gone into promotions is described in Jones, *The Advertising Business*, Chapter 31. The quotation from Ogilvy comes from *Confessions of an Advertising Man*, p. 103. The story of the Coca-Cola debacle is told in Jones and Slater, *What's in a Name?*, Chapter 2, Note 42.

Manufacturers' reliance on share of sales value to determine their advertising budgets is described in a historic paper by San Augustine and Foley, "How Large Advertisers Set Budgets." From my own observation, the system remains today as popular as ever, although many advertisers supplement it with more sophisticated techniques so that they can come to their budgeting from more than one direction. Advertising's inability to produce "macro" effects is demonstrated in Jones, *How Advertising Works*, Chapter 29; also in Broadbent, *Does Advertising Affect Market Size?* The response of sales to changes in price is described in Tellis, "The Price Elasticity of Selective Demand." The second myth in the chapter also comes from Kotler, *Marketing Management*, p. 22.

Chapter 2: The myth comes from Wells and colleagues, *Advertising Principles and Practice*, p. 89. The delightful idea that advertising can operate "subliminally" is discussed in Jones, *Advertising Organizations and Publications*, Introductory Essay. Estimates of the numbers of advertisements to which every member of the public is exposed every day are published regularly in the trade press. They are little better than guesswork. John O'Toole (a well-known advertising practitioner who ended his career as the head of the American Association of Advertising Agencies), quotes a number of 1,600. See O'Toole, *The Trouble With Advertising*, p. xiii. Selective perception is described by Brown, Hanc, and Pangsapa in Jones, *The Advertising Business*, Chapter 20. Low involvement is an important concept, first propounded by Herbert E. Krugman. See his article "Television Advertising: Learning Without Involvement," republished in Jones, *The Advertising Business*, Chapter 14. The word "nudge" expresses neatly how advertising prompts consumers to buy. It was first used in this sense by Andrew Ehrenberg, whose work is referred to later in this chapter. The estimate of the number of advertisements that stick in people's memories is based on experiments I have carried out among more than 3,000 students. The Harvard Business School research is described in Greyser, *Cases in Advertising and Communications Management*, pp. 628–637. The more up-to-date information on public attitudes to advertising can be found in Mittal, "Public Assessment of TV Advertising."

The quotation from the two journalists comes from Winters and Milton, *The Creative Connection*, p. 4. The Galbraith quotation comes from *The New Industrial State*, p. 213. The Simon quotation comes from *A Life Against the Grain*, p. 169. The question of whether advertising is in reality a powerful force is discussed by Jones, "Advertising: Strong Force or Weak Force? Two Views an Ocean Apart," in Luik and Waterson, *Advertising and Markets,* Chapter 6.

Ehrenberg's work is described fully in his monograph, *Repeat-Buying;* it is summarized in Jones and Slater, *What's in a Name?,* Chapter 5. Ehrenberg's classic essay "Repetitive Advertising and the Consumer" is also valuable, and it was republished in Jones, *How Advertising Works. The Role of Research,* Chapter 6.

Chapter 3: The myth at the beginning of the chapter comes from Reeves, *Reality in Advertising,* p. 54. The anecdote about Procter & Gamble is based on private information. The development of consumer goods markets and branding are both discussed in Jones and Slater, *What's in a Name?,* Chapter 2. The progress of Lever 2000 at the expense of Ivory soap is a fascinating story, but *how* it actually took place would call for me to reveal confidential information. Added values were first described fully by James Webb Young in his modest but important book *How to Become an Advertising Man,* Chapter 14. Gardner and Levy's article "The Product and the Brand" also made an important contribution to developing the concept.

Functional differentiation is reviewed fully in Jones and Slater, *What's in a Name?,* Chapter 1. This includes references, the two most important of which are to Peckham, *The Wheel of Marketing,* and to Davidson, "Why Most New Consumer Brands Fail."

The way in which added values can be demonstrated empirically is shown in Jones and Slater, *What's in a Name?,* Chapter 2. The latter chapter also describes the sources of added values. Lannon and Cooper's paper "Humanistic Advertising" is particularly interesting. The ways in which consumers reveal their perceptions of brand personality are illustrated in Jones, *How Much Is Enough?,* Chapter 8.

The way in which advertising can reduce the price elasticity of demand is described in Jones, *The Ultimate Secrets of Advertising,* Chapter 9. The prices of Cheerios and its generic competitor were picked up in the P&C supermarket in Fayetteville, New York.

Life cycle theory is discussed in Jones, *How to Use Advertising to Build Strong Brands,* Chapter 16. The Dial case is based on unpublished data. The Procter & Gamble quotation comes from Peters and Waterston, *In Search of Excellence,* p. 233. The Unilever quotation comes from Sir David Orr, chairman of Unilever from 1974 to 1982, in his Foreword to Jones, *Does It Pay to Advertise?* The final myth, the academic quotation, comes from Kotler, *Marketing Management,* p. 354

Chapter 4: The myth comes from O'Guinn et al., *Advertising,* p. 251. The relationship between a manufacturer's advertising expenditure and profit is illustrated by Jones, "How Clients Can Improve Their Advertising by Improving Their Decision-Making," in Kitchen, *The Future of Marketing,* Chapter 6.

Advertising strategy is described in detail in Jones, *How Much Is Enough?,* Chapters 7, 8, and 9. Chapter 7 is devoted to target groups, and demographics and psychographics are discussed there. Comparison advertising is described by Slater in Jones, *The Advertising Business,* Chapter 22.

Propositions are discussed in Jones, *How Much Is Enough?,* Chapter 8. The Unique Selling Proposition (USP) and Usage-Pull are the central concepts of Reeves, *Reality in Advertising.* They are examined critically in Jones, *The Advertising Business,* Chapter 23. The Role of Advertising is described in Jones, *How Much Is Enough?,* Chapter 8.

Chapter 5: The myth comes from Wells et al., *Advertising Principles and Practice,* pp. 251–252. Scale economies are a basic concept of microeconomics. They are discussed in most advertising textbooks, such as Samuelson, *Economics,* pp. 28–29. The original concept of brand segmentation is described in Schisgall, *Eyes on Tomorrow,* Chapter 9. The extremes of category and brand fragmentation are illustrated in Weilbacher, *Brand Marketing,* Chapters 4 and 5. There is persuasive evidence from ACNielsen that the success of new subbrands is not much influenced by a common brand name. What matters most is the advertising investment put behind each individual subbrand. See Peckham, *The Wheel of Marketing,* pp. 90–91.

The data on Budweiser, Cheerios, and Crest come from the 1998 MRI Annual Reports on consumers' use of brands and media. The information about Procter & Gamble's simplification of its product lines is based on personal observation of the retail trade. It was also noted by the business press, which published data (taken from the company's annual reports) on the reduction in the size of P&G's range of products and varieties, and this reduction was related to figures of total unit sales released by Paine Webber.

The 80:20 rule was formulated first by Ehrenberg and described by Jones and Slater, *What's in a Name?,* Chapter 5. The creative characteristics of successful advertising are illustrated in Jones, *When Ads Work*, Chapter 7. The importance of likability is demonstrated by Alexander Biel, in Jones, *How Advertising Works*, Chapter 10. Research into the Reading-and-Noting of press advertising is discussed in Jones and Slater, *What's in a Name?*, Chapter 6; and in Jones, *How Advertising Works*, Chapter 18.

Chapter 6: The introductory myth comes from Russell and Lane, *Kleppner's Advertising Procedure*, p. 532. The proportion of campaigns that have a positive effect on sales over the course of a year is detailed in Jones, *How Advertising Works*, Chapter 26. The evidence that a short-term effect of advertising acts as a gatekeeper to further effects is presented in Chapter 12 of this book.

The deficiencies of the Unique Selling Proposition are discussed in Jones, *The Advertising Business*, Chapter 23. The failings of Day-After-Recall testing are described in Jones and Slater, *What's in a Name?*, Chapter 6. The British doctrine that the effect of advertising gradually builds from a low start is discussed in Chapter 12 of this book. The quotation about a gradual buildup of "effects" comes from Hedges, *Testing to Destruction*, p. 12. David Ogilvy's views on creating advertising, particularly on the craftsmanship involved, are a prominent feature of his book *Confessions of an Advertising Man*. The Hierarchy of Effects and the various ways in which it has been described are reviewed in Jones and Slater, *What's in a Name?*, Chapter 6. Selective perception and cognitive dissonance are described by Brown, Hanc, and Pangsapa in Jones, *The Advertising Business*, Chapter 20. Festinger's article "Cognitive Dissonance" is an important work. The Groucho Marx anecdote can be found in O'Brien, "The Triumph of Marxism." The quotation from Bernbach comes from his speech "Beware of Arithmetic."

Young's notion that all new ideas are rearrangements of existing ones comes from his monograph *A Technique for Producing Ideas*, p. 25. Bisociative Fusion is a concept associated with Arthur Koestler and published in *The Act of Creation*. The De Beers advertising campaign for diamond gemstones is described in Jones, *Does It Pay to Advertise?*, Chapter 13. Other methods of generating ideas have been published by various authors, such as Edward de Bono and Roger von Oech. De Bono is a prolific writer, and a typical example of his work is *The Use of Lateral Thinking*. Von Oech's book is *A Whack on the Side of the Head*.

Young's five-step process is described in *A Technique for Producing Ideas*.

Evidence that experts cannot predict the effectiveness of advertisements can be found in Bogart et al., "What One Little Ad Can Do." The pre-testing system that can identify effective creative ideas is described in Chapter 14 of this book. The concluding myth is the work of an academic, Gillian Dyer, in *Advertising as Communication,* p. 184.

Chapter 7: The myth comes from Belch and Belch, *Advertising and Promotion. An Integrated Marketing Communications Perspective,* p. 315. The belief that advertising must be heavy enough to cross a threshold of exposure before it can work is examined by Erwin Ephron and also by Jones; both articles are published in Jones, *The Advertising Business,* Chapters 27 and 28.

The system of measuring sales in stores was introduced by ACNielsen, which began its retail audits in the early 1930s. The first consumer panel (started by J. Walter Thompson, New York) dates from the late 1930s. The technique of Pure Single-Source research is described in Jones, *When Ads Work,* Chapters 1 and 2; also in Jones, *The Ultimate Secrets of Advertising,* Chapter 2.

The anecdote about the professionals who counted the number of sales stimuli comes from Reeves, *Reality in Advertising,* p. 4. Diminishing returns to advertising pressure are described in Jones, *When Ads Work,* Chapter 4; and in Jones, *The Ultimate Secrets of Advertising,* Chapter 5. Both chapters emphasize the way in which advertising can work effectively on a single-exposure basis.

The exceptional cases in which advertising needs more than a single exposure for cognitive reasons are discussed in Krugman, "Why Three Exposures May Be Enough." Krugman's work refers to new brands and new advertising concepts. With familiar brands and concepts, a single exposure is effective.

Chapter 8: The myth comes from Kotler, *Marketing Management,* p. 623. The Budweiser case was published by Ackoff and Emshoff, "Advertising Research at Anheuser-Busch." The opinion about Anheuser-Busch "pouring money into advertising" comes from a private source. The Lux case was published in Jones, *Does It Pay to Advertise?,* Chapter 6 (supplemented by significant personal experience of the brand). Listerine case studies have been published in Jones, *Does It Pay to Advertise?,* Chapter 5; and in Greyser, *Cases in Advertising and Communications Management,* pp. 148–67. The Oxo case was published in Jones, *Does It Pay to Advertise?,* Chapter 8.

The budgetary division between advertising and promotions is reviewed in Jones, *The Advertising Business,* Chapter 31. The data on Procter & Gamble were published in Smith, "Keep an Eye on Expenses." The system of determining advertising budgets according to a percentage of sales is discussed in San Augustine and Foley, "How Large Advertisers Set Budgets." The method of using the SOM/SOV relationship to help determine a budget is described in Jones, "Ad Spending: Maintaining Market Share." The effect of large increases in SOV and how they can boost SOM are detailed in Schroer, "Ad Spending: Growing Market Share." My book of case studies is *Does It Pay to Advertise?* Average figures on advertising elasticities are published in Assmus et al., "How Advertising Affects Sales." The advertising elasticity for Andrex is discussed in Jenkins and Timms, "The Andrex Story."

The use of econometrics to set advertising budgets, in particular by calculating the financial productivity of advertising in different media, is discussed in Jones, *The Ultimate Secrets of Advertising,* Chapter 6. The broader aspects of budgeting are reviewed in Jones, *The Advertising Business,* Chapter 7. The substance of the latter chapter was published in 1990, in a widely read article: Jones, "Ad Spending: Maintaining Market Share."

Chapter 9: The introductory myth comes from Kotler, *Marketing Management,* p. 625. The estimates of expenditure on media advertising in the United States are made by Robert J. Coen of the Interpublic advertising agency group. Interpublic can supply the data direct, although until recently the estimates for any year were published in May of the following year by the trade publication *Advertising Age.* Trends are examined in Jones, *The Advertising Business,* Chapter 1.

The estimates of the division of funds between advertising and promotion are based on sample surveys of major advertisers. Trends in the figures are published in Jones, *The Advertising Business,* Chapter 31. The most recent data can be found in Jack Neff, "Accounting by New Rules," *Advertising Age,* July 15, 2002, pp. 4 and 27. Ogilvy's *cri de coeur* can be found in a speech entitled "Sound an Alarm!," included in *The Unpublished David Ogilvy,* pp. 106–111. The most authoritative book on Integrated Marketing Communications (IMC) is Schultz, Tannenbaum, and Lauterborn, *Integrated Marketing Communications.* See also Schultz's article in Jones, *The Advertising Business,* Chapter 32.

Growth in the buying power of the retail trade was first signaled by Schultz and Dewar, "Retailers in Control: The Impact of Retail Trade

Concentration." The concept of franchise-building sales promotions is examined in Prentice, "How to Split Your Marketing Funds Between Advertising and Promotion."

The arithmetic quantifying how sales promotions contribute positively to sales volume but negatively to profit is spelled out in Jones, "The Double Jeopardy of Sales Promotions." Estimates of the range of price elasticities can be found in Tellis, "The Price Elasticity of Selective Demand." The story of the travails of the detergents market in Denmark comes from my personal experience. The data about the big three American car manufacturers comes from "Storm Clouds Over Detroit," *The Economist*, November 16, 2002, p. 55. The concluding myth comes from Arens and Bovée, *Contemporary Advertising*, pp. 503–504.

Chapter 10: The myth comes from Arens and Bovée, *Contemporary Advertising*, p. 431. The figures showing the degree to which large advertisers concentrate on television come from the "*Ad Age* Special Report: Mega Brands," *Advertising Age*, July 22, 2002, p. S-2. (The figures refer to 2001.) The data published every year by *Advertising Age* show that each advertiser's distribution of its budget between different media remains remarkably stable. And the distribution of the media expenditures placed by leading advertising agencies, also published by *Advertising Age*, shows a similar stability. The anecdote about General Foods comes from a private source.

The description of Pure Single-Source research comes from Jones, *The Ultimate Secrets of Advertising*, Chapter 2, which also covers the short-term success rate for campaigns together with certain international comparisons. The important article "What One Little Ad Can Do" was written by Leo Bogart and two colleagues and is listed in the Bibliography. The Sales Deconstruction and payback estimates by Marketing Management Analytics (MMA) are published in Jones, *The Ultimate Secrets of Advertising*, Chapter 6. The most recent data—those comparing packaged goods and non-packaged goods—come from Ephron and Pollak, *The Curse of Lord Leverhulme*. The Giffen Paradox is described in Marshall, *Principles of Economics*, pp. 109–110. The application of the Giffen Paradox to media buying in the United States was first demonstrated by Erwin Ephron.

The skewed distribution of the television audience is rarely discussed in the advertising literature. The best data describing it are published in the annual MRI reports on consumers' use of brands and media. In these, the total television audience is analyzed into quintiles (i.e., units of 20 percent), ranked from the heaviest to the lightest viewers. The top three quintiles account for 85 percent of all viewing; the bottom two quintiles account for only 15 percent. Erwin Ephron demonstrated (in unpublished research) that it is now possible to reach tightly defined target groups through the use of specific television programs. The problems of TiVo are discussed in "The Future of Television: Heave Ho, TiVo!," *The Economist*, February 8, 2003, p. 60. The relative payback from different media is illustrated in Jones, *The Ultimate Secrets of Advertising*, Chapter 6. Ogilvy's criticism of agencies' lack of craft skills in print advertising can be found in Ogilvy, *Ogilvy on Advertising*, Chapter 7. See also Amico's independent investigation, *Breaking the Rules*.

Chapter 11: The two myths come from Wells et al., *Advertising. Principles and Practice*, pp. 106 and 304. The book devoted to the importance of three advertising exposures and the use of the purchase interval as a media planning tool is Naples, *Effective Frequency*.

The evidence from Pure Single-Source research that an effective advertisement can generate a sometimes substantial sales effect from a single exposure comes from Jones, *When Ads Work*, Chapter 4; and Jones, *The Ultimate Secrets of Advertising*, Chapter 5. I heard the words of the skeptical media director in private conversation. My cosmetics client was Chesebrough-Pond's, on whose business I worked in Britain and in a number of other European countries. The ARF statement about amputating the three-exposure rule of thumb was made in November 1997.

The estimates of net reach obtained by various quantities of weekly GRPs were made by Erwin Ephron. The Andrex example of successful Continuity Planning was published in Jenkins and Timms, "The Andrex Story." The second Andrex case is presented in Stow, "Sold on a Pup." The Ubiquity case and the MMA research into the efficiency of Continuity are published in Jones, *The Ultimate Secrets of Advertising*, Chapter 5. The ARS research into the superiority of Continuity is awaiting publication.

Chapter 12: The two myths come from Hedges, *Testing to Destruction*, p. 26. The week-by-week volatility of markets is illustrated in Jones, *When Ads Work*, Appendix A. It was first revealed by the veteran researcher Leo Bogart. See Bogart, "The Turbulent Depths of Marketing," in Jones, *How Advertising Works*, Chapter 3.

The description of Pure Single-Source research comes from Jones, *When Ads Work*, Chapter 2; and Jones, *The Ultimate Secrets of Advertising*, Chapter 2. The medium-term effect of advertising is described in Jones, *The Ultimate Secrets of Advertising*, Chapters 4 and 5; and the long-term effects in Jones, *The Ultimate Secrets of Advertising*, Chapters 6 through 10.

The large battery of cases published by the British Institute of Practitioners in Advertising is described by Chris Baker in Jones, *International Advertising*, Chapter 27. The British "Small Steps" theory is discussed (without the use of that name) in Hedges, *Testing to Destruction*. The concept of "Adstock" was originated by the late Simon Broadbent and was first described in Broadbent, *The Leo Burnett Book of Advertising*, pp. 91–94. McDonald's statement that a model is a "myth with numbers" comes from McDonald, "Myths, Evidence and Evaluation." Karl Popper's concept of the scientific method is described in his book *The Logic of Scientific Discovery* and is elegantly discussed in McGinn, "Looking for a Black Swan." The second myth comes from this article, and it is an extract from McGinn's criticism of Popper (which I personally endorse strongly).

Chapter 13: The myth comes from Levitt, *The Marketing Imagination*, p. 39. The supermarket I visited was a new store, P&C, in Fayetteville, New York. The previous store check mentioned in this chapter was carried out in 1984 in Wegmans supermarket in Dewitt, New York. Its findings were published in Jones and Slater, *What's in a Name?*, Chapter 2. Von Hayek's description of the competitive process appears in "The Meaning of Competition." The estimates of the sales volume and sales value accounted by manufacturers' brands are derived from product categories audited by ACNielsen.

Branding and added values form the substance of Chapter 3 of this book. The GCMB process (introduced in Chapter 12 of this book) is based on the measurement of the long-term effects of advertising that are described in Jones, *The Ultimate Secrets of Advertising*, Chapters 6 through 10. (These refer to many sources in the endnotes.) The Dove information comes from private sources. The "Small Steps" theory is examined critically in Chapter 12 of this book. The MMA data on the payback from large versus small brands come from Ephron and Pollak, *The Curse of Lord Leverhulme*. The whole question of waste in advertising is the focus of Jones, *How Much Is Enough?*

Chapter 14: The myth comes from Hedges, *Testing to Destruction,* p. 48. The article by Bogart et al. is "What One Little Ad Can Do." Direct-response practitioners are also unable to forecast the effectiveness of different advertisements, although they have excellent measures of such effectiveness after the event. See McCorkell, "When Experts Can Get It Wrong." The success rate of new brands is examined by Slater in Jones, *How to Use Advertising to Build Strong Brands,* Chapter 13. The proportion of campaigns that have an effect in the marketplace is detailed in Jones, *How Advertising Works. The Role of Research,* Chapter 26. The concept of low involvement is important. See Krugman's article, republished in Jones, *The Advertising Business,* Chapter 14. Account planning and the use of focus groups are discussed in detail in Cooper, *How to Plan Advertising;* and in Feldwick, *Pollitt on Planning.*

The discussion of quantitative pre-testing in this chapter is derived substantially from Jones, *The Ultimate Secrets of Advertising,* Chapter 3; and Jones, *Getting It Right the First Time.* Day-After-Recall-Testing is discussed critically in Jones and Slater, *What's in a Name?,* Chapter 6. The data comparing the sales effects of advertising campaigns in the United States and other countries can be found in Jones, *The Ultimate Secrets of Advertising,* Chapter 2, especially p. 25. The anecdote about Chiat/Day came from Lauren Brooks, one of my former graduate students.

Chapter 15: The myth comes from Reeves, *Reality in Advertising,* p. 10. The facts about brand KK come from private sources. The week-by-week volatility of sales is illustrated in Jones, *When Ads Work,* Appendix A. The results of the campaign for the Scottish Health Education Board are summarized in Jones, *The Ultimate Secrets of Advertising,* pp. 184–185. The effects of the Nescafé advertising are also shown in Jones, *The Ultimate Secrets of Advertising,* pp. 185–86.

The various techniques used for tracking research are described in McDonald, *Tracking Advertising and Monitoring Brands.* The story of Decoré is published in Sutherland and Sylvester, *Advertising and the Mind of the Consumer,* pp. 143–45. The Oxo case comes from Jones, *Does It Pay to Advertise?,* Chapter 8.

The information about Listerine comes from two case studies: in Jones, *Does It Pay to Advertise?,* Chapter 5; and Greyser, *Cases in Advertising and Communications Management,* pp. 148–167. The details of the De Beers campaign are published in Jones, *The Ultimate Secrets of Advertising,* pp. 186–188 and 193.

The growth in sales promotions is described in Jones, *The Advertising Business,* Chapter 31. The synergy between advertising and promotions is illustrated by two tracking studies of advertising, promotions, and sales in Jones, *The Ultimate Secrets of Advertising,* pp. 65–71.

Chapter 16: The myth comes from Belch and Belch, *Advertising and Promotion. An Integrated Marketing Communications Perspective,* p. 440. The advertising investments of leading advertisers are detailed in "Special Report: Leading National Advertisers," *Advertising Age,* June 24, 2002, p. S-2. (The figures refer to 2001.) Data on American advertising expenditures and how these are broken down by media have been published by *Advertising Age* since 1948. Young refers to lessons he learned from direct response in *How to Become an Advertising Man,* p. 80; Ogilvy did the same in *Confessions of an Advertising Man,* pp. 91–92. The Starch research is discussed in Jones, *How Advertising Works,* Chapter 18. The American advertising executive who spent his career in Europe is George Black, who until his retirement was creative director and chairman of J. Walter Thompson, Germany, Austria, and Switzerland. (His views came from a private communication.) Some of the most interesting advertising written by Bernbach can be found in Dobrow, *When Advertising Tried Harder;* much of Ogilvy's best work is shown in *Ogilvy on Advertising.* The loss of craft skills in constructing print advertising is lamented in *Ogilvy on Advertising,* Chapter 7. The same phenomenon was detected as long ago as 1983 by Tom Amico, a remarkable undergraduate student at Syracuse University, *Breaking the Rules.* Ogilvy's view on salesmanship in advertising is given in *Confessions of an Advertising Man,* p. 114. The best book on Integrated Marketing Communications is Schultz, Tannenbaum, and Lauterborn, *Integrated Marketing Communications.* See also Schultz's chapter in Jones, *The Advertising Business,* Chapter 32.

Many books have been written about direct-response advertising. The classic work is Caples, *Tested Advertising Methods.* The estimate of the volume of direct-mail advertising was made by Robert J. Coen of the Interpublic advertising agency group. The quotation about testing comes from Ogilvy, *Confessions of an Advertising Man,* p. 86. The example of the disastrous mail-order advertising campaign for the collectible item comes from private sources. The research derived from neuroscience is described by Erik Du Plessis in Jones, *International Advertising. Realities and Myths,* Chapter 26. The Kraft example comes from personal experience. (I was personally involved in evaluating the results of the tests.)

The best source of information on IMC is Schultz, Tannebaum, and Lauterborn, *Integrated Marketing Communications.* The continuous importance of penetration growth is demonstrated by Anschuetz, "Why a Brand's Most Valuable Consumer Is the Next One It Adds." The practical impediments to the widespread adoption of IMC are illustrated by research sponsored by the American Marketing Association, discussed in Clare Atkinson, "Integration Still a Pipe Dream for Many," *Advertising Age,* March 10, 2003, pp. 1 and 47. The various examples of direct-response campaigns for major advertisers are all in the public domain. My wife received the Dove mailings, and we buy Gevalia coffee.

Chapter 17: The first myth comes from Levitt, *The Marketing Imagination,* p. 27. The second comes from Belch and Belch, *Advertising and Promotion. An Integrated Marketing Communications Perspective,* p. 633. The Heineken example comes from my own personal experience. The senior agency executive who spent most of his career in international operations is Denis Lanigan, who until he retired was vice-chairman of J. Walter Thompson. (His views on international advertising came from a private communication.) Different classifications of international brands are described by Ashish Banerjee, in Jones, *International Advertising. Realities and Myths,* Chapter 2. The story of Lux will be found in Jones, *Does It Pay to Advertise?,* Chapter 6. (Lux also appears later in this chapter.) The two agencies that almost became insolvent were Interpublic and Saatchi & Saatchi. The data on the increase and then the decline in the popularity of international campaigns can be found in Jones, *International Advertising. Realities and Myths,* Chapter 1 (which quotes a number of sources in the endnotes).

Kenichi Ohmae's enlightening metaphor about transplanting brands comes from Ohmae, *The Borderless World,* Chapter 7. The evidence on the uniformity of response to direct advertising run in different countries is based on personal experience. The Timotei case appears in Jones, *Does It Pay to Advertise?,* Chapter 12. The different eating habits in different countries are a matter of simple observation. One of the few sensible analyses of psychographic differences between countries, based on good empirical work, is Marieke de Mooij, *Global Marketing and Advertising: Understanding Cultural Paradoxes;* see also de Mooij in Jones, *International Advertising. Realities and Myths,*

Chapter 6. The originator of the phrase "Global Village" was Marshall McLuhan. See McLuhan et al., *War and Peace in the Global Village.*

The Pan American case and the story of the anonymous brand of bar soap are both derived from my personal experience. The data on the incomes of Indian households come from Tata Industries, *Statistical Outline of India, 2002–2003,* p. 218.

What is said about the role of advertising agencies in international advertising operations is also derived from personal experience. I spent seventeen years in the field.

Chapter 18: When I worked at J. Walter Thompson, London, during the 1960s I spent three years on Beecham business. Henry Lazell had recently retired, although his view on the importance of advertising was widely known both within the Beecham organization and to its advertising agencies. However, I have not been able to find a written source of the myth that appears at the beginning of this chapter. Lord Heyworth's statement can be found in Heyworth, *Advertising.* FDR's interest in an advertising career was revealed in a letter he wrote to J. Walter Thompson. This has been preserved in the J. Walter Thompson archives, lodged in Duke University, North Carolina. A well-informed observer, Wally O'Brien, former head of the International Advertising Association, shares my view that CEOs today are remote from the advertising carried out by their companies. He can, however, name four CEOs of very important international companies who are exceptions to this rule. Not surprisingly, these organizations are highly successful in their fields. The issues of the nine business journals whose contents I analyzed were published in December 2002 and January 2003.

Sir David Orr's view of corporate cultures can be found in his Foreword to Jones, *Does It Pay to Advertise?* The best picture of advertising agencies during their heyday of the 1950s can be found in Mayer, *Madison Avenue: U.S.A.* The most interesting discussion of advertising agencies' loss of cachet is in Mayer, *Whatever Happened to Madison Avenue?*

The origins of the brand management system are described in Schisgall, *Eyes on Tomorrow,* Chapter 9. The deficiencies of the system are discussed in Jones, *How to Use Advertising to Build Strong Brands,* Chapter 10; also in Jones, "How Clients Can Improve Their Advertising by Improving Their Decision-Making," in Kitchen, *The Future of Marketing,* Chapter 6. Wally O'Brien has reminded me that when agencies received 15 percent commission, they practiced Integrated

Marketing Communications more widely than they do today. Agencies were often anxious to take the initiative in this and to show creative enterprise, for competitive reasons. This view represents an interesting reversal of received opinion.

Typical advertising to sales ratios are illustrated in Jones, *How Much Is Enough?*, pp. 306–308. Systems to pre-test advertisements and agencies' prejudice against quantitative methods are discussed in Chapter 14 of this book.

Chapter 19: The myth at the beginning of the chapter comes from Ogilvy, *Confessions of an Advertising Man*, p. 49. The six business books listed at the beginning of this chapter are detailed in the Bibliography. Their authors are Lasky, Katz, White, Mayer, Mann and Plummer, and Swasy. The four books about advertising—by Packard, Mayer, Reeves, and Ogilvy—are also listed there. The most informative view of advertising agencies during the 1950s can be found in Mayer, *Madison Avenue: U.S.A.* This book is strongly focused on the leading personalities running the advertising business at that time. The agency commission system is discussed by Said, in Jones, *The Advertising Business*, Chapter 10. Clients' early discontent with agency commission is demonstrated in Young, *Advertising Agency Compensation*. The method by which agencies produced radio shows is the background to the best novel ever written about advertising: Wakeman, *The Hucksters*. (Some of the personalities in the story are modeled on well-known advertising practitioners.) Hollywood turned this novel into a magnificent motion picture starring Sidney Greenstreet and Clark Gable. David Ogilvy's celebrated metaphor of the extinct volcanoes comes from *Confessions of an Advertising Man*, p. 26.

The changes that took place in agencies during the second half of the twentieth century, in particular agencies' loss of cachet, are discussed in Mayer, *Whatever Happened to Madison Avenue?* This talks much less about advertising agency personalities than Mayer's earlier book. Fox, *The Mirror Makers*, is very good on the agency business during the 1960s. The public flotation of agencies and the subsequent mergers and acquisitions are described in Millman, *Emperors of Adland*. The separation of media planning and buying from mainline agencies has not yet been seriously discussed in the advertising literature. The trends in agency compensation systems are outlined by Said, in Jones, *The Advertising Business*, Chapter 10. The data on the number of agencies that are members of conglomerates come from "Ad Age Special

Report: Agency of the Year," *Advertising Age,* January 13, 2003, pp. S10–15. The present low fortunes of the advertising industry are regularly discussed in business journals and the advertising trade press.

Advertising strategy is the main topic of Chapter 4 of this book. Agency income is discussed in Jones, *The Advertising Business,* Chapter 10. Incentive systems for agencies are regularly discussed by advertising trade publications. The earliest reference I can find is Julie Liesse, "Kraft G. F. Shifts Agencies, Pay," *Advertising Age,* October 22, 1990, pp. 1 and 58. I personally know of three large advertisers which have such systems successfully in place. Accountability is the main concern of Chapters 10 and 12 of this book. Additional data of considerable interest can be found in Ephron and Pollak, *The Curse of Lord Leverhulme.* The method of adding long-term productivity to the medium-term (end-year) productivity of advertising is described in Jones, *The Ultimate Secrets of Advertising,* Chapter 10.

Chapter 20: The myth comes from Toffler, *Power Shift. Knowledge, Wealth and Violence at the Edge of the 21st Century,* p. 322 and p. 368. Jones and Slater, *What's in a Name?,* Chapter 1, describes and discusses various classes of books about advertising according to their quality.

Bibliography

Ackoff, Russell L., and James R. Emshoff. "Advertising Research at Anheuser-Busch." *Sloan Management Review* (Winter 1975): 1–15; (Spring 1976): 1–15, 91–98. (Comment by Yvon Allaire and rejoinder by Ackoff and Emshoff.)

Advertising Age. Weekly periodical.

Amico, Thomas C. "Breaking the Rules: An Examination of Magazine Advertising Effectiveness and the Principles Which Govern It." Unpublished Honors Thesis, Syracuse University, 1982.

Anschuetz, Ned. "Why a Brand's Most Valuable Consumer Is the Next One It Adds." *Journal of Advertising Research* (January–February 2002): 15–21.

Arens, William F., and Courtland L. Bovée. *Contemporary Advertising,* 5th ed. Burr Ridge, Ill.: Irwin, 1994.

Assmus, Gert, John U. Farlet, and Donald R. Lehmann. "How Advertising Affects Sales: Meta-Analysis of Econometric Results." *Journal of Marketing Research* (February 1984): 65–74.

Belch, George E., and Michael E. Belch. *Advertising and Promotion. An Integrated Marketing Communications Perspective,* 4th ed. Boston, Mass.: Irwin McGraw-Hill, 1998.

Bernbach, William. "Beware of Arithmetic." Speech read at the Association of National Advertisers, New York, 1973.

Bogart, Leo, B. Stuart Tolley, and Frank Orenstein. "What One Little Ad Can Do." *Journal of Advertising Research* (August 1970): 3–13.

Broadbent, Simon, ed. *The Leo Burnett Book of Advertising.* London: Business Books, 1984.

———. *Does Advertising Affect Market Size?* London: Advertising Association, 1997.

Caples, John. *Tested Advertising Methods.* Englewood Cliffs, N.J.: Prentice Hall, 1974.

Cooper, Alan, ed. *How to Plan Advertising,* 2nd ed. London: Cassell, 1997.

Davidson, J. Hugh. "Why Most New Consumer Brands Fail." *Harvard Business Review* (March–April 1974): 117–122.

de Bono, Edward. *The Use of Lateral Thinking.* London: Jonathan Cape, 1967.

de Mooij, Marieke. *Global Marketing and Advertising: Understanding Cultural Paradoxes.* Thousand Oaks, Calif.: Sage Publications, 1998.

Dobrow, Larry. *When Advertising Tried Harder. The Sixties: The Golden Age of American Advertising.* New York: Friendly Press, 1984.

Dyer, Gillian. *Advertising as Communication.* London: Routledge, 1989.

The Economist. Weekly periodical.

Ehrenberg, A. S. C. *Repeat-Buying: Facts, Theory and Applications,* 2nd ed. New York: Oxford University Press, 1988.

Ephron, Erwin, and Gerry Pollak. *The Curse of Lord Leverhulme.* Publication forthcoming, 2003.

Feldwick, Paul, ed. *Pollitt on Planning.* Henley-on-Thames, Oxfordshire, UK: Admap Publications, 2000.

Festinger, Leon. "Cognitive Dissonance." *Scientific American* (October 1962): 93–102.

Fox, Stephen. *The Mirror Makers. A History of American Advertising and Its Creators.* New York: William Morrow, 1984.

Galbraith, John Kenneth. *The New Industrial State,* 2nd ed. Harmondsworth, Middlesex, UK: Penguin Books, 1978.

Gardner, Burleigh B., and Sidney J. Levy. "The Product and the Brand." *Harvard Business Review* (March–April 1955): 33–39.

Greyser, Stephen A. *Cases in Advertising and Communications Management,* 2nd ed. Englewood Cliffs, N.J.: Prentice Hall, 1981.

Hedges, Alan. *Testing to Destruction. A Critical Look at the Uses of Research in Advertising.* London: Institute of Practitioners in Advertising, 1997.

Lord Heyworth. *Advertising* (Statement accompanying Unilever annual report). London: Unilever, 1958.

Hopkins, Claude C. *Scientific Advertising.* Chicago: Crain Books, 1966. Originally published in 1923.

Jenkins, Evelyn, and Christopher Timms. "The Andrex Story—A Soft, Strong and Very Long-Term Success." In *Advertising Works: Papers From the Institute of Practitioners in Advertising (IPA) Advertising Effectiveness Awards,* edited by Charles Channon, 179–190. London: Cassell, 1987.

Jones, John Philip. *Does It Pay to Advertise? Cases Illustrating Successful Brand Advertising.* Lexington, Mass.: Lexington Books, 1989.

———. "Ad Spending: Maintaining Market Share." *Harvard Business Review.* (January–February 1990): 38–42.

———. "The Double Jeopardy of Sales Promotions." *Harvard Business Review* (September–October 1990): 145–152.

———. *How Much Is Enough? Getting the Most From Your Advertising Dollar.* New York: Macmillan–Lexington Books, 1992.

———. *When Ads Work. New Proof That Advertising Triggers Sales.* New York: Free Press–Lexington Books, 1995.

———. *Getting It Right the First Time. Can We Eliminate Ineffective Advertising Before It Is Run?* Henley-on-Thames, Oxfordshire, UK: Admap Publications, 1996.

———. *The Ultimate Secrets of Advertising.* Thousand Oaks, Calif.: Sage Publications, 2002.

Jones, John Philip, ed. *How Advertising Works. The Role of Research.* Thousand Oaks, Calif.: Sage Publications, 1998.

———. *The Advertising Business. Operations, Creativity, Media Planning, Integrated Communications.* Thousand Oaks, Calif.: Sage Publications, 1999.

———. *How to Use Advertising to Build Strong Brands.* Thousand Oaks, Calif.: Sage Publications, 1999.

———. *Advertising Organizations and Publications. A Resource Guide.* Thousand Oaks, Calif.: Sage Publications, 2000.

———. *International Advertising. Realities and Myths.* Thousand Oaks, Calif.: Sage, Publications, 2000.

Jones, John Philip, and Jan Slater. *What's in a Name? Advertising and the Concept of Brands,* 2nd ed. Armonk, N.Y.: M. E. Sharpe, 2003.

Katz, Donald R. *The Big Store. Inside the Crisis and Revolution at Sears.* New York: Viking, 1987.

Kitchen, Philip J. *The Future of Marketing. Critical 21st-Century Perspectives.* Basingstoke, Hampshire, UK: Palgrave Macmillan, 2003.

Koestler, Arthur. *The Act of Creation.* New York: Macmillan, 1964.

Kotler, Philip. *Marketing Management. Analysis, Planning and Control,* 5th ed. Englewood Cliffs, N.J.: Prentice Hall, 1984.

Krugman, Herbert E. "Why Three Exposures May Be Enough." *Journal of Advertising Research* (December 1972): 11–14.

Lannon, Judie, and Peter Cooper. "Humanistic Advertising: A Holistic Cultural Perspective." *International Journal of Advertising* (July–September 1983): 195–213.

Lasky, Victor. *Never Complain, Never Explain: The Story of Henry Ford II.* New York: Richard Marek, 1981.

Levitt, Theodore. *The Marketing Imagination.* New York: Free Press, 1983.

Luik, J. C., and M. J. Waterson. *Advertising and Markets. A Collection of Seminal Papers.* Henley-on-Thames, Oxfordshire, UK: NTC Publications, 1996.

Mann, Charles C., and Mark L. Plummer. *The Aspirin Wars. Money, Medicine, and 100 Years of Rampant Competition.* New York: Alfred A. Knopf, 1991.

Marshall, Alfred. *Principles of Economics.* London: Macmillan, 1988. Originally published in 1890.

Mayer, Martin. *Madison Avenue: U.S.A.* New York: Harper & Brothers, 1958.

———. *The Greatest-Ever Bank Robbery. The Collapse of the Savings and Loan Industry.* New York: Charles Scribner's Sons, 1990.

———. *Whatever Happened to Madison Avenue? Advertising in the 90s.* Boston: Little, Brown, 1991.

McCorkell, Graeme. "When Experts Can Get It Wrong." *Campaign* (February 15, 1985): 55–56.

McDonald, Colin. "Myths, Evidence and Evaluation." *Admap* (November 1980): 546–555.

———. *Tracking Advertising and Monitoring Brands.* Henley-on-Thames, Oxfordshire, UK: Admap Publications, 2000.

McGinn, Colin. "Looking for a Black Swan." *New York Review of Books* (November 21, 2002): 46–50.

McLuhan, Marshall, Quentin Fiore, and Jerome Agel. *War and Peace in the Global Village.* New York: Bantam, 1968.

Mediamark Research Inc. (M.R.I.). Annual reports on consumers' use of brands and media. New York: author.

Millman, Nancy. *Emperors of Adland. Inside the Advertising Revolution.* New York: Warner Books, 1988.

Mittal, Banwari. "Public Assessment of TV Advertising: Faint Praise and Harsh Criticism." *Journal of Advertising Research* (January–February 1994): 35–53.

Naples, Michael J., ed. *Effective Frequency: The Relationship Between Frequency and Advertising Effectiveness.* New York: Association of National Advertisers, 1979.

O'Brien, Geoffrey. "The Triumph of Marxism." *New York Review of Books* (July 20, 2000): 10.

Ogilvy, David. *Confessions of an Advertising Man.* New York: Atheneum, 1984. Originally published in 1963.

————. *Ogilvy on Advertising.* New York: Crown Publishers, 1983.

————. *The Unpublished David Ogilvy.* New York: The Ogilvy Group, 1986.

O'Guinn, Thomas C., Chris T. Allen, and Richard J. Semenik. *Advertising,* 2nd ed. Cincinnati, Ohio: South-Western College Publishing, 2000.

Ohmae, Kenichi. *The Borderless World. Power and Strategy in the Interlinked Economy.* New York: Harper Perennial, 1990.

O'Toole, John. *The Trouble With Advertising.* New York: Times Books, 1985.

Packard, Vance. *The Hidden Persuaders.* Harmondsworth, Middlesex, UK: Penguin Books, 1979. Originally published in 1957.

Peckham, James O., Sr. *The Wheel of Marketing,* 2nd ed. Privately published, 1981, but available from ACNielsen.

Peters, Thomas J., and Robert H. Waterman, Jr. *In Search of Excellence. Lessons From America's Best-Run Companies.* New York: Harper and Row, 1982.

Popper, Karl. *The Logic of Scientific Discovery.* London: Routledge Classics, 2003. Originally published in Germany in 1935.

Prentice, Robert M. "How to Split Your Marketing Funds Between Advertising and Promotion." *Advertising Age* (January 10, 1977): 41–44.

Reeves, Rosser. *Reality in Advertising.* New York: Alfred A. Knopf, 1960.

Revans, R. W. *Action Learning: New Techniques for Management.* London: Blond & Briggs, 1980.

Russell, J. Thomas, and W. Ronald Lane. *Kleppner's Advertising Procedure,* 13th ed. Englewood Cliffs, N.J.: Prentice Hall, 1996.

Samuelson, Paul A. *Economics,* 10th ed. New York: McGraw-Hill, 1976.

San Augustine, Andre J., and William F. Foley. "How Large Advertisers Set Budgets." *Journal of Advertising Research* (October 1975): 11–16.

Schisgall, Oscar. *Eyes on Tomorrow. The Evolution of Procter & Gamble.* Chicago: J. G. Ferguson, 1981.

Schroer, James C. "Ad Spending: Growing Market Share." *Harvard Business Review* (January–February 1990): 44–48.

Schultz, Don E., and Robert D. Dewar. "Retailers in Control: The Impact of Retail Trade Concentration." *Journal of Consumer Marketing* 1, No. 4, (1984): 81–89.

Schultz, Don E., Stanley I. Tannenbaum, and Robert F. Lauterborn. *Integrated Marketing Communications. Pulling It Together and Making It Work.* Chicago: NTC Business Books, 1993.

Simon, Julian L. *A Life Against the Grain. The Autobiography of an Unconventional Economist.* New Brunswick, N.J.: Transaction Publishers, 2002.

Smith, Terry. "Keep an Eye on Expenses." *London Sunday Telegraph,* Business Section (June 16, 2002): 4.

Stow, Mary. "Sold on a Pup." In *Advertising Works: Papers From the Institute of Practitioners in Advertising (IPA) Advertising Effectiveness Awards,* edited by Chris Baker, 53–74. Henley-on-Thames, Oxfordshire, UK: NTC Publications, 1993.

Sutherland, Max, and Alice K. Sylvester. *Advertising and the Mind of the Consumer,* 2nd ed. St. Leonards, NSW, Australia: Allen and Unwin, 2000.

Swasy, Alecia. *Soap Opera. The Inside Story of Procter & Gamble.* New York: Random House–Times Books, 1993.

Tata Services. *Statistical Outline of India, 2002–2003.* Mumbai, India: Tata Services Department of Economics and Statistics, 2002.

Tellis, Gerard J. "The Price Elasticity of Selective Demand: A Meta-analysis of Econometric Models of Sales." *Journal of Marketing Research* (November 1988): 331–341.

Toffler, Alvin. *Power Shift. Knowledge, Wealth and Violence at the Edge of the 21st Century.* New York: Bantam Books, 1990.

Underhill, Paco. *Why We Buy. The Science of Shopping.* New York: Simon & Schuster, 1999.

von Hayek, Friedrich A. "The Meaning of Competition." In *Individualism and Economic Order.* Chicago: University of Chicago Press, 1980.

von Oech, Roger. *A Whack on the Side of the Head.* New York: Warner Books, 1983.

Wakeman, Frederic. *The Hucksters.* New York: Rinehart, 1946.

Weilbacher, William M. *Brand Marketing. Building Winning Brand Strategies That Deliver Value and Consumer Satisfaction.* Chicago: NTC Business Books, 1993.

Wells, William, John Burnett, and Sandra Moriarty. *Advertising. Principles and Practice,* 3rd ed. Englewood Cliffs, N.J.: Prentice Hall, 1995.

White, Larry C. *Merchants of Death. The American Tobacco Industry.* New York: William Morrow–Beech Tree Books, 1988.

Winters, Arthur A., and Shirley F. Milton. *The Creative Connection.* New York: Fairchild Publications, 1982.

Young, James Webb. *Advertising Agency Compensation.* Chicago: University of Chicago Press, 1933.

―――. *A Technique for Producing Ideas.* Chicago: Crain Communications, 1972. Originally published in 1940.

―――. *How to Become an Advertising Man.* Chicago: Crain Books, 1979. Originally published in 1963.

Glossary

Added Values

See Brand

Adstock

See Econometrics

Advertising Agency

Business organization employed by advertisers of all types (e.g., consumer marketers, business-to-business marketers, and also governmental and political organizations) to plan, write, produce, expose, and monitor advertising for its clients.

Advertising Agency Account Group

Multidisciplinary collection of specialists employed by an advertising agency to produce its work for a specific brand, in the case of most large clients; with small advertisers, the account group may deal with all the client's advertising. This group normally embraces account managers to take care of client relations; strategy specialists; and creative writers, art directors, and television producers. Until the 1980s, the planning and buying of the media used for advertising was carried out by the account group; this function is now generally undertaken by media agencies, which are separate organizations. The account group is normally headed by a senior account manager (often called the "management supervisor"), who operates as *primus inter pares.*

Advertising Agency Remuneration

Traditionally, the agency received 15 percent of the value of all television and radio time and all newspaper and magazine space purchased on behalf of its clients. This commission was paid by the media. This system, known as *full commission*, is now extremely rare. Agencies today receive either commission at reduced rates (often on a sliding scale with the commission falling off as the advertising expenditure rises), or else fees based on the time of staff employed on the client's advertising, plus an agreed loading to cover overhead and profit. Many clients have introduced systems of incentive-based payment, by which agencies receive extra pay for demonstrably superior work.

Advertising Allowance

A type of trade promotion by which an advertiser provides funds to a retail organization on the understanding that the retailer uses part of the money to promote the advertiser's brand(s) in the retailer's own advertising.

Advertising and Promotional Budgets: Above- and Below-the-Line

A client's total expenditure on advertising and promotion is known as its *advertising-plus-promotional (A&P) budget*. Media advertising is called *above-the-line spending*; promotions are described as *below-the-line expenditure*. Above-the-line normally covers advertising time and space, mechanical production, agency fees, and advertising-related research. Below-the-line covers consumer promotions (e.g., price reductions, banded packs, coupons, sweepstakes/contests, self-liquidators, collecting schemes) and also trade promotions (e.g., volume discounts per brand, overriding volume discounts, slotting allowances, advertising allowances).

Advertising Audience Measurement

Data generated by quantitative market research into the audience delivered by a television station or network, a radio station or network, a newspaper, or a magazine. The measurement of the television audience both nationally and in regions is normally continuous, that is, at hour-by-hour or at even shorter intervals. The audiences for other media are measured at regular but usually infrequent intervals.

Estimates of the national television audience (and also that in certain regions) is derived from meters (called "Audimeters") attached to television sets. These are supplemented with People Meters, which call for people to identify who is in the room when the set is switched on. Passive Meters, which automatically detect the presence of people in a room, have been developed but are not used. Figures for the other media are derived from personal diaries and from interviews with consumers. Newspaper and magazine surveys, covering the numbers and characteristics of readers, are known as *readership studies*. Readership figures are always higher than circulation figures (which measure paid-for sales), because all publications have multiple readers per copy.

Advertising Elasticity

The response of sales of a brand to a change in advertising expenditure, normally calculated by estimating the percentage increase in sales that results from a 1 percent increase in advertising spending (excluding the influence of other sales stimuli). The calculation is difficult and must be carried out by using econometric techniques.

Advertising Intensiveness

A measure of the advertising investment in the brand, expressed in relative terms, that is, in comparison with other brands. It is normally measured by examining the difference between a brand's share of market and its share of voice. This provides powerful evidence of the scale economies associated with the advertising for large brands, because the latter generally manage to underspend and still maintain their sales.

Advertising Media

The message carriers for advertising. The five main (or measured) media in the United States are newspapers, magazines, television, radio, and billboards. In many countries, the cinema represents a sixth main medium. Note that the singular word is "medium"; the plural is "media."

Advertising Payback

A calculation, derived from econometric analysis, of the financial return (normally over the course of a year) from a dollar spent on advertising. It is based on the calculation of advertising productivity and is carried out by deducting the direct and indirect production costs of the extra sales generated by the advertising from the value of those sales. Separate calculations can be made for each main medium, and for each main below-the-line activity.

Advertising Productivity

Econometric calculation of the value of a brand's sales during a year that are directly generated by advertising, compared with the cost of the advertising. It is generally measured in sales per advertising dollar and is derived from econometric analysis.

Advertising:Sales (A:S) Ratio

The percentage of a brand's net sales value (NSV) that is applied to media advertising.

Advertising Strategy

A document produced as part of the process of managing brands. It is derived from judgment applied to quantitative and qualitative research. Advertising strategy is normally agreed on by both advertiser and advertising agency before work is begun in developing advertising, and it is used to set direction and objectives for the advertising campaign. Different organizations use slightly different systems, but they all contain two elements. First, the strategy identifies the target group, that is, the consumers at whom the advertising is directed; this group is defined in terms of what brands they use already and also by their demography and by their life styles (described as their *psychographics*). Second, the strategy has a statement of the advertising proposition, that is, the specific points of identification and positioning for the advertised brand in comparison with its competitors; these points of identification cover both rational and nonrational factors.

Animatic

Videotape used to describe the idea for a television commercial. It is based on drawings or rough photographs and is accompanied by a soundtrack.

Artwork

Advertising material prepared under the supervision of the advertising agency. In the process of print production, the artwork is put together in an assembly called a *mechanical* and is then sent to publications and production houses as the precise, detailed template for an advertisement. The artwork is transferred photographically onto the printing plates and cylinders. Artwork comprises typeset copy, photographs, and drawn illustrations, together with a detailed description of how the different elements are positioned. The actual artwork is normally prepared by outside specialists under the close direction of the advertising agency.

Atomistic Competition

See Oligopoly

Audimeter

See Advertising Audience Measurement

Banded Pack

Multipack unit sold in retail stores; for example, items sold as "Four packs for the price of three." This is an important type of consumer promotion.

Barter-Syndication

See Television Advertising Categories

Brand

A product or service that offers its users a competitive functional performance compared with other brands; successful brands offer functional superiority in at least some respects. Functionality can easily be demonstrated using objective measures. A brand also offers an additional benefit. It possesses added values: psychic preferences in the minds of its users. These can also be demonstrated. Brands are the main source of a manufacturers' continuous business, and they usually generate substantial profit in the long term. The strongest brands have great longevity if they are properly managed.

Brand Manager

See Management of Advertising

Bursts

See Flights

Category

A broadly defined product group, such as soft drinks.

Category Manager

See Management of Advertising

Circulation

Audited figures proving the average sales of a newspaper or magazine, normally calculated over a six-month period. Circulation figures are always smaller than readership (see Advertising Audience Measurement), because readership figures factor in a number of different readers per copy.

Comparison/Comparative Advertising

A style of advertising that names competitive brands, although in some circumstances the competitive brands are hinted at rather than named explicitly. Comparative claims must be robustly supported with evidence in order to avoid expensive lawsuits. Comparison advertising began to be used during the 1970s and was encouraged by the Federal Trade Commission (the most important regulator of advertising claims) because they foster competition. Comparison advertising accounts for at least 10 percent of all advertising on network television. It is normally used by second and third brands in a category and not by category leaders.

Concentration Ratio

See Oligopoly

Concept Board

See Market Research—Qualitative

Consumer Panel

A valuable but expensive type of quantitative research. The same panel members provide continuous information on their purchasing of brands. It is, therefore, easy to detect seasonality and also longer-term trends; and we can learn much about the patterns of consumer buying and the demography of buyers. Data were formerly collected by the use of paper-and-pencil diaries. Today, handheld scanners are used, and the information is passed every week to the research company over public telephone lines. The scanners themselves are highly automated.

Consumer Purchases Analyzed

A simple formula can be used to calculate consumer purchases in strictly consumer terms, over a defined period of time.

Consumer purchases = (a) population

$\times$ (b) penetration

$\times$ (c) purchase frequency

$\times$ (d) number of packs purchased per occasion

$\times$ (e) average size of pack (measured in volume or money)

For all brands in a category, item (a) does not differ; and (d) and (e) differ little between brand and brand. A brand's sales are therefore driven by items (b) and (c). Penetration is of universal importance. Purchase frequency matters most to large brands (as described in the entry for Penetration Supercharge). If the calculation made from this formula shows a higher figure than the client's own sum derived from ex-factory sales (i.e., those leaving the factory), retail inventories are being run down. On the other hand, if this formula shows a lower figure than the client's, then retail stocks are growing. This information is of great operational value.

Continuity/Recency

A media policy that came into widespread use during the late 1990s. The underlying principle is that concentrated flights of television airtime should be avoided, and the advertising should be planned on a week-by-week basis to provide on average one exposure (or slightly more) to a brand's target group. This single exposure is normally run during the period immediately before most consumers purchase the brand. The money saved by reducing the weight of the flights is used to close some of the gaps in the schedule, which enables advertising to be run more continuously than with a flighted schedule. This policy is now followed by an estimated two-thirds of major American advertisers and has been demonstrated to offer economic advantages over previous policies.

Cost-Per-Thousand/Cost-Per-Mil (CPM)

A universally used method of comparing the cost-efficiency of different television dayparts. The calculation is very simple. The cost of screening a thirty-second commercial is divided by the size of the audience, measured in units of a thousand homes. The CPM figure therefore compares the value for money provided by widely viewed and selectively viewed television dayparts and is the most important tool used in efficient media buying. It is common for widely viewed programs that are very expensive in absolute terms to be relatively inexpensive when measured in CPM. The same type of calculation can also be used for press advertising.

Coverage

See Reach

Database Marketing

See Direct Response

Daypart

Television stations divide the day into broad time segments, called *dayparts*. Each daypart represents an audience that is different from other dayparts, a difference measured in both audience size and demographic composition. For example, dayparts in the morning and afternoon tend to have a relatively small audience and one made up of nonworking women and retirees of both sexes; advertising during these dayparts is therefore an economic way to reach homemakers and older people. The advertising rates charged for the different dayparts vary in broad relation to the size of the audience delivered.

Deconstruction of Sales

See Econometrics

Direct Costs/Variable Costs

A manufacturer's costs that vary with the quantity of a brand manufactured. The most important element of direct costs is raw materials.

Direct Response

A type of advertising that has been important for more than a century. It sells merchandise directly off the page, off the television screen, and via the Internet. Less commonly, it generates inquiries, and manufacturers follow these up with the objective of producing sales. Direct-response advertising generates business through the use of a response device, such as a coupon, an 800 telephone number, or an Internet reply. The unique feature of this type of advertising is that it is a pure stimulus, and sales produced by it are not contaminated by other factors, such as in-store activity. Because of this, direct response has produced quasi-scientific lessons concerning the style and the length of copy that are most effective. There has been much controversy about whether the lessons of direct response apply to other types of advertising. Recent research suggests that they do.

Direct-response advertising is traditionally run in newspapers and magazines. It is also used fairly widely on television, although it does not appear to work on radio. However, the most important medium for direct response is direct mail. This is based on the use of address lists, many of which are assembled by the manufacturer whose goods are being advertised. The buying habits and the demographic characteristics of the people on these lists are therefore known. This type of activity is known as *database marketing*. It is an important element in Integrated Marketing Communications.

Display Allowance

Rebate given by a manufacturer to retailers to guarantee that the manufacturer's brand is displayed in-store, generally in a special position, such as in a gondola, or large display stand, at the end of an aisle.

Double-Head

See Film Production for Television

Econometrics

The use of high-order mathematics to establish the existence or nonexistence of statistical relationships between variables. Econometrics employs laborious computer calculations between different independent variables (e.g., separate causes of sales) and a single dependent variable (e.g., the sales of a brand over the course of a year). The technique used is known as *Multivariate Regression*, and the end product is a model that deconstructs the total sales value of a brand in terms of the specific drivers of those sales. These include advertising in each of a number of specific media and also various types of sales promotions.

Almost invariably, the largest single driver of sales is the brand's equity: the sales level that would have been achieved without any sales stimuli at all. A common figure for this is 75 percent, which is a statistical representation of the strength of the relationship between a brand and its consumers. Advertising Productivity and Advertising Payback are calculated with this type of econometric analysis.

A common type of input in models is a hypothesized stimulus known as *Adstock*. This presupposes that, week by week, the effect of advertising gradually grows. And when advertising stops, the effect declines week by week. The time taken for the effect to reach half the level it was at when advertising stopped is known as the half-life. The Adstock hypothesis is built on questionable foundations. Among other problems, Adstock itself cannot be detected with observed data; it must therefore be looked upon as a less reliable independent variable than a direct measurement of advertising and promotions.

Effective Frequency

See Flights

Fast-Moving Consumer Goods (FMCG)

See Repeat-Purchase Packaged Goods

Film Production for Television

Film production is the responsibility of the advertising agency, although the actual process is almost invariably carried out by outside filmmakers. The agency normally employs a staff film producer as supervisor of all details of the work. He or she hires an outside director—the actual filmmaker—and also the crew, facilities, and artistes. The agency needs to have close knowledge of the expertise of outside specialists so it can make the right choice of outside talent.

Filmmaking budgets are invariably high. It is common to spend more than $500,000 to produce a single thirty-second commercial, which means that the agency producer must keep a close watch on costs. There is invariably a great emphasis on the quality of the finished film, although a geometrical relationship exists between quality and price; for example, a 10 percent improvement in quality could boost the cost by 50 percent. High production values, however, can make a major contribution to the quality of an advertisement.

Films can be made using 35mm or 16mm film stock, or videotape. Commercials made by major agencies virtually always use 35mm film, although this means a considerable increase in expenses because of the larger size of the film crews. The lead times in film production are quite long. Agencies should allow six months between the first planning of the film and its appearance on-air. However, this sort of timetable is normally a great luxury.

Film editing (including amendments required by the client) takes place at an early stage of production, when the picture and the sound are on separate film tracks. The film at this stage is known as an Interlock or Double-Head. Until fairly recently, the editing of a film was carried out by hand, the rough prints being cut and pasted. However, the most common procedure today is for rough films to be put on videotape and the editing carried out electronically. When the two parts of the Interlock are brought together as a single film—known as a Married Print—no further editing is possible.

Fixed Costs

See Indirect Costs/Fixed Costs

Flights

Flights, known in Europe as bursts, are concentrations of advertising—generally television advertising—in relatively short periods, such as three or four weeks, separated by gaps during which the brand is unadvertised. The once-popular doctrine of Effective Frequency dictated that viewers should be exposed to an average of three advertisements during the period of the flight. To achieve such an average, substantial numbers of viewers had to be exposed to the advertising at a wastefully high amount of repetition. This is one of the reasons why the doctrine has been widely abandoned.

Focus Groups

See Market Research—Qualitative

Frequency

See Opportunities-to-See

Half-Life

See Econometrics

Indirect Costs/Fixed Costs

A manufacturer's overhead costs; a sum the manufacturer must pay no matter how many goods it produces. The most important items are expenses for the factories and offices.

Integrated Marketing Communications (IMC)

The doctrine of Integrated Marketing Communications dictates that all marketing activities, both above- and below-the-line, should be expressions of a common strategy so as to maximize the synergy between them. Everything should march to the same drum beat. Although the doctrine offers obvious advantages and has been widely propagated since the early 1980s, it is not widely implemented. This is because it is unclear who should actually control the various parts of the program. It is most logically a client responsibility, but brand managers are too low in the hierarchy to provide forceful leadership. The fields in which IMC has been applied fairly widely are those in which Database Marketing is used, such as credit cards and other financial products, travel and hotel services, and some retailing.

Interlock

See Film Production for Television

Involvement

Involvement is an important concept that was developed by the psychologist Herbert E. Krugman. It applies to both media exposure and the purchasing of brands.

With media, low involvement means a lack of full attention and is characteristic of television viewing. Communication is highly selective; many things pass by the viewers. High involvement means the opposite; it is characteristic of reading—a rational and sequential process.

In the buying situation, low involvement means a casual purchase decision, normally an instantaneous choice between the brands that are already in the purchaser's repertoire. This is characteristic of virtually all repeat-purchase packaged goods. High involvement means a planned, rational buying decision and is associated with purchasing items with a high ticket price.

One of Krugman's most important observations was the harmony he saw between how television advertising for repeat-purchase packaged goods is viewed and how those products are actually bought. Both processes are low-involvement decisions. This could provide a clue (which, to date, has not been clearly articulated) to how the television advertising for these products actually works in terms of the consumer's psyche.

Layout

A device used to present proposed press advertising to clients. A layout sketches the form of an advertisement, using drawings or rough (e.g., Polaroid) photographs. The copy is usually set out as a separate element and is sometimes pasted on the back of the layout so that it can be read aloud by the person presenting the advertisement.

Life Cycle Theory

This is a widely propagated doctrine that describes how brands, like animals and plants, go through the four stages of birth, growth, maturity, and decline. Although many brands do go through these stages, this in itself does not prove that the theory is valid. Brands are in effect a product of efficient—or inefficient—management. If they are managed well, there is nothing inevitable about their decline. The life cycle theory is a dangerous fallacy: dangerous because it is self-fulfilling. If managers believe in decline, they will lose interest in their supposedly declining brands, thus hastening the process of decline and causing their premature demise.

Management of Advertising

Two basic systems of management exist: brand management and advertising management. The brand management system was developed by Procter & Gamble to ensure that all aspects of advertising and promotional activities are coordinated. The brand is seen as the central focus of all marketing activities. But the system emphasizes coordination and not true management because brand managers do not have the operational authority to make decisions. They carry out a staff and not a line function. Brand managers are expected to make recommendations, and they must learn to steer these upward through the decision-making hierarchy of their companies. And because brand managers cannot make decisions, they do not have the authority to implement Integrated Marketing Communications. In a number of organizations, brand management has been broadened into category management, which exercises overall control over a manufacturer's portfolio of brands in a product category. This system suffers from a major disadvantage, although it reduces some waste in the system. Category management restricts the opportunity for individual brand managers to exercise their entrepreneurial drive, which many analysts believe to be the particular advantage of the system.

The older advertising manager system treats advertising as a self-contained activity, and an advertising manager has a much greater decision-making role than a brand manager. The advertising manager organization has an obvious drawback because advertising is not independent of other parts of a business. The system is used today mainly in companies that produce large amounts of collateral material, such as leaflets, brochures, and showcards. The advertising manager can control these sometimes complicated operations efficiently, but he or she will generally take a rather narrowly focused view of advertising proposals.

Market Research—Qualitative

A research method based on interviewing people in a detailed and often indirect fashion, in order to explore motivation and the reasons for preferences and actions. It answers the questions "why?" and "how?" This type of research is conducted in two ways: by individual interviews (known as *one-on-ones*), and by focus groups of eight to twelve people. The questions asked differ to some extent between different respondents because there must be some flexibility to stimulate people to give thoughtful and detailed answers. The interviewing is carried out by a moderator, who often has training in psychology, and whose job is to conduct the research and interpret the answers.

Qualitative research is expensive, so we must rely on small samples that do not allow the responses to be projected to represent the population as a whole. The research provides nothing more than selective insight, although this can be very valuable. Qualitative research is widely used in the development of advertising ideas. Respondents discuss advertising presented to them in a schematic form such as an animatic or a concept board (a visual depiction of one or two episodes in the commercial together with a script of the sound track).

Market Research—Quantitative

Broad scale research to elicit simple and relatively unambiguous information. The research is used to answer direct questions such as "what?" "how much?" "how often?" "who?" and "when?" Large samples, of 2,000 people or more, are employed, and the questions are uniform for all respondents. Data are collected by personal interviews, telephone interviews, the Internet, and in some cases through mechanical means, such as by using scanners. The large samples mean that the responses can be projected (with known margins of error) to represent the population as a whole. The main problem with this type of research is the difficulty of formulating questions that have no hidden bias. (This is not as easy as it sounds.) The questions cannot be modified once the interviewing begins, because it would then be unsound to aggregate the answers.

Market Share

See Share of Market

Married Print

See Film Production for Television

Mechanical

See Artwork

Media Agency

Media agencies have grown since the early 1980s and have taken over the media planning and buying for most large advertisers. Conventional advertising agencies are now mainly confined to producing creative work. By handling large volumes of advertising for many clients, media agencies can reduce costs for their clients by exercising downward pressure on media rates. Media agencies can also offer special professional expertise: in their use of research to plan media and in their detailed knowledge of the media marketplace to seek out buying opportunities.

Media agencies originated in Britain. Over the years, the conglomerate companies that have acquired advertising agency networks have bought or set up their own media agencies to handle all the media work for the advertising agencies in their networks. Media agencies are normally remunerated by fees.

Media Buying

Essentially an opportunistic process. All rates are negotiable.

Media Schedule

See Media Tactics

Media Strategy

The underlying principle of media planning is that the advertiser is buying people and not advertising time and space. The media strategy sets out the most effective overall plan to deploy television time, radio time, and space in other media, to expose an advertising campaign to its target consumers. It determines the proportion of the total advertising budget that is to be used in each medium. The media strategy lays down three constants on which all alternative practical plans must be based: (1) the budget for each medium; (2) the target group for the advertising, defined demographically; and (3) the main periods of advertising over the course of a year.

Media Tactics

Media tactics detail how the media strategy will be implemented. The tactical plan covers the specific number of insertions in each media vehicle, that is, television stations and dayparts, and specific newspapers and magazines. Alternative plans are reviewed after carrying out computer runs of each to measure their delivery of four major outputs: (1) reach; (2) opportunities-to-see (OTS); (3) cost-per-thousand (CPM); and (4) the continuity provided by the number of weeks on air. These four objectives cannot all be maximized (remembering that maximizing cost-per-thousand means a low and not a high figure), because more for some means less for others. The choice of the best alternative is made on judgment, using as a criterion the one offering the best optimization of the four variables. The final plan is presented with appropriate statistics and also as a media schedule, that is, a flowchart showing the distribution of the media exposures over the course of a year.

Media Vehicles

See Media Tactics

Monopoly

See Oligopoly

Multivariate Regression

An econometric technique used to estimate the relative importance of different independent variables in explaining a single dependent variable (e.g., a brand's sales). *See also* Econometrics.

Net Proceeds of Sales (NPS)

See Net Sales Value (NSV)

Net Profit

A residual; the amount of money that remains after deducting all direct and indirect costs from a brand's net sales value (NSV).

Net Sales Value (NSV)

A manufacturer's net receipts from the sales of each of its brands. This is measured after deducting normal trade margins but before deducting production costs. Some manufacturers measure their NSV by calculating their net proceeds of sales (NPS). This arrives at sales net of all trade rebates, including promotional allowances. The problem with this calculation is that it effectively conceals an important trend in the manufacturer's costs: the increasing amounts of promotional money that manufacturers are being forced to pay to their retail customers.

Oligopoly

This unattractive word describes the most common feature of markets: that they are dominated by relatively small numbers of major competitors, usually three or four. The proportion of total market sales that is accounted for by these dominant manufacturers is known as the *Concentration Ratio*, a figure that is normally in the 60 to 80 percent bracket. Oligopolistic competition is intense because manufacturers are not only conscious of the end-consumers to whom they sell their goods and services but they also feel the presence of their competitors, who will constantly react to any manufacturer's actions in the marketplace. Oligopolistic competition actively encourages product and brand differentiation, which means a major role for consumer advertising.

Pure, or atomistic, competition, which means a large number of competitors that manufacture undifferentiated products, is extremely rare despite the prominence given to it in the literature of economics. At the other extreme, monopoly, which means a single large manufacturer that dominates its market, is equally rare except in the cases of government-licensed businesses like public utilities. It also operates with new discoveries, such as in the pharmaceutical field, during the period when they are still protected by their patents.

One-on-Ones

See Market Research—Qualitative

Opportunities-to-See (OTS)

This measure represents the number of times that consumers will, on average, be exposed to a brand's advertising during the course of a week or a flight of advertising. This description is European and is more precise than the word Frequency, which is more commonly used in the United States. (An advertising exposure can only offer an opportunity-to-see; there is no guarantee that people will actually look at an advertisement, as is implied by the word Frequency.)

OTS is calculated in a reasonably simple way. We start with the estimated number of Gross Rating Points (GRPs) achieved for the period of advertising. These are a measure of the total number of advertising impressions during that period. We then estimate the net reach associated with this number of GRPs; there are standard tables published that will give accurate estimates. The net reach covers all households that will have been exposed to any of the advertisements: some will receive one advertisement, others will receive two, three, four, five, or more; in other words, the net reach figure covers duplication of viewing. We then divide the total number of GRPs by the net reach, and this produces the average OTS. This demonstrates that, say, 70 percent of homes will be exposed during a week at an average of 1.9 OTS (the total number of GRPs being 133). Another way of looking at this mathematical relationship is that net reach multiplied by average OTS equals the total number of GRPs.

The technique is most commonly used for television advertising, but it can also be applied to other media.

Passive Meter

See Advertising Audience Measurement

Penetration

The proportion of households that buy a brand at least once in a defined period. There is a direct relationship between penetration and share of market. Penetration is the main driver of market share.

Penetration Supercharge

A characteristic of the largest 20 percent of brands. For these large brands, not only do they have a high penetration, but they also have an above-average purchase frequency and repurchase frequency. This represents an important scale economy for large brands. The original concept of the Penetration Supercharge originated in Britain, although it was originally described with the use of a negative phrase. Small brands are described as suffering from Double Jeopardy—a low penetration allied to a low purchase frequency.

People Meter

See Advertising Audience Measurement

Pool-Out

When a commercial is made, it is normally fairly easy to film a number of alternatives of the individual sequences of which a commercial is composed. These make it possible for the film to be edited in a number of different ways to provide variations. These are known as Pool-Outs.

Pre-Testing of Advertisements

The procedure of researching advertising before it is exposed. Two types of research are carried out, although most advertisers use only one or the other; only the largest use both.

The first type is research conducted at an early stage to help generate and refine advertising ideas. The respondents see the advertising in schematic form, that is, as animatics or concept boards. The investigation at this stage is mostly qualitative. Focus groups are most commonly used, although they are ineffective for evaluating the communication of ideas; for this, one-on-ones are needed.

The second type of research aims to predict the actual effectiveness in the marketplace of a commercial in its finished form. It acts in the same way as an insurance policy: money paid out to avoid the loss of much larger sums through running ineffective advertising. The research is usually quantitative and there are a number of proprietary techniques. The best of these are supported by evidence that, with the majority of individual tests, the findings predict the eventual success or failure of the advertising.

Price Elasticity

The response of sales of a brand to a change in consumer price; it is normally calculated by estimating the percentage increase in sales that results from a one percent price reduction. Note the reciprocal relationship: sales go up when prices go down, and vice versa. Price elasticity is a common measure, but econometric analysis is needed to do the job.

Print Production

See Artwork

Production Values

The special magic provided by top-quality filmmaking talent. *See* Film Production for Television. A similar contribution is made to newspaper and magazine advertising by outstanding photographers and illustrators.

Proposition

See Advertising Strategy

Pulsing

A little-used method of distributing a television budget across the course of a year. There is a very low level of weekly exposure; occasional but regular "blips" are superimposed on this.

Purchase Frequency

The average number of times a household buys a brand within a defined period.

Pure Competition

See Oligopoly

Reach

An important variable in determining a brand's media strategy. It represents the number of households that are reached at least once during a period of advertising. The actual number of times they are reached varies from once to sometimes large figures. The word coverage is often used to describe the same concept.

Readership Studies

See Advertising Audience Measurement

Reading-and-Noting

See Recognition

Recall

Research conducted into the degree to which consumers recall advertisements. Various types of prompt are used. At one extreme, the measure is based on spontaneous recall, that is, with no prompt. At the other extreme, the measure becomes recognition, with a full prompt. Recall studies have a long history. The measure was once commonly used to investigate consumers' recall of television advertising within twenty-four hours of the appearance of an advertisement. This was called Day-After-Recall-Testing (DART). It suffered from a number of methodological problems, and it was abandoned during the late 1980s when it was finally discovered that the recall scores did not predict sales. *See also* Tracking Studies.

Recall studies are also used to evaluate newspaper and magazine advertising.

Recency

See Continuity/Recency

Recognition

Research based on an extreme type of prompted recall of an advertisement. The classic method was developed during the 1920s by the prominent early market researcher Daniel Starch. It is still in operation. The system, known as Reading-and-Noting, takes respondents through a newspaper or magazine that they claim to have read recently. For each advertisement in it, respondents are asked to indicate whether they had noticed it, then if they had registered the brand name, then if they had read most of the copy. In isolation, Reading-and-Noting scores have been shown to be inaccurate. When tracked over time, however, they can be valuable in detecting the wearout of individual advertisements. They also give a useful guide to the effectiveness of advertisements that stimulate readers to read large amounts of copy, such as advertisements containing recipes.

Repeat-Purchase Packaged Goods

Low-price branded goods that consumers buy regularly in food and drug stores, for example, branded foods, cigarettes, soft drinks, and proprietary drugs. Advertising in these categories remains very important, although they have lost their once-dominant position. (During the 1960s, they accounted for two-thirds of all the advertising of major brands.) Nevertheless, most of the hard information that we have acquired about advertising is derived from repeat-purchase packaged goods. In most overseas countries, they are known as fast-moving consumer goods (FMCG).

Repertoire of Brands

The majority of buyers—both households and individuals—do not confine their loyalty to a single brand. In most product categories, more than 80 percent of sales are made to multibrand buyers. The collection of brands that people buy is known as their *brand repertoire*. In various fields of repeat-purchase packaged goods, households buy on average at least three brands over the course of a year. These are made up of a primary brand (which accounts for about half of total purchases), a secondary brand (which accounts for about a third of all purchases), and a tertiary brand, which is much less important: some people experiment by making single purchases of a number of alternatives. The important point about the repertoire is that people have constant experience of competing brands. If one of these should receive functional improvements, this brand will increase its share of market at the expense of brands that have not improved. The repertoire of brands is, therefore, an artifact that ensures that functional improvements are rapidly copied within product categories.

The repertoire concept also holds for infrequently purchased goods and services, such as motor cars. In these cases, however, the time period over which the repertoire is revealed must be years and not months.

Retail Audit

An extremely important research device to measure the sales of brands in retail stores. The first retail audit was set up by the A. C. Nielsen Company in the early 1930s. The method is based on selecting a representative sample of stores of different types, and the research is carried out by measuring the presence of brands in these stores at intervals of two months. At the beginning of the period, the researchers measure all the inventories in the product categories that are being investigated. Two months later, the process is repeated. In the meantime, each store manager has been instructed to retain delivery notes for the product categories in question. In each store, by adding deliveries every two months to the stocks at the beginning of the period, and then deducting the stocks at the end, it is a simple matter to calculate the sales that have taken place over the two months. The research is presented by aggregating the figures for all the stores in the sample.

This type of research has an extremely rich history that has revealed trends and changes in the structure of markets. Important general lessons about the progress of a multitude of brands have been assembled by A. C. Nielsen. Many of them have been embodied in a book written by James O. Peckham, Sr., *The Wheel of Marketing* (see the Bibliography).

Besides revealing data on sales, retail audit research provides figures on deliveries, stocks, distribution, and out-of-stock items. The original system of collecting data was laborious, but hand counting has now given way to collecting sales data from scanners at the checkout of the stores.

Retail Distribution

A measure of the retail coverage of a brand. It is calculated in two ways, unweighted and weighted:

Unweighted (or numerical distribution)

1. Aggregate the number of stores in your retail "universe" (e.g., drug stores in the Eastern United States, or food stores in Syracuse, New York) (A).

2. Aggregate the number of stores in the universe that carry your brand at a particular time (B).

3. Percentage B on A.

Weighted (or dollar distribution)

1. Aggregate the annual total sales value (sales of goods of all types) in your retail universe (A).

2. Aggregate the annual total sales value (sales of goods of all types) in the stores carrying your brand at a particular time (B).

3. Percentage B on A.

"Ripomatic"/"Stealomatic"

A special type of animatic that employs existing film material either from commercials or from television programs. "Ripomatics" are used both for research and to present creative ideas to clients.

Scanner

A laser device used to record the bar code/Universal Product Code (UPC) printed on a brand's pack. This is used both to charge customers in-store and also to count sales for research purposes. Research uses both checkout scanners and handheld scanners in respondents' homes. The most sophisticated type of consumer panel research employs in-home scanners.

Segment

A narrowly defined product group (e.g., diet soft drinks). A *category* is normally made up of a number of segments.

Self-Liquidator

A type of consumer promotion that offers merchandise at a special price so long as consumers mail tokens proving purchase of the promoted brand. The financing of self-liquidators is calculated in such a way that the relatively small payment made by the consumer will cover both the cost of the merchandise and all mailing and handling expenses. A self-liquidator is therefore a zero-cost activity to the manufacturer who is promoting the brand in question, unless the manufacturer has been forced to buy a large quantity of the promoted merchandise that cannot be sold.

Share of Market (SOM)

SOM is by far the most important measure of the health of a brand. The effects of advertising and promotions are invariably measured in terms of a brand's share of market. It represents a brand's share of total consumer purchases in a category in a defined time period. It is calculated from either volume or dollar figures.

1. Aggregate total category purchases (in volume or dollars) (A).

2. Aggregate the brand's consumer purchases (in volume or dollars) (B).

3. Percentage B on A.

Share of Voice (SOV)

A brand's share of total measured media advertising in a category in a defined time period. It is calculated from dollar figures.

Short-Term Advertising Strength (STAS)

A calculation of the immediate effect of advertising on sales. This is derived from Pure Single-Source research. It is based on product categories and measures the difference in the share of purchases of a brand in the households that had received advertising for it during the seven days before they bought it (Stimulated STAS), and the share of purchases in the households that had not received such advertising (Baseline STAS). The difference between the two is called the "STAS Differential." It is presented as an index figure, the Baseline having a value of 100.

Single-Source Research

A market research technique that collects data in individual households and that relates two things: (1) each household's purchasing of specific brands; and (2) the advertising of those specific brands that was—or was not—received by the household immediately before the purchasing. The pure method of single-source research specifically identifies the advertised brand and relates this to the purchase of that same brand. The diluted method is much weaker and relates the purchasing of brands to various patterns of television viewing. *See also* Short-Term Advertising Strength (STAS).

Slotting Allowance

An important type of trade promotion that takes the form of a special rebate paid by manufacturers to retailers to persuade them to carry new brands that have no track record of success. The phrase is also occasionally used to describe allowances paid to retailers to carry ongoing brands.

"Stealomatic"

See "Ripomatic"/"Stealomatic"

Stock Cover

The number of days' or weeks' supplies of a brand that are held in a retail store, calculated at the normal rate of sale. Out-of-stock poses a significant problem because demand for a brand will be frustrated and sales will be lost because consumers cannot buy it. Large retailers often demand that manufacturers should install computerized systems to monitor the stock levels in individual stores for each of the manufacturer's brands. The purpose of this is to reduce stocks to minimum levels so as to achieve just-in-time deliveries. This reduces demands on the retailers' working capital and in effect passes the costs of stock control onto the manufacturer. This is the equivalent of a further increase in trade rebates.

Store Checking

A simple method of estimating the composition of a product category. This is done by visiting a small number of typical stores, often as few as three. The procedure is to count the number of shelf-facings of each brand and variety in a product category; a *facing* is the front pack on the shelf, ignoring the packs that are stacked immediately behind it. We then aggregate the facings in all the stores visited and percentage the number of facings of each brand and variety on the total of all facings. The resultant estimates will give a serviceable approximation of market shares. The only consistent bias in the procedure is that it tends to underestimate the shares of market of large brands and overestimate those of small ones.

Storyboard

A large board containing the script of a proposed television commercial, accompanied by drawings or rough photographs of the action. A storyboard is commonly used to present the idea of a commercial to a client. Directors also often prepare their own storyboards to help them frame their shots when carrying out filming.

Syndicated Research

Large-scale quantitative research providing data on consumer purchasing in a wide range of product categories and also information on the audiences for the main advertising media. Individual clients and advertising agencies pay a subscription to give them access to the data, and they can also pay for special analyses. The overall cost of syndicated research is extremely high, and many hundreds of clients are needed to make this type of research service profitable. The leading syndicated services are Mediamark Research Inc. (MRI) and Simmons Market Research Bureau (SMRB).

Target Group

See Advertising Strategy

Television Advertising Categories

Four main categories of television advertising exist:

Broadcast Network: This provides national coverage, with no possibility of separate regional coverage. Six main broadcast networks exist in the United States; ranked by volume of advertising, the largest is NBC, followed by CBS, Fox, ABC, WB and UPN. Networks operate by hooking up chains of local stations. Network advertising is only suitable for national advertisers. It offers very little demographic selectivity.

Spot: Advertising on stations in the 150 local regions in the United States. Spot advertising uses the stations that are local affiliates of the networks. Spot advertising, which offers little demographic selectivity beyond its geographical limits, is used by local advertisers and also by national advertisers that wish to reinforce their local efforts.

Cable: There are cable networks and also local cable stations. These all offer a greater deal of demographic selectivity than broadcast advertising. The classic cable station is MTV, which reaches a young audience. Many others now exist, appealing to the special interests of groups of consumers.

Barter-Syndication: A system, which came into use during the 1970s, by which advertisers and advertising agencies produce television programs. They make these programs available to television stations and in return receive free airtime that can be sold to clients. The barter-syndication system is highly entrepreneurial and is subject to constant negotiation. Certain accounting scandals have emerged as a result of it.

Television is quantitatively the most important advertising medium, and its share of media advertising continues to rise gradually. But the increases are exclusively due to cable and barter-syndication.

Television Ratings

In the United States, these are known as Gross Rating Points (GRPs); in Europe, as Television Ratings (TVRs); and in Australia, as Target Audience Rating Points (TARPs). One GRP represents 1 percent of all homes with the television switched on to a specified program. High-rating programs provide a GRP level of more than 10, and often as high as 25; the usual rating of the Super Bowl is much higher.

GRPs describe the weight of a television schedule, and it is important to remember that they cover duplicate viewing. Homes exposed to two programs are counted twice; those exposed to three are counted three times, and so forth. The following is an example. Four television shows with a cumulative rating of 50 GRPs could attract the following audience:

71 percent of homes would be exposed to no programs (0 GRPs)

16 percent of homes would be exposed to one program (16 GRPs)

7 percent of homes would be exposed to two programs (14 GRPs)

4 percent of homes would be exposed to three programs (12 GRPs)

2 percent of homes would be exposed to four programs (8 GRPs)

In this example, the net reach of the schedule would be 29 percent. If this figure is divided into the figure of 50 GRPs, the average number of Opportunities-to-See is 1.7. In other words, advertising in these four shows would deliver an audience of 29 percent, who would, on average, be exposed to 1.7 commercials.

Tracking Studies

Quantitative research carried out on a continuous basis to measure consumers' awareness of advertising, awareness of brands, awareness of the attributes of brands, and recent purchasing. Investigations into awareness and purchase are often called Usage-and-Awareness (U&A) surveys. Some controversy surrounds tracking studies, although they are widely used in many countries. The controversy revolves around whether awareness drives brand usage, or whether the causality is the reverse one, with usage driving awareness. Tracking studies are sometimes carried out on a weekly basis and reported monthly; sometimes they are carried out at less frequent intervals, when they are referred to as "Dipstick" studies. In tracking studies, different people are interviewed during each survey, although all the samples have the same demographic composition. In this respect, tracking studies are different from consumer panels, which are based on receiving repeated information from the same consumers. The leading tracking service is provided by the Millward Brown organization.

Usage-and-Awareness Surveys

See Tracking Studies

Variable Costs

See Direct Costs/Variable Costs

Wearout

A signal that a television commercial is reaching the end of its useful life. Wearout is not so much a result of the period of time over which the commercial is used as the outcome of heavy media expenditure. As a general rule, wearout is detectable after a commercial has been used for a total weight of exposure represented by 2,000 Gross Rating Points, or GRPs. Note that wearout applies to single commercials and not to campaigns. Wearout can be prevented if a campaign uses a number of Pool-Outs of a single creative idea. With advertising in other media, wearout is less of a problem than with television, because in general the weight of exposure is much less.

Index

About the Author

John Philip Jones was born in Wales and graduated in economics from Cambridge University (B.A. with Honors; M.A.). From 1953 to 1980, he worked in the advertising agency field. This experience included twenty-five years with J. Walter Thompson—as a market research executive in London (1953–55); advertising account executive in London (1957–65); account supervisor and head of television in Amsterdam (1965–67); account director and head of client service in Scandinavia, based in Copenhagen (1967–72); and account director in London (1972–80).

He worked with a wide variety of advertising clients and was most concerned with major brands of packaged goods. His responsibilities included many brands marketed by Unilever, Chesebrough-Pond's (before its acquisition by Unilever), Beecham, Gillette, Nestlé, Pan American, Pepsi-Cola, Quaker Oats, and Scott Paper. He was international account director on Lux Toilet Soap (the largest selling bar soap in the world) from 1972 to 1980. As a result of his professional experience, he became a specialist in the development and monitoring of brands.

He was extensively involved with advertising education both within and outside the agency. He conducted his last agency seminar in January 1981, just before he became a full-time educator upon joining the faculty of the Newhouse School of Public Communications, at Syracuse University. He is a tenured full professor and was chairman of the Advertising Department in the Newhouse School for seven years. He has taught a wide range of advertising classes, at both the graduate and undergraduate levels.

Since the beginning of his teaching career, John Philip Jones has spent a good deal of his time supervising postgraduate education. He has taught postgraduate seminars every year. He has supervised more than 100 masters' theses, both at the Newhouse School of Public Communications and at Syracuse University's School for Visual and Performing Arts. He has also supervised Ph.D. theses and has served as a member of many Ph.D. committees, including recent ones at the University of South Australia and the University of Navarre, Spain.

For three years, he edited the university's interdisciplinary journal of ideas, *Syracuse Scholar*. He was a member of the Mellon Foundation project group, which spent two years exploring the connection between liberal and professional education and which published a book, *Contesting the Boundaries* (Syracuse University Press, 1988).

The author has published widely in the professional press, with articles in *Admap, Commercial Communications,* the *Economist Media & Marketing Europe,* the *Harvard Business Review, International Journal of Advertising, Journal of Advertising Research, Journal of Marketing Communications, Marketing & Research Today, Marketing Management, Market Leader,* and many other publications, including journals in Australia, Britain, the Czech Republic, Germany, India, the Netherlands, Scandinavia, and Switzerland. He has also been responsible for a number of pieces of journalism in the *New York Times* and other publications.

His books *What's in a Name? Advertising and the Concept of Brands* (1986); *Does It Pay to Advertise? Cases Illustrating Successful Brand Advertising* (1989); *How Much Is Enough? Getting the Most From Your Advertising Dollar* (1992); and *When Ads Work. New Proof That Advertising Triggers Sales* (1995) are widely used in the advertising profession in the United States and overseas. His books have been translated into German, Spanish, Japanese, Korean, Chinese, Portuguese, Turkish, and Arabic. A new book, *The Ultimate Secrets of Advertising,* was published by Sage Publications in 2002. This propounds a general theory of advertising, embracing long-term effects. A substantially revised second edition of *What's in a Name? Advertising and the Concept of Brands* was published in early 2003.

He was the editor and part author of five major handbooks, also published by Sage. The handbooks dealt with all major aspects of advertising practice, with volumes coming out in 1998, 1999, and 2000. They cover more than 2,000 printed pages. These books are entitled: *How Advertising Works—The Role of Research; The Advertising Business; How to Use Advertising to Build Strong Brands; International Advertising: Realities and Myths;* and *Advertising Organizations and Publications.*

He has developed certain measurement devices based on robust quantitative research. These include STAS (Short-Term Advertising Strength) and AIC (Advertising-Intensiveness Curve). These are used in professional practice and are described in his books. He is employed as a consultant by many leading consumer goods companies and advertising agencies in the United States and abroad. He also regularly addresses major professional conferences.

In 1991, John Philip Jones was named by the American Advertising Federation as the Distinguished Advertising Educator of the Year. In the same year, he became a member of the Council of Judges of the Advertising Hall of Fame. In 1994, he was elected a member of the National Advertising Review Board. In 1996, he received a major award from Cowles Business Media and the American Association of Advertising Agencies for leadership in the media field; the one other prize winner was NBC Sports. He received the Telmar Award in 1997, for extending the concept of Short-Term Advertising Strength from television to print media. In 2001, he received the Syracuse University Chancellor's Citation for Exceptional Academic Achievement. In 2003, he was named by American Demographics as one of the twenty-five leaders in the fields of demography, market research, and statistics during the past quarter century.

He presents his work to professional and academic audiences in many countries around the world. As an adjunct professor at the Royal Melbourne Institute of Technology, Australia, he teaches there every May. He is also a visiting professor at the Copenhagen Business School.

He has worked on evaluating advertising copy, has acted as an expert witness, has given opinions to attorneys, has been deposed, and has also testified in court. As a member of the National Advertising Review Board, he has judged competing copy claims.

Footnote on Action Learning

During his academic career, John Philip Jones has found it extremely productive to incorporate elements of *Action Learning* into his teaching. This technique is described in Revans, *Action Learning* (see Bibliography). This present book has been planned with Action Learning in mind.

The technique stresses strongly the importance of literacy and numeracy. It gradually moves the responsibility for how learning actually takes place from one-way, professor-to-student communication, to two-way mutual communication. It means that students must make increasing demands on themselves and become self-starters. They are, of course, carefully and continuously supervised.

Action Learning is very beneficial to the people being taught, and it is fairly clear that the students who have passed through the author's hands and have gone on to positions near the top of their professions owe some of their success to the inculcated habit of Action Learning. They continue the learning process after they have left the university.

If anyone in the teaching profession wishes to know more about how *Fables, Fashions, and Facts About Advertising (FFFAA)* can be used for Action Learning, they should write to the following e-mail address: *jpjones@syr.edu*